Also by Alva Johnston

THE GREAT GOLDWYN
THE CASE OF ERLE STANLEY GARDNER

The Legendary Mizners

The

Legendary Mizners

By ALVA JOHNSTON

ILLUSTRATED BY REGINALD MARSH

FARRAR, STRAUS AND GIROUX
NEW YORK

Farrar, Straus and Giroux
19 Union Square West, New York 10003

The material in this book appeared originally in *The New Yorker*
in somewhat different form.

Library of Congress Cataloging-in-Publication Data

Johnston, Alva.

The legendary Mizners / by Alva Johnston ; illustrated by Reginald Marsh.
    p.   cm.
ISBN 0-374-51928-5 (pbk. : alk. paper)
    1. Mizner family.   2. Mizner, Addison, 1872–1933.   3. Mizner, Wilson,
1876–1933.   4. United States—Biography.   5. Benicia (Calif.)—
Biography.   I. Marsh, Reginald, 1898–1954.   II. Title.
CT274.M57J64 2003
929'.2'0973—dc21

                                                    2003045214

www.fsgbooks.com

1   3   5   7   9   10   8   6   4   2

CONTENTS

The Legendary Mizners

Chapter One

A BEGINNING IN BENICIA

THE LEGENDS OF WILSON MIZNER and Addison Mizner ran parallel through most of their lives, but now and then, with outrageous results, the lines converged. Wilson was by profession a conversational artist, Addison an architect, but neither was that easily classified. Addison was born in 1872, in Benicia, California, the second youngest of seven children. Wilson was born in the same town four years later.

The Mizners, in addition to being one of the most eccentric families this country has produced, were the oldest of the old families of Benicia, which is twenty-five miles northeast of San Francisco on a strait through which the waters of the Sacramento and San Joaquin Rivers enter San Francisco Bay. The Mizners went back to the beginning of things in Benicia. It was founded in 1847 by Dr. Robert Semple, a great-uncle of Addison and Wilson and a stirring figure in California history. Elsie Robinson, the author and columnist, was a Benicia girl, and she has written of the awe the Mizners inspired by their antiquity and elegant ways, particularly their habit of taking tea in the afternoon. Benicia was the center of high-toned education for young ladies and a bright spot on the social map of California. The pusillanimous artifice of understatement was unknown a couple of generations ago, and the old accounts of Benicia give it the glorious title of the Athens of the Pacific, because of the number of boarding schools there. Gertrude Atherton received her polishing at a Benicia academy. Mills College, now in Oakland, California, is an offshoot of a Benicia seminary. Benicia was enlivened by military officers from Benicia Barracks, which was ruled over during the town's halcyon days by Colonel Julian McAllister, brother of Ward McAllister, the oracle and dictator of New York society, and son of Matthew Hall McAllister, a lawgiver of the early San Francisco aristocracy. The Mizner house, a cottage that had been enlarged into a kind of rambling hotel, was the headquarters of fashionable Benicia. It was normal for the family to have twelve or fourteen head of select prep students and young lady seminary students at dinner. The plentifulness of sea food around San Francisco Bay made it comparatively inexpensive to run the place like a country club. "When the tide was out, your table was set," Wilson Mizner once said. There were three cooks in the Mizner household during the family's heyday, the most important being Ying Lee, who started with Wilson's grandmother and was with the family for sixty years. The intense affection the members of the family had for one another extended to Ying. Addison in later life always had a pet named Ying Lee, and Wilson gave the name of Ying Lee to one of his characters in a Broadway play called "The Greyhound."

Ida M. Tarbell, historian of Standard Oil and author of a biography of Addison, describes Mama Mizner, the mother of Addison and Wilson and the five other Mizners, as "a *grande dame*," and there is ample corroboration for her statement. The late Arnold Genthe, the society photographer, wrote that he became a social rage in San Francisco through the recommendations of Mama Mizner, her daughter Minnie, and a few other influential San Francisco women. Mama Mizner's personality was so authoritative that during the San Francisco fire she commandeered a passing fire engine to drive her to a place of safety and departed from the burning city on a steam yacht. Papa, or Lansing Bond, Mizner was a lawyer, politician, railroad promoter, land speculator, and presiding officer of the California Senate for many years, and was often suggested for Governor. He was a major during the Mexican War, and went to San Francisco after the war at the urging of Dr. Semple, who had settled in San Francisco several years before the discovery of gold. The elder Mizner made one major miscalculation. He believed that the coming great city of the Pacific Coast was Benicia, not San Francisco. He acquired enormous real-estate holdings there and waited in vain for Benicia to become the California metropolis and make him the John Jacob Astor of the West. An old letter among the family papers describes him as "the original Benjamin Harrison man," and on taking office in 1889 President Harrison appointed Papa Mizner Envoy Extraordinary and Minister Plenipotentiary to five Central American nations—Guatemala, Nicaragua, Honduras, El Salvador, and Costa Rica. That more or less broke up the Benicia household. Addison, then seventeen, and Wilson, thirteen, went to Guatemala City. Addison's natural appetite for high life was sharpened by the social splendor and martial gorgeousness that surrounded the Minister Plenipotentiary. He and Wilson shared a valet and a Spanish tutor. A cousin of Addison's states that a young Guatemala priest, who took a liking to Addison, first roused his lifelong enthusiasm for Spanish art and architecture. Among the family souvenirs of Guatemala is a photograph of Addison painting a full-length portrait of a gilded and feathered Latin-American general. Addison was already over six feet, and the fact that he was fundamentally a fat boy was concealed by the enormous development of his arms, shoulders, neck, and chest, as a result of heaving his two hundred pounds about on crutches for many months after an accident.

In 1890, Addison was sent back to San Francisco to resume his education. Private schools around San Francisco fell down on the job of preparing him for the University of California. They couldn't cope with the problem of a youth brimming over with non-academic culture but defective in spelling, arithmetic, and other rudiments. The family met the problem by sending him to Spain for a few months at the University of Salamanca. His

Spanish instructors did little to overcome his academic weaknesses, but "Educated at the University of Salamanca" sounded as impressive as three doctor's degrees after his name. On his return to San Francisco, he mortified his parents by talking of taking up art as a profession. The Mizners had been in the diplomatic service for three generations, and collateral branches of the family teemed with governors, judges, generals, and cotillion leaders. One ancestor was the first governor of Illinois, another gave Abraham Lincoln his first political appointment, another practically founded California, and another married into the Rutgers family, which once owned the land that is now the Bowery and which gave its name to Rutgers University. The four older Mizner brothers were professional men and seemed on their way to eminence. The parents expected Addison and Wilson, two exceptionally knowing youths, to become illustrious figures in national life. "I thought they were going to be at least bishops or ambassadors," Mama Mizner later told Ethel Watts Mumford, the artist and writer. The family couldn't bear the idea that a Mizner should be an oaf in a paint-spattered smock and Latin Quarter tie, so Addison was bundled off to China, in the hope that a change of scene would give him a healthier outlook. He returned with several chows, a fondness for Chinese art, and a conviction that silk pajamas were correct street attire. He found work in San Francisco, in the office of Willis Polk, later famous for his skyscrapers and World's Fair buildings in San Francisco but then a starving young architect known as Whistler, because of his genius for making enemies.

Papa Mizner died in 1893, on Addison's twenty-first birthday, leaving the family land-poor. Polk was not making enough money to pay Addison's salary, so he took him into partnership, and they lived together in a wooden pueblo that had been built in upside-down fashion on Russian Hill. One entered the seventh floor from the street; the rest of the house consisted of six basements clinging to the side of a precipice. One of Addison's friends of this period was Wallace Irwin, poet and author of the famous "Letters of a Japanese Schoolboy," who says that

Addison and Polk used to save their tin cans and hurl them down the rocks to welcome visitors threading their way up the cliff. Addison wrote in his autobiography, "The Many Mizners," that he and Polk were so poor at times that they lived on canned beans and kept warm by stealing fuel, with the help of a complicated grappling apparatus, from a woodyard some distance below their lowest sub-basement. They invaded the fringes of literature, becoming volunteer workers on the *Lark,* the house organ of the Pacific Coast intelligentsia of the Cleveland-McKinley era. There was no intellectual accolade in the West equal to that of being connected with the *Lark,* and after half a century *Who's Who* still has a surprising number of venerable authors who boast that they once wrote for it. The magazine was in its time a vehicle of great new thoughts and revolutionary art movements, but its chief link with history today is probably the fact that it was the first magazine to publish Gelett Burgess's four-line stanza about the purple cow.

Addison picked up some knowledge of architecture in San Francisco, but he never learned how to draw detailed plans or write a set of specifications. Willis Polk was considered the father of the California bungalow. Addison, working on bungalows and other modest structures, laid the foundation for his recognition in Palm Beach as an incomparable Jack-of-all-trades. He picked up crafts as a born linguist picks up languages, and soon had more than a smattering of carpentry, house painting, bricklaying, masonry, plastering, plumbing, and kindred lines. He was saved from being a dilettante by a genuine love of toil and saved from being a complete snob by his admiration for anybody who could do good work with his hands. These enthusiasms were secondary, however, to his ambition to be a gilded juvenile in the wealthy and sprightly set. It took money to travel with the Nob Hill crowd in San Francisco. Addison couldn't finance his scale of living on his income as an architect. A refugee from collection agencies, he fled to northern California in 1897 and became a day laborer in a gold mine near the town of Delta.

In his autobiography, Addison connects his flight with one

of the great disappointments of his life. President José María Barrios, of Guatemala, had commissioned him, he says, to build a two-million-dollar government palace and had promised him a twenty-five-thousand-dollar cash retainer, but was assassinated the day before Addison was to sail from San Francisco, so the young architect had no alternative but to dash to the mines. Addison's memory seems to have played him false in his account of this great disappointment. Barrios apparently had reason to be grateful to Addison and may have once planned to give him a big architectural job, but he died more than a year after Addison's flight to the mines. Miss Tarbell, who wrote her account of Addison as a foreword to a magnificent volume on his Palm Beach architecture, relates that on one occasion he had saved the life of Barrios and that Richard Harding Davis used the exploit as the basis of "Soldiers of Fortune," a record-breaking best-seller of 1897, dealing with the adventures of a couple of Gibson girls and a tall, clean-cut Gibson man against a background of bananas and tin soldiers. The Addison Mizner tale is that while he was running the American Legation at Guatemala City in his father's absence, he learned of a plot to execute his young friend Barrios, who had been imprisoned, without trial, after a coup engineered by his political rival Manuel Barillas. He induced Barillas, who had assumed dictatorship, to sign an order to release Barrios; the dictator, however, talking in a dialect, directed an Indian servant to dash to the prison and countermand the release order before Addison arrived. Barrios' wife reported the dictator's duplicity, and Addison, sparing no horses, outraced the bearer of the death sentence, carried Barrios to safety under the Stars and Stripes that waved over the Legation, and later smuggled him out of Guatemala. This romantic episode has no particular relation to the plot of "Soldiers of Fortune," but Addison did meet Richard Harding Davis at the Chicago World's Fair of 1893 and may have inspired his interest in the *coup-d'état* belt as the setting for a novel. Addison was only one of the scores who were pointed out as the original Soldier of Fortune. Lloyd C. Griscom, the diplomat, who accompanied Davis on his search

for local color in Central America, said that the novelist got
his background of politics and graft from a civil engineer he
met down there and that the fine, upstanding young Gibson-
type hero was, like all other Richard Harding Davis heroes,
Richard Harding Davis.

Failing to thrive as a gold miner in Delta, Addison joined
his brothers Wilson, William, and Edgar in the Klondike rush
in 1897. Addison hurled himself frantically at the frozen gravel.
He boasted in a letter to his mother that he had hauled up two
hundred and fifty-six buckets of ore from his shaft in one day.
According to his account, he washed out two hundred thousand
dollars' worth of gold dust, but, with the exception of thirty
thousand dollars, which he concealed in an old boot, it was
all stolen from him by Canadian officials, on the pretext that
his mining operations had encroached on government land.

Addison's "The Many Mizners" has brilliant passages, but
it is hazy in spots. He returned from the Klondike to San
Francisco late in 1899 with, he states, enough money to leave
him a modest fortune after his debts were paid. But, instead
of practicing architecture in San Francisco, he went on a two-
year odyssey in the Pacific and Indian Oceans. His explanation of his wanderings is that he had tied up his money in
a trust fund, was lured to Honolulu by the mistaken belief
that he could make a fortune building houses for rich Hawaiians,
and spent two years beachcombing in the tropics rather than
return home with a confession of failure. The probability seems
to be, however, that Addison was lying low in order to give a
San Francisco social storm time to blow over. His career as a
San Francisco society man can be traced in the newspaper art
of that city. In 1893, at the age of twenty-one, he was already
enough of a man-about-town to have his bulky physique cari-
catured by the great Homer Davenport, then in his first year
on the San Francisco *Examiner*. During the nineties, the horse
show was the field day of society in San Francisco and in all
other communities that claimed the rank of city. In its sketches
of the celebrities at the horse show of 1896, the *Examiner* presented a fat, highly tailored figure doffing a silk hat. This draw-

ing, entitled "Mr. Addison Mizner Greets a Friend," was the
work of Jimmy Swinnerton, who startled San Francisco with his
purple-and-white check suit and yellow vest and who, according
to the Dictionary of American History, helped to found the comic
strip, in 1892. But it was in the San Francisco *Call* of March 7,
1900, that Addison made his most sensational appearance in
pictorial journalism. He was the central figure in four drawings of the climax of a vendetta between him and the social
tyrant of the town—Edward M. (Ned) Greenway, the Hero
of a Thousand Cotillions. Greenway, a red-faced, bullet-headed
man with popeyes and a white mustache, was a carpetbagger
from Baltimore, but he made himself the most powerful champagne agent and ballroom bully in the West. Evelyn Wells,
author of "Champagne Days of San Francisco," writes that he
boasted of having drunk twenty-five bottles of champagne a
day, with beer chasers, and originated the expression "No gentleman ever feels well in the morning." Another carpetbagger,
William H. Chambliss, had attempted to rule San Francisco
society but had been run out of town by the Greenway faction.
He took revenge by writing "The Parvenucracy," which sought
to prove that there was no such thing as San Francisco society.
Greenway was famous for his Friday-night dances, which were
called the Greenways, to distinguish them from some rival affairs known as "chippy dances." Every season, he distributed
what he called Greenway garters, as though they were birthday
honors. His enemies charged that these coveted decorations were
often found on unselect legs and that Ned made a business of
selling social position to debatable débutantes for two thousand
dollars apiece. Nevertheless, Greenway was firmly established as
the Judge Lynch of the fashionable world when Addison incurred his disapproval. Greenway could put on the black cap
and sentence a man to be hanged by his exclusive neck until
he was socially dead. He indicated capital punishment for Addison by causing his name to be stricken from the list of guests
for the Mardi Gras Ball of the San Francisco Art Association.
The young fellow's crime is not quite clear; a tentative newspaper explanation in 1900 was that he went around saying that

Widow Clicquot's product beat Mumm's Extra Dry, which Greenway represented. The *Call's* narrative, with its four action pictures, indicated that Addison died game. He cornered Greenway in a café, where the old autocrat was having a beer chaser, and challenged him to come out and fight. When Greenway declined, Addison called him a coward, spat in his beer, and stalked haughtily out of the café. He spent the next two years hanging around the equator.

There was only a limited demand for Addison's architecture in the Orient and the coral isles, and he was reduced to variegated hustling. In Hawaii, he did miniatures on ivory and made charcoal enlargements of photographs; in Samoa, he painted magic-lantern slides for a travelogue man; in Shanghai, he sold coffin handles to replace doorknobs; from Tokyo to Bangkok, he picked up commissions selling antiques; in Melbourne, he thrashed about the prize ring under the name of Whirlwind Watson; in Hawaii, he was fired from a job with the Inter-Island Steamship Company for nicknaming its ships "the Inter-Island pukers;" in Hawaii, also, he was created an extinct Polynesian nobleman by the deposed Queen Liliuokalani, who struck him with her royal yellow feathers and dubbed him Sir Addison as a reward for restoring the portraits of her ancestors.

After more than two years in exile, Addison reappeared in triumph in San Francisco. He was now a literary lion. In Honolulu, he had become acquainted with Ethel Watts Mumford. Starting with the parlor game of grafting surprise twists on old quotations, they developed a long list of debauched proverbs and, with help from Oliver Herford, published "The Cynic's Calendar," which gave America its baptism of early-twentieth-century sophistication. Goose pimples were raised on the nation by "Where there's a will, there's a lawsuit," "Many are called but few get up," "The wages of gin is breath," "Be held truthful that your lies may count," "God gives us our relatives; thank God, we can choose our friends." As an intellectual cannon ball of the highest calibre, Addison was now able to defy Greenway and rotate once more in the vortex of society. He couldn't live, however, on the royalties from the funny almanac, so he

planned to become the new Lumber King of the West. The old
Lumber King, S. S. Dolbeer, had died in 1902, leaving his
forests and sawmills to his only daughter, Bertha. She was
worth five million dollars in the newspapers and nine hundred
and seventy-six thousand dollars according to the official ap-
praisers, and Addison was deeply smitten. He was thirty and
felt that it was high time to espouse visible means of support
and settle down. In his later years, Addison was never considered a Romeo, but he may have been different in his burning
youth. He represents himself as an eagle among the doves of
the Yukon dance halls, a dragon among the expensive Jezebels
of San Francisco, and an occasional martyr to true love. His
fastidiousness was the only thing that saved him from suicide
on one occasion; unrequited affection had driven him to a
lonely spot in Golden Gate Park to shoot himself, but he spared
his life because, suddenly remembering a hole in his under-
drawers, he was horrified at the impression he would make
on the coroner's helpers. He became very much in earnest
about Miss Dolbeer. His courtship did not prosper, and he lived,
he said, in agonies of jealousy. Miss Dolbeer's ideal was a strong
man like her father, and she gave Addison to understand that
she couldn't be interested in a putterer and trifler, even though
he was the premier Joe Miller of the epoch. But she told him
that she might consider him seriously if he made something
of himself, so he decided to become a Coffee King. He had
ideas for packaging and marketing the product, and he went
to Guatemala to sign up a few plantations. While in Guatemala,
he received word that Miss Dolbeer had killed herself on July 7,
1904, by jumping from the seventh floor of the Waldorf-Astoria.
Her suicide apparently had nothing to do with her lukewarm
romance with Addison. Her cousin and travelling companion,
Miss Etta Warren, told reporters that Miss Dolbeer had been
brooding over the death of her father and had spent hours
gazing at his picture. In the tenderness of an old passion, Addison, in his autobiography, describes his lost sweetheart as "an
orphan with several million dollars in her hip pocket" and mis-

spells her name. The tragedy caused him to forget coffee and become the most stupendous old-clothes man of the era.

Guatemala was rich in ancient and splendid priestly vestments. Earthquakes and confiscation had ruined many of the religious establishments. In some cases, there was only one priest to two churches, but there were quantities of venerable paraphernalia, and deals could be made because of the need of money for the relief of half-starved parishioners. Addison, like most raconteurs, was always ready to assassinate his own character to improve a story, and he delighted in picturing himself as an unconscionable skinflint. He never led off, according to his account, with an offer of more than one per cent of the value of an object. He claimed to be the greatest cathedral looter in the world and asserted that he used whiskey, poker, and droll stories to lubricate his negotiations. He dealt with laymen as well as churchmen, many of the old church estates having passed into private hands. Centuries-old ceremonial robes and other sacred needlework were his specialties at first, but he bought altars, carved woodwork, crucifixes, candlestands, paintings, and other relics. For six hundred dollars paid to a plantation owner, he obtained some monastery altars decorated with twelve thousand dollars' worth of gold, which had been mistaken for gilt. He reported that it took eight or ten donkeys to carry off the noble merchandise he obtained from the half-ruined Cathedral of Antigua. In his Palm Beach days, Addison told Miss Tarbell that his lifetime plunder from cathedrals, churches, and palaces in Latin America and Europe could be measured only in shiploads.

Arriving in New York late in 1904 with his ecclesiastical swag, Addison was a social and commercial success. Comstock Lode millions and other Western wealth had gravitated to Fifth Avenue and Newport, and many of the old Nob Hill friends of the Mizners were high up in the Eastern social hierarchy. His first patronesses were Mrs. Hermann Oelrichs and Mrs. William K. Vanderbilt, Jr., who had been the two biggest silver-and-gold heiresses in San Francisco. The celebrated Mrs. Stuyvesant Fish and her eccentric favorite, Harry Lehr, gave him their stamp of approval. One of Addison's San Francisco cronies, Peter Martin (Addison had been arrested with him twice, once for treating a milkman's horse to beer and pretzels in Los Angeles and once for resisting a bouncer at the Waldorf-Astoria), had married a niece of Mrs. Oelrichs and taken a house in Newport. Addison was launched in style. "The Cynic's Calendar" made him a somebody. His wit, gaiety, and Klondike and South Seas background gave him a vogue. Mrs. Oelrichs set him up in a shop on Fifth Avenue and helped to popularize altar cloths and religious robes as wall decorations and as throws for tables and pianos. Mrs. Oelrichs was the former Tessie Fair, daughter of James Fair, the Nevada prospector who located the Big Bonanza, a hundred-million-dollar treasure chamber in the Comstock Lode. Edgar Mizner, older brother of Addison, had fallen in love with Tessie in spite of her money, but she rejected him and other native sons in favor of Hermann Oelrichs, known as the Dutchman, a popular society man and all-round athlete. According to the New York *Times*, Fifth Avenue sports once offered John L. Sullivan a purse of twenty thousand dollars to meet the Dutchman in a Fifth Avenue basement, but Sullivan declined. Oelrichs was one of the group that introduced polo into the United States, but he was best known as the marathon swimmer who had gone out many miles to greet Atlantic liners, taking with him a small watertight knapsack containing his lunch, a bottle, and, according to Cleveland Amory, a little light reading matter. By the time Addison arrived in New York, the Dutchman had become a serious drinker, punner, and rhymer, and Mrs. Oelrichs usually contrived to keep a continent or two between them. Mrs. Stuyvesant Fish had her court jester in Harry Lehr, and Mrs. Oelrichs now adopted Addison for a similar role. Other matrons and dowagers of the New York aristocracy made a pet of Addison, and he might have blossomed out as a society architect in 1905 or a little later, but he was always dashing about the country in private railroad cars and swaggering around at fashionable watering places, so he had no time to establish himself in his future profession.

In 1906, Wilson Mizner married the rich widow Mrs. C. T. Yerkes and moved into her mansion at Fifth Avenue and Sixty-eighth Street. *Town Topics* began to suspect a little later that Addison was about to marry a still richer widow and move into a mansion at Fifth Avenue and Fifty-eighth Street, as well as into Roseclyffe, a two-million-dollar cottage at Newport. Hermann Oelrichs had just died. During his lifetime, *Town Topics* had been persistently spiteful toward the Oelrichses. Colonel William d'Alton Mann, owner of *Town Topics,* regarded his journal as a Heralds' College that gave and took away aristocracy at will. His American peerage consisted chiefly of people who lent him money and never tried to get it back. He was the scourge of all pretenders who assumed to draw a breath of genteel air without lending him money. He was frightfully disappointed in the Oelrichses, who, with their vast wealth, had never taken out a patent of nobility in the form of one of his promissory notes, and he paragraphed away at Mrs. Oelrichs for years. He reported that Tessie looked like the chandelier of a Broadway lobster palace in a rhinestone gown she wore at the opera; that she had fallen in the esteem of bank clerks because she failed to tip them for helping her cut her coupons; that a clambake given by her nephew-in-law Peter Martin inaugurated a reign of vulgarity that threatened to depopulate Newport; that she was plump as a partridge; that she screamed and shouted and fought with Mrs. Stuyvesant Fish; that she had discarded her protégé Addison and was now the leader in "roasting him," but that Addison had, with the help of his mother, become so firmly entrenched in society that she couldn't hurt him. After the death of the Dutchman, the attitude of *Town Topics* toward Tessie underwent a complete change. One of the Colonel's fantasies was a belief that the *Town Topics* office was the heaven in which marriages of the Four Hundred were made. His greatest hobby was interbreeding the great American fortunes. He had a strong sociological conviction that one colossal estate should always be mated to another colossal estate, but he was sometimes suspected of slipping an impecunious pal into the list of entries for great matri-

monial prizes. As one of the richest widows in America, Tessie
became an important element in Colonel Mann's lonely-hearts
work among the moneybags. After a decent period of mourn-
ing, he began to nominate husbands for her. He proposed can-
didates by the platoon, filling *Town Topics* with glowing tributes that read like convention speeches for favorite sons. When
the campaign was at its height, news reached the *Town Topics*
office that Colonel Mann's whole slate was smashed, because
Tessie and Addison were beginning to go steady. In Newport,
they were seen everywhere together. Colonel Mann sent out
one of his best men to shadow them. The result of this inves-
tigation relieved the old matchmaker considerably. *Town Topics*
reported that its research man, finding the couple tête-à-tête,
had been able to creep close enough to overhear them. Tessie
was addressing Addison as Brother, Addison was calling her
Sister, and the conversation was about a bum steer somebody
had given her on the stock market. Tessie spoiled Colonel
Mann's plans, and possibly Addison's, by not remarrying at all,
and Addison became an invincible bachelor.

Addison was widely known in New York as a big, breezy
fellow who was usually accompanied by two handsome chows.
He generally aired them on Fifth Avenue, and often tied them
to a hitching post on Forty-fourth Street, just off the Avenue,
when he went to lunch at Sherry's. He was particularly breezy
in his language. One of his close friends for many years was
the late Philip Boyer, a well-known New Yorker, whom he
shocked at their first meeting. Boyer was having lunch with
Harry Markoe in Louis Martin's, at Fifth Avenue and Twenty-
third Street, when Addison strolled in alone after a promenade
on the Avenue. He shouted across the restaurant, "Hey, Harry!
I know a woman who wants to be bred to you!" Addison had
a way of sounding correct and innocent no matter what he said,
and his surprised and hurt attitude when anybody took exception to his language is said to have been most artistic and dis-
arming. Nearly everybody liked him. He had intimates among
theatrical stars and prima donnas as well as among the mature
women of social eminence. Mme. Emma Eames, the opera celeb-

rity, got him his first important work as a society architect—a
commission to remodel and decorate the half-finished house of
Mrs. Stephen Brown. Addison and Donald Brian, star of "The
Merry Widow," started a little dancing club at Addison's apartment under the auspices of Mrs. William K. Vanderbilt, Sr.
Addison ruefully recalls in his memoirs that he rejected a two-
thousand-dollar bribe from a social climber who wanted to crash
it. Addison and Marie Dressler became lifelong friends. He
took her and Jerome Kern, then her accompanist, to perform
at one of Mrs. Fish's parties. Addison wrote that he believed
this was the first social amalgamation of headliners of the stage
and of fashion, but the files of *Town Topics* show that Mrs.
Fish was giving home vaudeville parties as early as 1900, when
Colonel Mann publicly commended Mr. Fish for asserting his
authority and cancelling a scheduled performance at the Fish
home by Lily Langtry, who had starred in naughty French
shows and was suspected of having slipped cracked ice down the
neck of the Prince of Wales, later Edward VII.

As he made it a point of honor to live beyond his means,
Addison was overwhelmed by debt from time to time, but he
was always able to borrow money for an antique-buying tour
in Latin America or the Old World. On such expeditions, one
of which took him as far as Persia, he mixed his vocations. Between bouts of haggling over old robes, furniture, art, and religious relics, he sketched and photographed architectural monu-
ments, added to his store of anecdotes by pumping the local
antiquarians, and occasionally jotted down light thoughts for
future conversations or for "The Cynic's Calendar," which reappeared eight times in revised editions. Epigrams and drawings are found in about equal numbers in some of Addison's old
sketchbooks. There are studies of a huge iron lock in Cluny
Castle, a balustrade in Seville, a staircase in Valencia, street
lamps in Barcelona, and the façade of a castle in Bohemia;
these are mingled with random phrases and wisecracks—"maca-
roni legs," "porch chairs painted with mayonnaise," "Louis Fourteenth Street furniture," "teeth set out by a landscape gardener,"
"Two ideas in his head at once would constitute an unlawful

assemblage," "The Yukon grows lazy and finally stops flowing," "My mother thinks it is by the merest accident that I am not President," "He's old enough to sleep alone," "A cow couldn't find its calf in this room," "He has no manners—he just has customs," "Don't make those Madonna eyes at me," "Talking as though the Standard Oil Company was the smallest thing he owned."

Addison now bought the Baxter homestead, built about 1775 on the waterfront in Port Washington, Long Island, and re-modelled it into a home for himself, a private museum for his relics, and a zoo for various pets he had. He soon had a flourishing truck garden and kennels with forty or fifty chows. He lived there most of the time, commuting to a studio he had set up in New York. One of his Long Island neighbors was H. K. Landis, who put out a house organ for a gas company and amused himself by printing a bi-weekly called *Plain Talk*. Landis wrote enthusiastic accounts of Mizner's antiques, contracted the antique fever himself, and then ran the Landis Valley Museum, at Lancaster, Pennsylvania, noted for its collection of Pennsylvania Dutch objects. *Plain Talk* printed interviews with Miko, the capuchin monkey; Ying, the Maltese cat; Honeybuggy and Lambypie, two chows; and other members of the Mizner animal kingdom. It listed a few items in the Château Mycenae, as *Plain Talk* called Addison's house—a Japanese ceremonial banner; an illuminated manuscript of a Spanish-convent musical service of 1551; a carved wooden candlestick made in 1535 for the first cathedral in the Western Hemisphere; the terrible spurs worn by Alvarado, chief lieutenant of Cortez and first governor of Guatemala; a gorgeous twelfth-century Moorish stirrup; an eighth-century Fu porcelain dog; a thirteenth-century ivory archbishop; a papal bier; Aztec stone carvings; ancient Spanish page caps; an altar made in 1501; and a variety of wood and metal crucifixes.

Addison established a modest practice as a landscape architect on Long Island. He was noted for his Japanese landscapes, with dwarf trees among midget mountains and pygmy rivers. He planted and terraced the Great Neck estate of Raymond

Hitchcock, the famous comedian, and built a baroque staircase leading to the water. He beautified the Sands Point estate of Bourke Cochran, the volcanic Tammany orator, but was in such consternation because his paths and vistas converged on nothing in particular that Cochran let him build a Greek theatre to provide an intellectual destination for the revised landscape. J. J. Floherty, the writer, has said that Addison was in seventh heaven when a client gave him carte blanche to landscape an estate, build a house on it, decorate it, furnish it down to the table linen, and hire the servants. Addison built in several styles at this period. *Plain Talk* printed engravings of a Mizner Japanese house and a Mizner English house, asserting that the latter was an exact reproduction of an English inn in which William the Conqueror slept. He did a Spanish house for I. Townsend Burden near Roslyn and a Chinese teahouse for Mrs. O. H. P. Belmont at Sands Point, which later became a studio for Ethel Watts Mumford, Addison's literary partner. One of Addison's best productions was White Pine Camp, Archibald S. White's place for roughing it in luxury in the Adirondacks.

The architect was a puzzle to his neighbors. He startled them by shopping in his dressing gown and sometimes in his pajamas. Now and then, the town was kept awake until 3 or 4 A.M. by frightful uproars in his house, and he was thought to have been entertaining the riffraff of Hell's Kitchen until the local newspaper came out with a list of the guests, most of them from the higher echelons of the *Social Register*. Addison had an outburst of civic spirit on one occasion. He was outraged to learn that it was proposed to vulgarize Port Washington by allowing a circus to invade the place for one night. He circulated petitions, made speeches, and hired lawyers, but was unable to avert the horror. Late on the night of the circus, pandemonium broke loose in Addison's house and lasted till daybreak. The sleepless neighbors learned later that Addison had thrown one of his tremendous parties for the circus people.

During the last few years of her life, Mama Mizner lived with Addison in Port Washington. Addison's friends regarded her as a grand old matriarch and admired him as a most devoted son. His attitude toward her was that of an impresario showing off a famous imported star. He always shaped the conversation to bring out her wit, penetrating insight, and sharp judgments. Her death, in 1915, in her eightieth year, prostrated Addison and was deeply felt by the scapegrace Wilson. Addison wrote to San Francisco relatives that while he was broken with grief, Wilson nursed him and attended to all his affairs. A little later, Wilson was in a sanatorium himself. Addison said that for a year after her death any reference to Mama Mizner would cause Wilson to burst into tears. The great ambition of Addison's life, according to Miss Tarbell, was to build a cathedral in Florida in memory of his mother.

The First World War ruined Addison's practice. Late in 1916, he was broke and a very sick man, with necrosis of the bone resulting from his old leg trouble and with other serious ailments. Phelan Beale, the lawyer, who had represented Wilson in his occasional legitimate endeavors, went to Port Washington to see what could be done. He saved Addison's house from his creditors by organizing a corporation to take it over. Mrs. O. H. P. Belmont, Jules Bache, and several others bought bonds of the corporation in the belief that they were doing charity under the guise of business, but the property was later sold at a good figure and the bonds were paid off. Through this deal, Beale raised about twelve thousand dollars for Addison. Fully expecting to die in the near future, Addison planned to spend his last days in Antigua, Guatemala, which he considered the most beautiful spot on earth, but friends persuaded him that he would be better off in Palm Beach. There he began his great career.

Chapter Two

THE PALM BEACH ARCHITECT

ADDISON MIZNER had suffered for years from a complication of ambitions, and it took a complication of diseases to cure him. When he had the use of his legs, he was perpetually busy with small things and neglected his creative talents. But, bedridden in his forties, he was forced to daydream for lack of anything else to do, and he began to live in visions of Addison Mizner castles in Addison Mizner landscapes. Until then, he had not been able to decide whether he was an artist, architect, interior decorator, landscape designer, curio peddler, fortune hunter, antiquarian, society ladies' pet, chow raiser, heiress chaser, or literary man. His various professions and enthusiasms tended to destroy one another. He was too bohemian to be a fixed star in Newport or on Fifth Avenue; too much of a scholar, artist, and pleasure lover to be a very successful antique dealer; too changeable in his objectives to capture any of the rich prizes of literature, art, or matrimony. But his long illness caused his various talents to stop fighting among themselves and work in harmony. After he regained his health, all his old occupations, sidelines, and follies played their part in making him the fashionable architect of the bull-market period. As an antiquarian, he had a sure touch in adapting the architecture and decoration of past ages to the Mizner Palm Beach period. As a landscape expert, he had a feeling for the melodramatic botany of Florida and knew how to mount his show places against thrilling backdrops. As an artist, he handled color with bold and attractive effects. As a veteran wit, courtier, and social comedian, he possessed the best qualities of showmanship and salesmanship for recruiting a billion-dollar clientele. Even his hobby of breeding chows had its value. His retinue of high-lineaged pets was part of his scenery and added something to the impression he made on the golden holiday town. His more or less misspent life turned out to be the perfect preparation for his Florida career.

Addison's illness was the result of a boyhood injury. At a Fourth of July celebration in Benicia, in 1888, at the age of fifteen, he was the leader in the childhood ritual of leaping over the dying fireworks. As he landed on the other side, his foot caught in a hole, and all the other patriots jumped on him. He was treated for a sprained ankle, but when his leg turned black, he was found to be suffering from a greenstick fracture. He was operated on repeatedly because of gangrene, and spent about a year in bed. His older brother Henry, later a High Church clergyman, gave him a set of water colors, and Addison spent most of his waking hours painting. It was a law of his nature to scatter his energies and obscure one objective with another; he had to paint with a minimum of motion, because he was utilizing the heat of his body to hatch eggs, and any ill-advised change of position was likely to ruin a lot of unborn chickens. In later life, Addison always surrounded himself with a sort of royal court whenever he had the money to support it, and this taste was probably developed while he was an invalid. One of Addison's Benicia contemporaries has said that it was considered a sort of social triumph to have tea in Addison's bedroom. During his months as a star patient, the spoiled darling of young and old ladies, he gradually became a promising painter, a confirmed prima donna, and an experienced veteran at tea and scandal. His chief aim in life from then on was to shine in society, and his most highly cultivated talent was entertaining fine ladies.

In the twenties, Addison became one of the four pillars of the Palm Beach community, the others being Henry M. Flagler, railroad and hotel builder; Colonel E. R. Bradley, roulette king and civic leader; and Paris Singer, social disciplinarian and patron of the arts. Addison Mizner is mentioned by Dixon Wecter, historian of high life in the United States, as one of our three great society architects, the others being Stanford White and Richard M. Hunt. Addison blossomed late. He had dawdled away most of his life in miscellaneous pursuits. Early in 1918, at the age of forty-five, he arrived in Palm Beach from New York City on a stretcher, suffering from necrosis, lung symptoms, heart symptoms, and a general breakdown. He had, he said, sixty thousand dollars in debts and only a few months to live. In borrowing money to get to Palm Beach, he offered his imminent death as gilt-edged security against bothering his benefactors again. At the winter resort, he fell in with Paris Singer, a wealthy architectural amateur and all-round dilettante, who had also come to Palm Beach to enact a big deathbed scene. The moribund Mizner put in his dying hours sketching gay and beautiful pleasure domes for the expiring Singer. Suddenly, they both got bored to death with dying and decided to turn their energies to building. With Singer's vast sewing-machine wealth to launch him, Addison in a few years transformed Palm Beach from the rich man's Coney Island into a perpetual world's fair of architecture.

For several years, Addison's life in Palm Beach was an architect's heaven. He had the Golden Horde for a clientele and practically no competition. A Wall Street magnate imported Joseph Urban and set him up as a rival to Addison, but Wilson Mizner blasted Urban out of the picture with one wisecrack— "Harry Thaw shot the wrong architect." Some New Yorkers assert that Percy Hammond, the drama critic, invented this well-known line and applied it to a movie palace. In Dallas, they say that Harry Thaw, on seeing a local hotel, exclaimed, "My God, I shot the wrong architect!" There are probably scores of other claimants. But great numbers of Palm Beach people are ready to swear that Wilson first said it of a Joseph

Urban palace and that they circulated it so well that it has since been applied to half the buildings in the world. Addison devoted a large part of his life to the uphill task of trying to reclaim and make something of Wilson. Now and then, Wilson was valuable to Addison.

Addison was not a regular architect. He never attended a professional school or even took a correspondence course in architecture. New York State maintained at one time that he wasn't an architect. A leading Palm Beach architect of the present day has called Addison a quack, adding that he had a great sense of beauty and sometimes produced splendid work. Mizner architecture has been furiously attacked and lavishly praised. Some authorities have classed his Everglades Club, in Palm Beach, and his Cloister, in Boca Raton, among the most beautiful buildings in America. The late Royal Cortissoz, the *Herald Tribune* art critic, previewed Addison's Joshua Cosden house, in Palm Beach, and bracketed it with Kubla's country place in Xanadu. A critic in *Arts & Decoration* paid Addison the pretty compliment of comparing him, with some modest reservations, to Michelangelo and the architects of the Acropolis. Paris Singer, a connoisseur, lived in an apartment designed by Mizner and explained his not living in a Mizner villa or *palazzo* by saying, "Each house that Addison builds is more beautiful than the one before, so I am waiting to get the last of them." Addison received favorable comments from some unexpected sources. Frank Lloyd Wright, who denounced all Washington as seedy and derivative, praised Mizner's work. Harvey Wiley Corbett, one of the Rockefeller Center designers and an enthusiast for the functional skyscraper, said that Addison had a remarkable gift for creating loveliness. Jo Davidson described Addison as an architectural genius, and added that he was even greater as a personality. Davidson and José María Sert, the Spanish muralist, were once guests of Addison in Palm Beach, and the two artists were hypnotized. Under Addison's domination, the painter and sculptor were soon furiously working on sketches for an artistic scheme that was entirely new to them. Addison was creating the paper city of Boca Raton, a happy combination of Venice and Heaven, Florence and Toledo, with a little Greco-Roman glory and grandeur thrown in. He wanted the two famous artists to decorate a theatre that would do justice to the mirage metropolis. Davidson and Sert were to blend their talents; the sculpture and painting were to shade into each other, so that the casual observer couldn't tell the work of the chisel from the work of the brush. The artists surrendered themselves to the experiment, but the busting of the Florida boom annulled this marriage of the arts.

Addison's architecture is usually called Spanish. Alexander P. Moore, once American Ambassador to Spain, on being shown Mizneresque Palm Beach by a member of Addison's staff, declared, "It's more Spanish than anything I ever saw in Spain." Other critics denied that it was Spanish at all. It has been called by many names, adding up to the Bastard-Spanish-Moorish-Romanesque-Gothic-Renaissance-Bull-Market-Damn-the-Expense Style. Rich clients poured scores of millions into Addison's experiments at Palm Beach, and he turned the twentieth-century sandspit into a strange medieval city. His architecture was strictly functional. The typical Mizner client wanted grandeur as an index to his wealth and social position; he also wanted a combined amusement park and country club for his houseparties and other festivities. Addison's massive plaything-houses, formidable but gay, answered the purpose. Lilias Piper, an interior decorator, called him the Hans Christian Andersen of architects; she regarded his work as three-dimensional illustrations for storybooks about enchanted castles, ogres, princesses, and magicians. Addison would probably have preferred to be called the Scott or Dumas of architects, because he tackled his work in the spirit of a historical novelist. He claimed that he invented a cycle of ancient romance, legend, scandal, and tragedy and then designed buildings to go with it. In his wild fancy, he saw his American oil, steel, railroad, chain-grocery, and straight-rye kings ambling about in ancestral halls that their noble Spanish and Moorish forefathers had trodden for generations. He even had men in hobnail shoes walk up and down staircases as the cement was setting, to imitate wear and tear caused by the spurs of knights of Castile and the Holy Roman Empire. He invented a kingdom for himself. His Palm Beach was a Graustark located on the old Spanish invasion route, where the Christians and Moslems fought it out in the Dark Ages. The town lots and subdivisions of Palm Beach and Boca Raton formed the gory background of the Charlemagne epics. Addison's ideal building, as he explained it, was based on Romanesque ruins that had been rebuilt by the triumphant Saracens, added to by a variety of conquerors bringing in new styles from the Gothic to the baroque, and picturesquely cracked up by everything from battering-rams to artillery duels between Wellington and Napoleon's marshals. If the Florida boom had not collapsed, Addison would eventually have summed up a thousand years of Spanish history in one Boca Raton castle, but as it was, he never had a chance to throw more than two or three ages and three or four styles into a single structure. He mixed up his centuries with some caution, always being true to just one period in any one section of a building.

Addison admitted that he took liberties with the Spanish style. A severe building was picturesque in Spain, he explained, because of its contrast with the landscape and skyline, but the flatness of Palm Beach required bolder architecture to give character to a house. He also admitted that he used large, or non-Spanish, windows. The small, high, barred windows prevailing in old Spain were dictated, Addison said, by conditions; they were constructed against bandits, burglars, rioters, guerrillas, amorous cavaliers, and night air. In Palm Beach, however, the policing was good, amorous cavaliers were taken for granted, and night air was recommended by doctors; hence, Addison went in for big windows, light, and ventilation. A slight inconsistency in his reasoning was detected by Mary Fanton Roberts, managing editor of *Arts & Decoration*. She asked why, if Addison was changing the old architecture to fit Palm Beach conditions, he continued to fortify certain houses so heavily. She couldn't see why it was necessary to top off holiday pavilions with warlike arrangements—battlements with notches for the crossbowmen, parapets for pouring down flaming pitch and

molten metal on the enemy, and towers and turrets for domi-
nating the medieval conflict. The big scenes from "Ivanhoe" or
"Macbeth" could be played on a life-size scale in some of Addi-

son's houses. The architect admitted that the editor had caught
him in a flaw in logic. His only justification was that Palm
Beach had become, in his imagination, a stronghold on the

Christian-Mohammedan frontier and that he couldn't leave his clients defenseless. The collapse of the Florida boom prevented Addison from getting into high gear in his military architecture. The house he planned for himself at Boca Raton would have been the most martial of all his fortress-homes. His designs for it included not only oubliettes, hidden staircases, trapdoors, battle towers, and a donjon keep but also a huge drawbridge over a great moat, and Addison said that he was going to post Pop Weed, an aged attendant on his staff, in the high turret to hurl down strange missiles on sightseers and uninvited guests, who were already invading his Palm Beach home in embarrassing numbers.

Addison was a blond giant, six feet two inches tall; he was fat but brawny. When he was approaching middle age and weighed two hundred and fifty pounds, he would startle social gatherings on Long Island by walking up and down the dance floor on his hands. He delighted in showing off his strength by seizing the leg of a moderately heavy chair or table with one hand and holding it out at arm's length. When he was working on his first big job in Palm Beach, he grabbed a bathtub away from two slow workmen, swung it over his back, and carried it into the half-completed building and up the stairs. When he weighed two hundred and fifty pounds, his chest measurement still exceeded his waist measurement. It was only in his later years, when he tipped the scales at three hundred and ten, that he developed a marked bulge. Ordinarily, he was an epidemic of good humor, radiating bonhomie as far as he was visible or audible. Almost without exception, his employees and associates were devoted to him and remained devoted to his memory. For a while, Mizner ran a factory in West Palm Beach, where he produced furniture, tiles, wrought iron, and so on. There was usually a little insubordination at the Mizner plant because each workman considered himself the particular pal of the big boss and had a disdainful attitude toward his foremen and supervisors. Many of the hands at the Mizner plant were Spanish-speaking Negroes. Addison always traded insults with them in Spanish, and this created a fraternal feeling that practically destroyed the authority of subordinate executives, who, not understanding Spanish, were social outcasts. Addison had a big, *bon-vivant* face, with a baby complexion, brilliant baby-blue eyes, and a peculiar expression that combined joviality, authority, childlike innocence, and worldly wisdom. The personality that fascinated Davidson and Sert usually took charge of lesser individuals with ease. For several years, his popularity in Palm Beach was unbounded. He was the outstanding celebrity. He seemed to have almost a legal title to the seat on the hostess's right. He was taken aback on one occasion when he found his accustomed place usurped by a well-fed authoress. There was general raving over the guest's literary talents. "No talent at all," said Addison later. "She ought to be cut up for bait."

Except when talking to a few women he revered and to a few men he disliked, Addison's speech was a lingo he had picked up in the Klondike and on San Francisco's Barbary Coast. He rarely gave offense. His drawing-room conversation was such an artless dance of bad words that he was considered at his winsomest when he was at his bawdiest. "His mastery of Tavern English is a joy to everybody within hearing," wrote Paris Singer. A designer named Alex Waugh, a carefully reared English boy, joined the Mizner staff. He could hardly believe his ears when he was within range of the boss's conversation. While still a new hand, he happened to hear Addison and Wilson discussing a third party. His first thought was that this person must be the wickedest man on earth. He thought that the language of the brothers would inevitably mean bloodshed, or that the miscreant must instantly be dropped from all clubs and party lists—the death penalty in Palm Beach. As the awful words continued, Waugh gradually made the discovery that the Mizner boys were talking affectionately about a dear old friend. He used to wonder why they had to drain all the cesspools of their vocabulary in discussing the beauty of the sunset, the balminess of the weather, the size of a building lot, and other innocent topics. Finally, he decided that the Mizners alone understood the King's English and knew how to make the most commonplace fact sparkle with obscene execration. Addison was to some extent a respecter of persons. Waugh accompanied him on a trip to Spain to buy old furniture, objects of art, and architectural relics. One day, Addison was having an unusually violent bout with stomach ulcers in a hotel in Madrid. The telephone rang. "Tell 'em I can't see anybody," said Addison.

"This fellow insists on seeing you," said Waugh.

"Tell him to go to hell," said Addison.

Waugh did as he had been told and then hung up. A couple of minutes later, King Alfonso burst into the room. "Why, you old son of a bitch!" said Addison. "How the hell are you?" That was pretty formal and respectful compared to the reception Addison would have given an uncrowned intimate.

When Addison was really excited and in need of wild expressions, his flow of language seemed to dry up. When he reached the boiling point, his best effort was "in the name of summer squash." Scurrilities from Addison were generally accepted as encomiums, and he was deeply hurt one day when a pint-size contractor turned on him and called him a fat bastard. After brooding a few days, Addison decided that it was an anecdote with an amazingly comical twist, and began telling it everywhere. The contractor became one of his few trusted confidants.

Addison had uncommon powers and odd weaknesses. He knew his profession at the top and at the bottom but not in the middle. At the high level, he had an imagination that teemed with beautiful façades and interiors, with striking vistas and splendid theatrical effects. At the low level, he was a master artisan, skilled in nearly all the building trades, from carpentry and cabinetmaking to ironwork and plastering. About the middle, or technical, part of his profession, he was strangely defective; he knew little about plans and specifications, stresses and strains. His mind was almost a blank on the sciences to which the architectural student of today is required to devote four or five years. Addison had an eye for beauty, a creative instinct, and a gift for inspiring his craftsmen, but he had to hire other brains for everything between the conception and the finishing touches. His methods gave considerable justification to the charge that he was not an architect but a painter, a façade sketcher, a scene designer. He had an enormous collection of photographs, sketches, and engravings of noble old buildings. When he received a commission, he would mull over his pictures and assemble a set of them; those pictures would be the basis of his new design. His sense of proportion and harmony was rarely at fault; he nearly always selected the right pictures for his purpose. Sometimes the house was strictly a reproduction; sometimes his pictures were simply points of departure. The first part of Addison's work was finished when he had turned out a magnificent set of colored-crayon sketches of the new place; it was up to his assistants and the contractors to work out the construction problems. At the height of his activity, in 1925, Addison said that he was working on a hundred jobs at once, and, according to an assistant, he would sometimes make sketches for two new buildings in a day. After the photographs had been assembled and translated into color drawings, Addison became a word-of-mouth architect. Distrusting blueprints, preferring metaphors to diagrams, he would explain and reëxplain the effects he was seeking to his aides. He liked phrases such as "about so high" or "right about here," rather than exact measurements. He watched the eyes and expressions of his employees to make sure they had the mental picture he was seeking to convey.

"Do you understand it now?" he once asked E. C. Peters, who has since operated a stone-casting plant Addison founded.

"Yes," said Peters hesitantly.

"You're a liar," said Addison amiably, and he proceeded to explain again. He was infallible, according to Peters, in sensing whether a man had a thorough grasp of an idea.

One remarkable phase of Addison's architecture was the expensive dress rehearsals he held at buildings nearing completion. He would dash out to the site, climb all over the walls and scaffolding like a two-hundred-and-eighty-pound cat, ordering costly structural alterations with the casualness of a Broadway play doctor ordering cuts and changes in a script. He caused completed walls to be partly wrecked in order to change the size and position of windows. He rebuilt one tower three times, throwing aside the plans and shouting directions to the bricklayers and masons until the work satisfied his eye. The grimmest and fiercest of all Addison's citadel-villas is The Towers, which he built in Palm Beach for the late William M. Wood, head of the American Woolen Company. Wood had said that he liked towers, and Addison built him a turreted castle that could resist a year's siege. It has a feature that is said to be unique—an immense wood-burning fireplace in a bathroom. Mr. Wood was highly satisfied and declared The Towers to be "a livable home." Addison ripped and tore and rebuilt at a great rate while working on The Towers. "This is going to cost a lot of money, Mr. Mizner," said one contractor, on getting orders for a major alteration. "Listen," said Addison, "these people can't stand the sight of anything that doesn't cost a lot of money." Another contractor who was working on a building for Addison telephoned to New York to William Helburn, publisher of architectural works, in great excitement. He said he was stumped. Instead of furnishing him with plans and specifications, Addison had handed him an architectural book, pointed out a picture of a building on the island of Minorca, and directed him to reproduce a window from the Minorcan house in the wall of a half-constructed Palm Beach edifice. The contractor wanted to know the dimensions of the window, which he couldn't figure out from the picture. Helburn cabled a representative in Spain and had the window measured.

Addison's methods were a surprise to contractors in more than one respect. They were used to architects who made a great point of locating "the center" and "balancing" the building around it. Addison had no centers and he didn't like buildings that balanced. Favorable critics have said that his symmetries were "subtle," "elusive," and "rhythmic;" at any rate, they were not obvious. Addison hated any building that looked like a mathematical formula with a roof on it. He wanted his structures to give the impression that they had evolved from century to century, not that they had sprung ready-made from a blueprint. His first sketches and his final editorial touches were all meant to confound the crude eye that expected the right front of a building to agree with the left front. Addison's dress rehearsals are said to have been especially effective in introducing happy accidents that kept his buildings from smelling of the drawing board. He has been compared to the medieval architects who collected their guilds of artists and artisans about them and relied heavily on the word-of-mouth and trial-and-error technique. Addison told, with a certain amount of glee, one story illustrating his casual attitude toward blueprints. He was building a house, considered one of his best works, for William Gray Warden, of Philadelphia, in Palm Beach. Shortly after construction had started, the client asked if he could have a set of blueprints to show his friends. "Why, the house isn't built yet," said Addison. "Construction first, blueprints afterward" was the idea, like "Sentence first, verdict afterwards" in "Alice." Addison was probably just making an excuse to prevent Warden from seeing the detailed plans, which often inspired a client with suggestions for changes. He never actually tried to get along without blueprints, but he treated them as rough drafts rather than sacred things.

Addison's thirteenth-century, off-the-cuff architecture didn't always work out perfectly. He used to tell, as a joke on himself, how he forgot to put a door in a boathouse he built onto a home on Lake Worth. At the housewarming, his clients glided in on their motor yacht and then found that they had to glide out again, make a landing, and walk back to the house. In building the famous Boca Raton hotel, the Cloister, one of Addison's final impromptu touches was an arched doorway intended to insert some character into one wall; he wasn't bothered by the fact that if you walked through the door, you bumped into the back of a chimney. His medievalism occasionally proved inconvenient to a client. Pipes would sometimes burst. One client exclaimed "Damn that half-witted genius!" when he was told that an entire wall had to be torn out to locate a leak, since the layout of the pipes was not in the blueprints. Perhaps the best-known charge against Addison is that he forgot to put a staircase between the first and second floors of a house. George S. Rasmussen, a wealthy Midwest grocer, came to Palm Beach from Chicago to see a house Addison was building for him. He was surprised to find no staircase, and asked the contractor about it. "The plans don't call for a staircase," said the contractor. Hugh

Dillman, former president of the Everglades Club, has said that the Chicago man's story was that Addison was annoyed at himself for the oversight but resolutely refused to spoil the beauty of his rooms with an interior staircase, so he built one on the outside of the house. This caused no particular hardship in balmy weather, but the Rasmussens had to put on raincoats to go up and down stairs on rainy days. The painting contractor who worked on the house said that Addison had planned it that way. The architect was greatly taken, according to the painter, with an Old World castle that had an exterior staircase and no interior one, and he decided to experiment with this device at the expense of the Chicago grocer, whom he didn't like anyway. The disputed staircase is an ornate hanging structure of wrought iron, partly enclosed by masonry to protect the Rasmussens from the arrows of the Saracens. The effect is impressive. It looks more like carefully planned work than a trick to cover up forgetfulness.

Addison's taste was faultless, according to Alex Waugh, who said that all examples of over-ornamentation in Mizner architecture were the follies of the people who hired him. When in good health and spirits, Addison was able to overawe or kid his clients out of their odd inspirations. Waugh was with the architect when a wealthy couple came to him with the idea of substituting an ornate staircase for a simple one. Addison tried to impress on them that the room was one of austere elegance, and that a fancy staircase would be completely out of harmony. "It would look like a whore at a christening," he said.

It was only when Addison was suffering from his ulcers that he allowed clients to spoil his work. When the ulcers tormented him, he would attempt to subdue them by excessive eating. He loved rich food and rich sauces. In fighting ulcers, he would have enough food for three men heaped up before him on a silver platter that a Guatemalan dictator had presented to his father in 1890, and he would ram down great quantities, like a fire chief smothering a fire. His usual dessert was ice cream, which he had specially made for him because the caterers didn't make it rich enough. He would cover the ice cream with ginger, which he imported from China in blue glazed jars, and shovel in helping after helping until the ulcers were ready to say uncle. He always kept a box of bicarbonate of soda on the dining-room table and would take a spoonful now and then as he ate. At times, this treatment would confound the enemy, and Addison would appear next day at the top of his form. At other times, the ulcers would rally and return to the attack. A contractor was in Addison's office one morning at eleven o'clock for a conference with Addison and a Palm Beach queen who had ordered a Mizner house. Addison arrived, dishevelled and wan, in a bathrobe. "How are you, Addie?" asked the client. "Oh, dearie, terrible," said Addison. "I feel as if I'm about to give birth to a litter of horned toads." On days like this, Addison would say yes to anything, and his clients could mess up his best work with their worst whims. One day, a painting contractor was doing a room in a house Addison had designed for a rising Palm Beach hostess. She told the contractor that she had some ideas of her own, and that she was going to tell Addison about them. The contractor happened to know that the ulcers were in the ascendant, and he sped to the architect's office in his car. "She's on her way," he said. Addison told his secretary to say he was out for the day. "It would kill me to talk to her," he told the contractor. He said that the great lady was a former chambermaid who had hooked a senile multimillionaire. A great lover of gossip, Addison was beginning to tell the startling details of the romance when high voices were heard in the outer office. "She's here," said the contractor. Addison jumped up, rushed into an inner office, and hid in a shallow closet. The client burst in. Addison had been unable to close the door on his huge proportions, and three or four inches of his stomach were visible. "Don't you hide from me, Addie!" cried the client. Addison emerged. "Dearie, we were just discussing you," he said. He gave in without argument to all her architectural inspirations.

Before going to Florida in 1918, Addison had practiced architecture in New York without a license. The Florida law required that an architect pass the Florida examination or prove that he had legally practiced architecture in some other state. The New York authorities refused to admit that Addison had ever legally practiced architecture in their state, but in 1919 Phelan Beale, Addison's New York lawyer, succeeded in obtaining a license "by exemption"—meaning that Addison had been exempted from taking an examination for a license, because of proof that he had done satisfactory work before examinations became compulsory. That gave Addison the green light, as far as Florida was concerned. But in 1930 he wanted to practice in California. The California law recognized architects from other states who had obtained licenses by examination but not those who had obtained them by exemption, so Addison had to go up to Tallahassee and face an examination by the Florida State Board of Architecture. He was scared to death, according to one of his assistants, Byron Simonson. The great man had dotted the enchanted island of Palm Beach with masterpieces, but he couldn't pass the most elementary examination in his profession. Although cultured to his fingertips, he couldn't compete with a seven-year-old schoolboy on any academic topic. He couldn't add or subtract, and he had long before given up the struggle to spell. When he made longhand notes, he would make a wild stab at the first syllable and represent the others by a long dash. His employees had to figure out that "foun–," "wane–," and "bal–" meant "foundation," "wainscoting," and "balustrade." With such shortcomings, plus his illiteracy in the scientific side of architecture, Addison had reason for consternation when he heard that the Florida examination lasted two days and ran the candidate through a savage gantlet of technical questions. Seeking to smother the State Board of Architecture under an avalanche of documents, Addison shipped several hundred pounds of sketches, paintings, blueprints, and other data to Tallahassee. He braced himself for a frightful ordeal, but it turned out to be a pleasant experience. He exhibited some of his sketches, explained his methods, and was recorded as having passed a Senior Examination—the first of its kind in Florida. The secretary of the board wrote that the examination "confirmed the opinions of the board members that, while Mr. Mizner had no formal educational training as an architect, he had a happy faculty of combining the illustrated works of other countries with the draftsmanship of his associates to bring about a most pleasing and successful architectural renaissance which suited the Palm Beach taste of the period." Before he left Tallahassee, however, Addison did face a technical examination. At a luncheon in his honor, he treated profound and intricate matters that went right to the heart of the science—how the hell you land a multimillionaire client, how you get to be a great society architect, how you put over a two-hundred-thousand-dollar house on a client who only wants a fifty-thousand-dollar one. Early in his Palm Beach period, Addison looked on business-getting as the chief of the seven branches of architecture, and he regarded salesmanship as a form of poetry. He was the first to hear of it when a socially ambitious matron with a silo of money arrived in Palm Beach. The most accidental of meetings, some lyrical conversation on the glories of Old Spain, a personally conducted tour of Miznerland, and Addison would soon be heaving and hacking at the new bank roll. A contractor making a late call on Addison about an emergency was startled to see him in a dinner jacket. As he had never before seen the architect in anything except ravaged working clothes, he mentioned the transformation.

"I'm going fishing," said Addison.

"In that outfit?" demanded the contractor.

"These are my fishing clothes," said Addison. "I do my fishing at the swell parties. Tonight I'm going to land a whale of a contract."

Addison was adept at egging on feuding social leaders to fight it out with Mizner architecture, and he stirred up terrific duels in which great ladies delivered tremendous blows with new Moorish patios and frescoed porticoes, only to receive savage counterthrusts in the shape of neo-Byzantine loggias, baroque staircases, and colonnaded orangeries. Architecture has been described as frozen music; much of Addison's architecture was solidified social ambition. The secretary of the State Board of Architecture reported that Addison had told of "somewhat lurid and almost unbelievable experiences in getting clients and 'satisfying' their somewhat unique desires in an atmosphere such as was Palm Beach in the days of the Florida Boom."

One principle of the profession on which Addison had the strongest possible grasp was the ancient architectural triangle—wife, architect, and injured husband. The wife is usually the aggressor in matters of residential architecture. She is born with the instinct for creating a home. In a place like Palm Beach, the instinct runs wild, and a hummingbird wants to build a roc's nest. It often takes infinite patience and tact to overcome the misgivings of the male. Addison's extraordinary social prestige and his hypnotic eloquence were sometimes invaluable in causing a husband to put a reluctant pen on the contract. Addison was a wizard at proving that it was an economy to spend two hundred thousand dollars instead of a hundred thousand dollars and at comforting a client when the final bill was four hundred thousand. He was an honest architect. He played no unethical games, such as taking kickbacks from contractors. In fighting against his natural enemy, the husband, he was, however, capable of hitting below the belt. In one case, the wife wanted a big, eye-filling mansion; the breadwinner wanted a modest one. He was in the money and not worried about costs, but he just didn't want people to think that he was a pretentious fellow. Addison sketched a house; the husband was worried about its size. Addison then got his assistant Byron Simonson to do a trick landscape showing how the house would look in its environment. Part of the environment was a cottage on a neighboring property. The cottage was exaggerated to vast proportions; the proposed new house was drawn on a reduced scale. It flattered the husband's modesty, and he signed the contract. It is stated that after his house was built the old gentleman would walk about, gazing at his own palace, then peering at the neighboring cottage, then scratching his head in a dazed way.

Success finally went to Addison's head, and he discarded his early business-getting ideals. He quit going to parties, except for an occasional royal-command affair. He rejected one big commission because of a difference of opinion about roofing materials. Alleging ill health, he refused to design a costly church for the Baptists of Jacksonville. When he received a letter saying that the congregation was praying for his recovery, he exclaimed, "I'll have to build it in self-defense," and he set to work designing a handsome Spanish and Byzantine edifice. Addison was the architect of houses for Harold Vanderbilt in Palm Beach and for George Vanderbilt in Biltmore, North Carolina, and Mrs. William K. Vanderbilt, Jr., commissioned him to build a Palm Beach house for her. She annoyed him by changing her mind two or three times about one small detail, and Addison told her in the crudest of terms that it was time for her to make a decision. For once, his choice of language was not regarded as quaint and charming, and the deal for the house was cancelled. According to one interpretation, Addison's arrogant methods were in reality business-getting arts, since his fame was brightened by tales of how he had slapped down big names and kicked around great American fortunes. Others think that Addison liked to make scenes, and that at the height of his success he felt he could afford to make the biggest possible scenes with the biggest possible people. He didn't like the client, or "the sucker," as he sometimes called him, to have ideas of his own. In an interview with John Taylor Boyd, Jr., a writer on architecture, Addison once said that he envied the doctor because he had the sense to throw the patient on the operating table, clap a cone of chloroform over his nose, and go to work without interference.

Chapter Three

THE SILENT TOUCHES OF TIME

K ID MC COY (Norman Selby), a prize-ring sensation of two generations ago, was instrumental in launching Addison Mizner on his architectural career in Palm Beach. It was the Kid who, in a roundabout way, inspired Addison to build the Everglades Club, the first masterpiece in his Saracen-Spanish style. The courts and galleries, tower and dome of the Everglades Club started an aesthetic revolution. Lorenzo the Magnificents were a dime a dozen in Palm Beach in the twenties, and most of them wanted to mount themselves in the new Addison Mizner settings. The publicity wizard Harry Reichenbach pronounced Addison "the Aladdin of architects." Mizner imitators appeared in swarms. Florida broke out with "the Spanish itch," which grew into a national affliction. Addison was mortified by his own vogue. He used to avert his face when he motored past other architects' lollipop-colored stucco houses that were said to belong to the Mizner school.

Kid McCoy was innocent of any intention of foisting neo-Spanish on America. He became mixed up with some startling personalities in Palm Beach and unwittingly created an emotional crisis that took the form of a new style of architecture. The Kid, a startling personality himself, was the original "real

McCoy." The phrase was coined by a San Francisco sport in 1899, when the Kid defeated Joe Choynski shortly after Joe had knocked out an old-time gladiator named Pet McCoy. A hero for a while, the Kid began to lose favor when, after a syndicate of gamblers had bet large sums that he would fold up in the fifth round of a fight with Jim Corbett, he did happen to fold up in that very round. Quitting the ring for the theatre, McCoy became, literally, a road-show Barrymore. Lionel Barrymore played Kid Garvey in "The Other Girl" on Broadway; McCoy played Kid Garvey on the road. The part was a lifelike picture of McCoy himself. Augustus Thomas, who wrote the play, said that he had originally called it "The Parson and the Prizefighter" but had dropped the name when a storm of protest against coupling the two professions came pouring in from prizefighters. Barrymore tried, in building up the part of Kid Garvey, to imitate the irresistible McCoy smile and the irresistible McCoy dimples, the Kid being one of the champion lady-killers of the era, with nine legal wives and a moderate-sized nation of sweethearts. After leaving the stage, the Kid became a drawing card for cafés and gymnasiums. Addison Mizner went to Palm Beach for his health in 1918, and McCoy was established there a little later as physical instructor at Gus's Baths. It was no social degradation to be connected with Gus's Baths; an authentic Italian count handed out the towels there. The Kid was working hard with his physical-culture classes and trying to mind his own business when he found himself entangled with some cyclonic characters and accidentally boosted Addison to greatness.

Paris Singer, the iron-fisted social dictator of Palm Beach and the great patron of Addison Mizner, was deeply involved in the Kid McCoy imbroglio. Singer, one of the youngest of the twenty-four children of the sewing-machine magnate Isaac Merrit Singer, was the last of the universal men—an artist, athlete, scholar, scientist, art patron, sports patron, philanthropist, and amateur in architecture, medicine, and music, with approximately a million dollars a year to finance his various roles. He became the master of the revels at Palm Beach when, before the First World War, after ransacking the world for radiant health and gorgeous sunsets, he settled in the Florida resort in the conviction that it was supreme in both departments. Paris was named after the city of his birth; his mother, Isaac's third, and last, wife, was a Frenchwoman. The family lived in England for a time. While still in knee pants, the boy, who was evidently born with a wonderful property sense, went to a British judge with a hunch that his mother was mismanaging his estate, and he was made a ward of the British Court. The Royal Family interested itself in the wellheeled waif, and Paris was practically raised in Buckingham Palace, where he came to look on Queen Alexandra as his royal stepmother. As a young man, he was a glittering figure—six feet three inches tall, of fine physique, handsome, highly educated, with a Court of St. James's air and a nest egg of fifteen million dollars. He became a liberal patron of worthy young poets, artists, playwrights, and soubrettes. Occasionally ambition seized him, and he hurled himself at professional studies. He steeped himself in architecture until splendid edifices and stately cities ran out of his pen. Dedicating himself to the search for a compound to abolish all diseases, he swallowed a new drug called aspirin in such quantities that for a time his life was despaired of. Deserting art and science for beauty, he became a celebrated international Romeo. Any disappointment in a romantic matter always caused him to console himself with architecture. A tiff was enough to start him on a villa or a harbor improvement. A broken heart inspired a project for a great medical-research institute, but a reconciliation cancelled it.

The heroine of Singer's epic romance was the celebrated dancer Isadora Duncan, who describes Paris in her autobiography under the name of Lohengrin. Paris and Isadora carried on for more than a decade over three or four continents and as many oceans. Only hearsay to the younger generation, Miss Duncan was, according to high contemporary authorities, the greatest of artists and the most volcanic of personalities. She communicated enthusiasm like a Mohammed. She apparently adored Paris Singer, both as a man and as a meal ticket. In her autobiography, she said that she spotted him at their first meeting as the ideal multimillionaire of her girlish dreams. He sank a fortune in her tours, cultural projects, artistic academies, and expensive gestures of all kinds, and she was as true to him as was compatible with the absolute freedom of spirit that was her ruling principle. At times, they bickered ideologically; she was a radical and he was a faithful Plantagenet in politics. Their chief differences arose, however, over her enthusiasm for handsome young fellows. She had a weakness for prizefighters, according to John Dos Passos. Mary Desti, one of Isadora's biographers and close friends, wrote of scolding her for flirting with a chauffeur. "He's a Greek god in disguise," explained Isadora. The dancer said that she had upset Paris Singer on two occasions, once because she forgot to scream when a French poet lost his head, and once when Paris found her teaching a beautiful Argentine youth one of the cozier versions of the tango. Now and then, Singer would get out his blueprints and for a while love would play second fiddle to architecture, but he usually wound up by making amends to Isadora with a rich gift. He loved to surprise her with rich gifts. One day, he surprised her with the old Madison Square Garden. He planned to remodel it into an arena for her art, but for some reason the Garden failed to please the tempestuous dancer, and Singer lost two hundred thousand dollars, which he'd put up as an option on it. The curtain was finally rung down on the world-famous romance when Isadora, during a vacation in Palm Beach, happened to catch a glimpse of the handsome physical instructor of Gus's Baths. Paris, returning to Palm Beach from a business trip, discovered that Kid McCoy not only had ousted him from his place in Isadora's heart but had formed the habit of throwing big champagne parties and charging them to Paris Singer's account. The sewing-machine heir told the dancer that he was discarding her forever. She retorted with an Irish curse guaranteed to make him lose all his money. He called in Addison Mizner and started to build and build and build. He didn't stop until the skyline and landscape of the enchanted isle were completely changed. The new Palm Beach—the Golden Littoral, as Joseph Hergesheimer termed it—was Paris Singer's substitute for Isadora Duncan.

The Palm Beach Mizner and Singer devised was acclaimed as one of the wonders of the world. Some of Addison's critics contended, however, that he owed a good deal to luck. They asserted that the third-rate architecture of early Palm Beach would have made any moderately good architect look like a Sir Christopher Wren. The big wooden hotels were examples of the house-of-correction, or Blackwells Island, period. The pretentious cottages were lace valentines in wood, belonging to the jigsaw school of architecture. Aside from the landscaped areas surrounding the funny hotels and funny cottages, Palm Beach was still a stretch of sand, swamp, and jungle, of which a few small acreages were under cultivation. The place had a curious evolution, which was important in preparing the foundation for the brilliant work of Mizner and Singer. The permanent settlement of the little sandbar started in the seventies, when blizzard-swept Middle Western farmers began reading articles and pamphlets picturing Florida as an inexpensive, steam-heated paradise. *Harper's* of October, 1870, described the carefree life of a farmer whose Garden of Eden had cost him less than a nickel an acre. Literature of this kind incited M. W. Dimick, an Illinois patriarch, in 1875 to lead three generations of his family out of the snow and ice to settle on the unnamed island that later became Palm Beach. Four members of the original Dimick migration are still valuable, living items in Florida's Fountain of Youth publicity. The conquest of Palm Beach was not all fun and frolic. The subtropical wilderness was particularly tough to clear for farming. The food problem, however, almost solved itself. Five-hundred-pound turtles of excellent flavor volunteered themselves for the Dimick table. Facing Lake Worth, the lagoon between Palm Beach and the Florida mainland, the Dimick house was within a few feet of some of the finest fishing waters in the world. According to Ziska, a Florida correspondent of the New York *Sun* in the seventies, it was sometimes difficult to navigate a small boat through what seemed to be an almost solid mass of fish. Fresh-killed venison could be had from the Seminoles for a few colored beads. Mrs. Belle Enos, of West Palm Beach, the youngest member of the Dimick colony, still recalls hunts in which men and boys blew horns and pounded tin pans to drive the bears into open spaces, so they could be shot. Bear steak was an ordinary article of diet, and bear fat a substitute for cooking butter.

Panthers, alligators, rattlesnakes, mosquitoes, fleas, and red bugs were the worst enemies of the Palm Beach colonists. Hurricanes were their greatest friends. Destroying quantities of shipping and washing a great variety of items ashore, a hurricane was practically a mail-order house to the Swiss Family Robinsons of Palm Beach. Drygoods, canned goods, salt, meat, furniture, and even cookstoves came riding in on the surf after a big blow. Ziska called on Charlie Moore, an old sailor and professional beachcomber, whose Rag Castle, the first Palm Beach estate with a name, was built and furnished largely with flotsam and jetsam. Over the door of Rag Castle, which was about twelve by twelve, was a sign from a ship's lifeboat that read, "Certified to Accommodate 36 Seamen." Built into two gables were a full-breasted lady and a mythological serpent—figureheads from wrecked ships. The old sailor's favorite beachcombing prizes were a small sawmill and a packing case full of women's underwear. The *Sun* man wrote that the settlers along the southern Florida beaches used to thank God for His goodness when a vessel sank but that they had recently taken to grumbling about the poor quality of the wrecks and they suspected skippers of scuttling empty hulks in order to rob insurance companies. The section was in great need of a couple of honest wrecks, according to one Floridian interviewed by Ziska. The *Sun* listed some of the merchandise from a disappointing disaster—two hundred gross of razors, several thousand yards of printed calico, five hundred pairs of women's stockings, and a hundred sticks of whisker pomade. The correspondent told of a "bull-driver," or cowboy, who had traded a mare for a hundred and twenty-five pairs of shoes, a peck of buttons, a bushel of spool thread, and a pint of fishhooks. The better grade of catastrophe was often looked on as an immediate response to the prayers of the faithful. A lady whose pioneer home became the site of a great Palm Beach hotel said that seven barrels of lard came ashore after pious settlers had begun to hint that the supply of cooking fat was running low. As soon as the oil shortage was pointed out, the beach was dotted with cans and drums of kerosene. Divine Providence was reminded that the rain barrel had gone to pieces; a large iron cistern came floating in with the tide. The biggest Palm Beach party that any hurricane ever threw was a sequel to the wreck of a Spanish ship with a cargo of sherry. The most important of all the wrecks was that of the Providencia in 1879, a misfortune that paved the way for the grandiose future of Palm Beach. The Providencia sank while sailing from the West Indies to Spain with a cargo of coconuts, thousands of which floated up on the sands of Palm Beach. Settlers planted them, in the hope that a coconut crop might prove a source of income. In a few years, the coconut groves were the pride of the island. In the early nineties, Henry M. Flagler, scouting a couple of hundred miles of the southern Florida coast in search of the best site for a smart winter resort, chose Palm Beach because of the graceful and lovely skyline of its coconut plantations.

Flagler, the biggest man in Standard Oil next to John D. Rockefeller, Sr., had discovered Florida on a vacation, and he started building a railroad and hotel chain that eventually reached Key West. Towns and cities, citrus groves and winter-vegetable farms sprang up in Flagler's footsteps. Drifting southward in his wake came wealth, society, anglers, invalids, heiress chasers, gamblers, confidence men, real-estate men, and Methuselahites. The city of St. Augustine became, after it had been Flaglerized, the high-society and the con-man capital of the United States during the winter season. Flagler put his magic touch on Ormond, and it became a center of high life and, for a time, one of the most flourishing green-goods and gold-brick headquarters in America. Flagler called St. Augustine the Winter Newport on the American Riviera when he opened the Ponce de Leon Hotel there in 1889. In 1894, he moved Newport and the Riviera a couple of hundred miles south, to Palm Beach, where he opened the Royal Poinciana, a gigantic wooden box holding about thirty billion dollars' worth of population.

The great early settlers of the Flagler empire were the invalids. Chronic sufferers had discovered southern Florida before, in the pre-Flagler days. Taking care of suffering Northerners was one of the earliest occupations in the Palm Beach region. It became a fixed idea that all visitors were "sick Yankees," and the Flagler hotels were at first regarded as colossal infirmaries for the ailing rich from the North. The business of taking boatloads of vacationers out fishing was known as "haulin' sick Yankees." Tom Wallace, editor emeritus of the Louisville *Times,* said that the established Floridians in the nineties regarded all non-Floridians as "sick Yankees." No matter how healthy a man might look, the fact that he came to Florida proved that he was sick. Even if he had a strong Southern accent, he was still classed as a "sick Yankee;" the Floridians ignored the Mason and Dixon Line and divided the South from the North at Jacksonville. Georgians, Alabamans, Virginians, and Carolinians were "sick Yankees," just as if they came from Maine or Vermont.

Flagler rapidly mastered the secrets of the hotel business. He had the big spenders of America falling over one another to get to Palm Beach when they learned they could pay as much as a hundred dollars a day for a double room at the Royal Poinciana. He opened still another immense wooden hotel for the aristocracy—the Palm Beach Inn, later the Breakers—in 1895. Some solid justification was built into the phrase "the American Riviera" when Colonel E. R. Bradley started the Beach Club, the most celebrated gambling hell in the New World, near the Royal Poinciana. Flagler, a typical Standard Oil puritan, was dismayed, and vainly offered Bradley three hundred and fifty thousand dollars to move elsewhere. Veteran lawyers of Palm Beach County say that Flagler at one point threatened to close his hotels in order to wipe out gambling, but he was frightened into silence by a counterthreat to indict him for promoting a lottery at a church fair—a nefarious felony under the Florida statutes. Bradley finally succeeded in convincing Flagler that you can't have a Riviera without having a Monte Carlo. The hotels and the casino settled down to existence on a mutually profitable basis. "All the world goes to our little principality of Monaco," said *Town Topics.* Karl K. Kitchen, the *World* columnist, wrote, "The real reason for the popularity of Palm Beach is not its climate or its hotels; it is Bradley's." Flagler felt some remorse, but he finally made peace with his conscience by building a chapel at the Royal Poinciana and hiring an eloquent preacher to knock games of chance.

A ticket to Palm Beach was believed, with reason, to be a free pass to society. The conditions there were perfect for social climbing. Palm Beach was high life in a boarding house. It is hard to keep the castes separate when they live, eat, and sleep under the same roof. Boarding-house politics were favorable to climbing. Women of modest social standing were eager to become social leaders. To become a leader, it is necessary to have followers, and nearly everybody was welcomed into the retinue of one rising young boarding-house queen or another. Partly because of the heiresses and other big game, Palm Beach was peculiarly rich in imported swells, and my-lording and your-gracing reached new peaks. "We've had more titled people in Palm Beach than were ever concentrated in one spot before," said John Holliday Perry, Sr., a Florida publisher. Magazine writers complained of the upstarts. According to one, some of the hostesses in flaming tiaras had only recently made the leap "from the washtub to diamonds." Colonel William d'Alton Mann, a moralist with a delicate streak of larceny, disapproved of the wild gambling and the vulgar display, but he was forced to recognize Palm Beach as an outpost of the Four Hundred. In his *Town Topics,* Colonel Mann scolded females who played roulette in public and sneaked into the dressing room at Bradley's to puff cigarettes. He reproached women for coming down to breakfast at the Royal Poinciana in cascades of jewels, counselled duchesses against wearing their coronets to the West Palm Beach prizefights, and censured Mrs. George Gould for distributing jewels as tips to the hotel help. "On every side," he complained, "one hears the jingle of money, and in all the 1,600 rooms of the Royal Poinciana that sprawls for a quarter of a mile of Florida, nothing counts but lucre." He asserted that J. Pierpont Morgan quit the place because of the constant twittering about lucre. Objecting to any relaxation of the caste system, he criticized countesses for exchanging repartee with the colored hotel employees, denounced the Duke of Manchester for awarding the prize at a waiters' cakewalk contest, and arraigned thoughtless young dudes for allowing themselves to be seen at the lifeguards' ball.

Henry James, who visited Palm Beach in 1904, described it as "a hotel civilization." It was also a yacht and private-railroad-car civilization. The nearest thing to a real aristocracy in America was the private-car peerage, and Palm Beach had the world's most snobbish railroad yard—a Newport-on-wheels, an exalted trailer camp for the gold-encrusted Pullmans of the New World nobility. An occasional Midas arrived in Palm Beach by a special train. August Belmont and a couple of friends once completed the trip in the cab of a locomotive, which was chartered at Jacksonville after Belmont's car developed wheel trouble. The greatest of the barons had yachts as well as private cars, the most talked of being Pierre Lorillard's, which was said to carry a small herd of Jerseys to provide fresh milk for the guests, and Isaac Emerson's, which had a huge wood-burning fireplace on the deck. The patent-medicine aristocracy came into its own in Palm Beach. The best-known men in America were the discoverers of sovereign remedies, pink pills, and painkillers. Their whiskered faces appeared daily in their advertisements at a time when presidents and kings had to be shot at in order to get their pictures in the papers. Years of display advertising caused the discoverer and the discovery to become merged in the public mind, and in Palm Beach the princes of science were always named after their cures and compounds. Dr. Pierce and his sloop were both familiarly referred to as Golden Medical Discovery; Dr. Kilmer was Swamp Root, and so was his yacht; Dr. Fletcher was Castoria, and so was his launch. The wife of the headache-and-morning-after king became so accustomed to being identified with the hangover powder that, according to *Town Topics*, she would beat strangers to the draw by saying, "I am Mrs. Bromo-Seltzer Emerson." There was considerable excitement when a distinguished-looking marquis began besieging the charming widow of Little Liver Pills. One of the pillars of Palm Beach was Dr.

Munyon's Remedy, a pleasant old gentleman who owned Munyon's Island, just north of Palm Beach. The custom of naming men after their products extended to other lines of endeavor. A. T. Snider and the yacht in which he followed freshly ripening tomato crops over a twenty-five-hundred-mile itinerary were both known as Snider's Catsup; Adams, the chewing-gum magnate, and his boat were both Tutti Frutti; Francis Marion Smith, celebrated for his Twenty Mule Team Borax, quit Palm Beach in anger, according to *Town Topics*, because he was persistently called Borax.

Fishing was the chief sport, but not far ahead of bicycling, which was at the height of its popularity when the Royal Poinciana opened. Many men wore cycling caps, sweaters, tight-fitting knee pants, and stockings, and the brains that ran the country were wildly bobbing up and down over handle bars along the Palm Beach bicycle paths. Franklin Leonard Pope, the ace bicycle manufacturer, was one of Palm Beach's biggest celebrities. There was some shooting; herons, pelicans, and other water birds were fired at with rifles from the decks of yachts for the sport of seeing them fall; pigeons, so tame that colored boys had to throw coconuts at them to make them fly, were targets for shotguns at shoots. Drinking was light in comparison with what went on in later decades, but one long corridor in the Royal Poinciana was known as Hypocrite's Alley because reputed teetotallers, the pillars of Northern communities, were always double-quicking along it on the way to the bar. Swimming, golf, and croquet were important pastimes. Literature was represented by the Fortnightly Club, one of whose programs consisted of an essay by a clergyman on the evolution of clothes and the recitation by the authoress of a poem called "She Confesseth Cupid's Secret." A Browning Society came along later, but literary inquirers found that the members chose that name because they were in the habit of browning themselves in the sun on the roof of the Breakers. There was a donkey-drawn streetcar between Lake Worth and the ocean, but most of the travelling was done in two-seater wicker chairs built into tricycles, which were pedalled by Negroes. These vehicles were equipped with lanterns at night; *Town Topics* reported that they were "conducive to tender sentiment." The favorite ride was to Joe's Alligator Farm, to see Joe wrestle with his tremendous reptiles. Another popular ride was to Melville Spencer's truck farm and citrus grove, which had a genuine windmill. Hotel guests invaded the farm in chattering swarms, according to Henry James, to congratulate Spencer and his family on their peace, quiet, seclusion, and privacy.

Flagler died in 1913, but the Flagler period continued in Palm Beach until 1919, when Addison Mizner and Paris Singer started to remake the town physically and socially. For twenty-five years before Paris took charge, Palm Beach had been getting its values mixed up. The old aristocratic ideals had gone to hell. Men of leisure were not what they used to be. Loafers with impressive family names were hardly superior to wealthy, free-spending, self-made fellows. Society was practically run on the merit system; people got into it by the sweat of their brows. After Addison and Paris had built the Everglades Club, Paris reformed all that. He owned the Everglades Club outright. The Everglades Club was Palm Beach society. Thus, Paris owned Palm Beach society outright. He was in a position to make or unmake society people at will; it was merely a matter of regulating his own household. Singer's system of running the club was devised to keep society riding on his coattails all the time. He allowed nobody to belong to the club on a permanent basis. Every club card expired at the end of the season, and whether a member got back into the club and into society the following year depended solely on Paris Singer's caprice. Everybody was kept on the anxious seat by this system of perpetual probation; nobody could draw a breath of aristocratic air except through Paris Singer's bounty. He thinned out Palm Beach society ruthlessly. He dropped one woman for laughing out loud, and threatened to drop a great Newport celebrity for daring to intercede for her. Colonel Bradley had developed into a philanthropist, racing-stable owner, and social lion, and was considered the grand old man of Palm Beach; Singer was outraged when Bradley was suggested for membership in the club. "A professional gambler

in a gentleman's club! Never!" he exclaimed. He dropped people
for getting into scandals, forgetting that he was himself a hero
of one of the scandals of the century and that he and Isadora
had once been bounced from the Royal Poinciana. He dropped
people for the disgrace of being "in trade," forgetting that he was
a despicable commercial character himself; he had manufactured
electric automobiles and concrete ships in England, and was
now deeply involved in Palm Beach real estate. Singer was delighted when A. W. MacDougall, the Everglades Club manager,
brought news that a world-famous jeweller had rented one
of the Singer properties. "That's splendid," said Singer. "You
know, I was a friend of his father, who was a great artist. In fact,
I brought him to the attention of Queen Alexandra, and he
made some exquisite pieces for her." MacDougall suggested that
the world-famous jeweller be invited to join the Everglades
Club. Singer's face fell. He twisted his mustache and shook his
head sadly. "Why, you know," he said, "his father came into
Buckingham Palace by the servants' entrance. These people are
servants. They're in trade."

Singer was never wholly successful in keeping trade and
scandal out of the club. Captains of industry and ambassadors
of commerce managed to sneak in. It was even harder to sift the
women than the men. At one Everglades reception, a vibrantly
beautiful woman turned pale at the sight of Wilson Mizner
and then greeted him with hysterical effusiveness. Arthur
Somers Roche, the novelist, later asked Wilson about the incident. "Confidentially," said Wilson, "the last time I saw her,
she was crying in a police station in New York after being arrested for rolling a drunk." In spite of some shortcomings, the
reign of Paris Singer was widely regarded as the most glorious
chapter in Palm Beach history. Many veterans of the resort look
back on the Paris Singer days as the golden age when the plebeian and the bourgeois were put in their places and severely
kept there.

In earlier life, Addison had not greatly distinguished himself
as an architect, but when the door of opportunity was opened
to him by Paris Singer, he jumped through it with frantic en-

terprise. The conditions during and immediately after the First World War made it impossible for Addison to obtain technical experts or architectural materials; he therefore set up his own workshops, where he taught craftsmanship to local workmen. Addison made a Spanish-wrought-iron expert out of the village blacksmith of West Palm Beach. Because of the impossibility of getting ornamental cast stone, Addison, assisted by Dayton J. (Pop) Kort, a painting contractor, became a pastry cook, baking powdered rock and glue in a back-yard oven and racing the hot mixture to an icehouse to make it solidify in a mold. The Everglades Club had been planned by Paris Singer as a hospital for wounded officers, but art and architecture gradually superseded patriotism. With both Singer and Mizner having new visions and inspirations every few days, the place began to be more of an Alhambra or a Midway Plaisance than a hospital. The increasing elaboration of the plans made it impossible to complete the structure until a year after the war was over, and it was decided to let the veterans recuperate somewhere else, so the projected nursing home could become the most iridescent of international peacock alleys.

One reason for the brilliance of the place was that for twenty years Paris Singer had collected beautiful old tiles from ruined buildings around the Mediterranean. One day, a party of Tunisians entering the lobby of the Everglades Club instantly assumed attitudes of worship. The explanation was that Singer's yacht had happened to touch the coast of Tunisia when an ancient mosque was being demolished, and he had bought several tons of sacred decorations from it. Over the years, he had acquired such quantities of magnificent old glazes that their weight broke the floor of a warehouse in West Palm Beach. Addison made dazzling use of ancient tiles in his pavements, courts, fountains, galleries, and portals. Developing an architectural style that called for the lavish employment of ceramics, he started to bake his own hand-dipped tiles; he built an amateur kiln, the chimney of which collapsed twice in the early stages of operation. He hired common laborers and taught them how to mold wet clay against their thighs to shape roof tiles in the

Spanish manner. He had to teach hollow-tile wall construction to men who had never seen hollow tiles and mistook them for skunk traps. Palm Beach artisans couldn't ever get used to Addison's Old World effects. Pop Kort argued in favor of painting some exterior woodwork that Addison had ordered stained; Kort contended that paint was necessary for protection. "To hell with protection!" said Addison. "I want effect." One workman couldn't see the sense of running an ornamental iron rod from a balustrade to the ceiling of a hall. "It's the first time I ever heard of putting a lightning rod on a staircase," he grumbled. Masons thought that it defied common sense to erect columns with large capitals and small bases, and they built them upside down at first. Addison hated anything that looked new or machine-made. In one structure, the roof tiles were being laid too symmetrically to suit him. Finding two men who had never laid a roof tile in their lives, he said, "You're the men I want. Hustle up the ladder and lay those tiles." A proud roofing contractor threatened to brain anybody who tampered with his work; Addison waited until the contractor had departed, cracked up the tiles with a sledge hammer, and had the broken pieces cemented together to give the roof a seen-better-days look. He practically bought out drugstores in his search for chemicals that would give a mellow, time-honored appearance to the gold dome of the Everglades Club. The club cesspool was the worst problem of all. It couldn't be built in an excavation; the site of the club being at water level on the shore of Lake Worth, any hole that was dug immediately became flooded. Addison hit on the idea of casting the cesspool in cement on dry land, sinking it in Lake Worth, and filling in around it; the great tank slid smoothly into the water, but instead of sinking it cruised around Lake Worth like a concrete ark, and had to be captured, towed back, and scuttled.

Other things went wrong. Not being completely familiar with the nature of Spanish roof tiles, Addison had arranged them in such a way that they conducted smoke from the kitchen all through the interior of the building, and the table linen became covered with a black snow. As world conditions made it impossible to furnish the club with actual old Spanish furniture, Addison fabricated ancient Spanish chairs. He used quicklime to antique the leather seats and backs. The quicklime refused to wash out, so he covered it with shellac. The morning after the housewarming of the club, Addison said to Kort, "We're in serious trouble, Pop. I spent the whole night pulling dames out of those goddam chairs, and half their gowns are sticking to the chairs now." Owing to the heat of the bodies and of the quick-lime, the shellac had softened, and the sitters found themselves stuck in the leather like figures in a high relief. In spite of fail-ures and fiascoes, Addison finally learned enough to organize the Mizner Industries, Inc., which supplied furniture, tile, terra cotta, cast stone, wrought iron, carved wood, stained glass, and other equipment for scores of Mizner houses.

Nobody was more enthusiastic over the Everglades Club than Mrs. E. T. Stotesbury. Pop Kort, who was along when Addison showed her over the building, said that she kept repeating, "Oh, Addie, it is beautiful, beautiful." Addison was the fashionable architect of America as soon as he had Mrs. Stotesbury's stamp of approval. She was the greatest of the Palm Beach institutions. According to upper-class historians, she had had a hard time hacking her way into society in her home town of Philadelphia, but she had been the leading hostess of Palm Beach since the time of McKinley. Her nickname was Queen Eva, and gossip writers of forty years ago said that being able to address her as Eva was enough to raise a woman socially from sea level to a moderate elevation. The Washington's Birthday Ball was the great event of the Palm Beach season, but Washington's Birth-day was gradually eclipsed by E. T. Stotesbury's Birthday. Old E. T., a partner of J. P. Morgan & Co., was, like many other Palm Beach husbands, a dignified hole in the atmosphere, the invisible hand that wrote the checks, but once a year, on his birthday, he was allowed to receive recognition as a member of the human race. The old gentleman went wild with excite-ment at having his existence acknowledged, and he always enter-tained his guests by beating a drum and singing "The Old Family Toothbrush That Hangs in the Sink." On the three hundred and sixty-four other days of the year, E. T.'s chief function was paying the biggest architectural and entertainment bills in the country. In 1916, Mrs. Stotesbury built her hundred-and-fifty-four-room Philadelphia house, Whitemarsh Hall, now the laboratory of the Pennsylvania Salt Company. Whitemarsh Hall was designed by Horace Trumbauer, then the leading architect of châteaux, villas, and mansions in the United States. Mrs. Stotesbury was so pleased with the great Trumbauer that she commissioned him to design a winter palace for her in Palm Beach. The plans were drawn and approved, but they became wastepaper when Queen Eva saw the Everglades Club. King Horace went into the discard, and King Addison reigned. El Mirasol, the Stotesbury mansion that Addison built at Palm Beach, is still one of the imposing architectural exhibits of the island. Mrs. Stotesbury entertained guests there by the hundreds; according to the New York *Times*, she once borrowed eight footmen from friends to assist her own forty-nine servants in handling one of her big affairs. There were servants to wait on servants in the Stotesbury ménage, and Karl Kitchen, the columnist, reported that among the features of El Mirasol was a reception hall for the chauffeurs of Mrs. Stotesbury's guests. One of the gems of interior decoration was the boudoir library, where Queen Eva worked every morning on her archives, studying a complete file of photographs of her jewels, gowns, shoes, and headgear, so that she could decide on the four or five outfits that were to be worn during the day. People were breathless about the façades, the interiors, and the landscaping of El Mirasol. As the royal architect of the Court of Stotesbury, Addison entered on a career of money and glory.

Addison altered the business as well as the social landscape of Palm Beach. With the backing of Paris Singer, he bought Joe's Alligator Farm and replaced it with Worth Avenue, Via Mizner, and Via Parigi—a shopping district that still collects its share of the world's loosest pocket money. As his prestige grew, Addison dominated not only the architecture but the art, furniture, and interior decoration of Palm Beach. His whims and hobbies became the fundamental laws of aesthetics. Addison was an antiquarian, a lover of the rust and decay, the wear and tear of the ages. "Pop, I want to make this look a thousand years old," he told Kort as he used a bucket of burning tar paper to smoke up the ceiling of the first house he built for himself in Palm Beach. "Take it away! Throw it away!" he shouted when he saw a lot of modern furniture that had been sent to Mizner Industries, Inc., for repairs after a hurricane. Addison didn't, of course, mind faking "the kiss of centuries" and "the silent touches of time" when he couldn't get hold of the real thing. He loved fine old worm-eaten timber for his ceilings, and if he was short of venerable beams, he used pecky cypress—the pitted and riddled surface of ancient cypress trees. Addison would plug up the holes with crimson, azure, lavender, and other pigments and then scrape the stuff out, to produce the effect of deteriorated magnificence. "Bert," said Addison one day to Albert Ives, a young architect who had recently joined the staff, "do you want to see how we antique a room?" Addison drove him to the Joshua S. Cosden house and took him to a newly frescoed dining room, a copy of a room in the Davanzati Palace, in Florence. Using Flit guns, several workmen sprayed the painted plaster walls with condensed milk and then gave the damp surface a rubdown with steel wool. This treatment was repeated several times before Addison was satisfied that he had the faded and melancholy tone of the late fourteenth century. He liked to give a room a good soot bath, and pointed out that the people of the Middle Ages smudged things up to rich, sombre hues with lamps, candles, open fireplaces, and charcoal-burning braziers. Addison outraged the feelings of many fine craftsmen by his defacing of their work in the interest of antiquity. The head of Addison's stonecutters thought his boss had gone crazy when he seized a sledge hammer, cracked up a handsome mantelpiece, and ordered him to get the fragments plastered together; Addison explained that he wanted the mantelpiece to convey a sense of the earthquakes, riots, rebellions, and bombardments of several centuries. A contractor claimed that one of his wood carvers quit on the spot when Addison took a large penknife and started to inflict a few centuries of damage

by whittling away detail from the carvings on an oak door.
Robert Ellis, a cabinetmaker, was putting the finishing touches
on a room in a Palm Beach mansion when Addison came in
with a hammer, knocked the nose off a grotesque stone dwarf
by the fireplace, and then knocked off the long, turned-up toes
of the little figure. Seeing Ellis's astonishment, Addison said,
"You see, this house is supposed to be four or five centuries old.
Hundreds of cords of wood have theoretically been carried into
this room and dropped by this fireplace. Now, it's perfectly obvious that that long nose and those curled shoe tips must have
been broken off long ago." Any glaring color offended Addison.
A room in one of his mansions was ornamented with sculptured
and painted figures of celebrated ecclesiastics. Their vestments
were too vivid to suit Addison, and he ordered them smoked
and sandpapered. Visiting the room a couple of days later, he
pointed a disapproving finger at one historic prince of the church
and said, "That son of a bitch's hat is too red." In one of Addison's workshops, brand-new furniture was scarred, bruised, and
acid-bitten into antiquity in a few hours. Men rubbed it with
broken beer bottles, then battered it with chains attached to a
stick, then painted it with chemicals to give it the complexion
of ages past. Fresh-made chairs and benches were planed and
filed to simulate erosion by the plush flanks of generations of
Castilian noblemen. The wormholes in the Mizner furniture
were usually jabbed in with an icepick, but Wilson, a perfectionist, insisted on shooting them in with a Daisy air rifle. Showing two friends over the antiquing factory, he gave them air
rifles and set them to popping away at a dining-room set. "Don't
shoot straight at it!" shouted Wilson. "Shoot from the side. Remember, a worm always charges at a piece of furniture from an
angle."

Addison lived for only brief periods in three of the houses
that he built for his own occupancy. He was practically dispossessed from the first by Harold Vanderbilt, who insisted he
must have the house and finally got his way by offering a colossal price. Addison's next two homes went to other wealthy people by the same process. His fourth, and last, house was a

massive square structure, five stories high, joined, by a bridge
over Via Mizner, with his architectural offices. Karl Kitchen
said that Addison spent more than three hundred thousand dollars furnishing it. The living room was forty by forty feet, and
had a twenty-foot ceiling. The place, rattling with Spanish
armor and rich with Spanish art, was maintained as an open
house and was always swarming with friends and sightseers.
Addison was on public exhibition nearly all the time, but he
nevertheless acquired the reputation of being a mysterious and
eccentric old bachelor. He deliberately made a zoo of whatever
establishment he was in. Albert Ives has told of the confusion
that Addison threw his office into when he came in, preceded by
two chows, with a small monkey named Ethel on one shoulder, a
macaw named Agatha on the other, and leading two large monkeys, Deuteronomy and Johnny Brown, who jumped on the
drawing boards and began throwing plans around. These formed
only one department of the Mizner menagerie. He had to be
surrounded by pets, selected impartially from the human race
and the animal kingdom. He did his best work with macaws
screaming, monkeys chattering, and his favorite human companions rattling off the lowdown on the latest Palm Beach
scandals. Addison had been mad about animals since 1889,
when his father was United States Minister to five Central
American states. His first monkey, which was also named
Deuteronomy, came to an untimely end at a waterfront reception in Costa Rica when it jumped from Addison's shoulder to
seize the plumes on a Latin-American general's hat and was
knocked off the pier with a trombone. Grace von Studdiford, the
light-opera star, sued Addison for four thousand dollars, alleging
that his monkey Mikko had wrecked all the art and bric-a-brac
in her New York apartment when Addison was calling on her.
Addison's second monkey named Deuteronomy made the trip
from New York to Palm Beach in a private railroad car with
Marie Dressler and Isabel Pell for nursemaids. Marie Dressler,
who became a house guest of Addison's, once found her bathtub
occupied by a chow and half a dozen newborn puppies. Addison's best-known pet in Palm Beach was Johnny Brown, now

buried in a patio in Mizner Alley under a slab with the inscription "Johnny Brown, the Human Monkey." Johnny Brown was famous for, among other things, his feud with Miss Dressler and for following the milkman around in the morning in order to jab his thumb in the necks of bottles for the fun of seeing the milk spurt up. Addison had two anteaters in Palm Beach; an earlier anteater of his had broken into print in San Francisco in 1890, when it bit a friend of the Mizner family. Addison's Palm Beach pets included, at one time or another, an otter, a raccoon, and a denatured skunk.

E. Harris Drew, one of Mizner's lawyers, said that his client had a historic effect on men's wear as well as on architecture and interior decoration. Living in China and the South Seas for long periods during his early life, Addison became addicted to Oriental dress. Wallace Irwin, the poet, as he was learning to drive a car on Long Island three or four decades ago, knocked down a gigantic mandarin in silk pajamas and tasselled hat, and was startled when his old San Francisco pal Addison jumped up, shouting, "Give me back my pound of flesh!" When Addison lived in Port Washington, he depopulated the streets on Saturday mornings, modest women fleeing at the sight of a man shopping in his pajamas. But his great contribution to the American wardrobe grew out of his going around Palm Beach with his shirttails sticking out. Too bulky to fit an ordinary automobile, he drove around in an old stripped-down White, perched on a bucket seat with his shirttails fluttering behind. He attracted attention at movie theatres by carrying a Flit gun to kill mosquitoes and wearing his shirttails out. In the early twenties, these things shocked Palm Beach. The winter colony was still conservative in dress. Lawyers, merchants, and the rest of the year-round population always wore the conventional professional-mourner attire and never dreamed of taking off their coats in public. Addison had become the great star of Palm Beach, and his example gradually set a new style. Palm Beachers experimented with leaving off their coats, then with discarding their neckties, and then with leaving their shirts unbuttoned at the neck. Then some haberdashery stylist came along and completed

the trend toward Addisonian informality by slashing off part of
the shirttails, putting a neat hem at the bottom of the garment,
and calling it a sports shirt. The style spread from Addison to
Palm Beach, and from Palm Beach to the rest of the world.

Chapter Four

THE SPORT

WHEREAS ADDISON MIZNER had many ambitions, Wilson Mizner seemed to have none. Conversation was Wilson's hobby, profession, and neurosis. His fame as a wit has grown steadily since his death, at the age of fifty-seven, in 1933. Although he wrote practically nothing, he is probably quoted more than any other American of this century. His chance remarks have been organized into a literature by his disciples. Like the character in Stendhal who became a noted wit on the strength of six or seven pleasantries inherited from an uncle, scores of men have won recognition as sparkling conversationalists because they have made small private collections of Mizner sayings.

Shortly before he died, a publisher asked him to write the story of his life. "It would be blowing a police whistle," replied Mizner. This was a reasonable excuse. The crime chapters would have occupied a large part of his autobiography. He was fundamentally a confidence man whom circumstances occasionally induced to go straight. But his real reason for refusing to write an autobiography was that he hated to write; he said, "Writing is too damned lonesome." He regarded it as an occupation for starvelings. Jim Tully once badgered him into writing a short story, which appeared in the *Liberty* of May 3, 1930. Mizner received a check for $1,000. He was incensed. "It took me eight hours to write it!" he exclaimed.

The short story is rather poor, although it contains a few typical Mizner lines. After a description of the long, tapering fingers of a cardsharp named Bert, Mizner added that Bert "could do more with fifty-two soda crackers than any other ocean grafter could with a new deck." The last paragraph of the story describes a tombstone erected over the grave of the hero, showing him kneeling, with hands clasped in prayer; the last line is "If you pried his hands open, four dice and a pearl necklace would fall out." Mizner was a little shamefaced over his literary effort. "I wanted to see something of mine in print except my thumbs," he said.

As a wit, Mizner belonged to two distinct schools—the scientific and the O. Henry. His scientific method consisted of bringing a calm spirit of inquiry to bear on boiling emotion. When an excited man rushed up to him exclaiming, "Coolidge is dead," Mizner asked, "How do they know?" The O. Henry school was the school of fantastic exaggeration. During Mizner's formative years, smart conversation consisted mainly of tired hyperboles. A majority of the familiar quotations from Mizner are extravagant figures of speech. He described a thin man as "a trellis for varicose veins." He told a conceited motion-picture producer, "A demitasse cup would fit over your head like a sunbonnet." Regarding a long-nosed Hollywood magnate, he said, "He's the only man who can take a shower and smoke a cigar at the same time" and "I'd like to take him by the feet and plow a furrow with him." Telling of a Klondike pal who had frozen to death in the act of tying his shoelaces, he said, "We had to bury him in a drum." A strutting little fellow went through bankruptcy and then strutted more than ever. "Failure has gone to his head," said Mizner. Describing his own flight from a madman armed with a revolver, he said, "I got up enough lather to shave Kansas City."

A man with a flourishing head of hair once joined his table at the Brown Derby restaurant in Hollywood, uttered several solemn platitudes, and left. "Now I know," said Mizner, "that hair can grow on anything."

A famous stage beauty, who had risen by five marriages to wealth and a title, attempted to bandy insults with him. "You're nothing but a parlayed chambermaid," he said. "You've compromised so many gentlemen that you think you're a lady," he added.

Talking about Tom Sharkey, the great heavyweight prize-fighter, who kept a saloon with the old-fashioned swinging doors, Mizner said, "He was so dumb that he crawled under them for two years before he found out that they swung both ways."

He disapproved of San Francisco at the time when Hiram Johnson was sending grafters to jail in large numbers. "They learn to say 'Guilty' here before they can say 'Papa' and 'Mama,'" he said.

He was asked by Lew Lipton, stage and screen writer, if a certain actress wasn't a little "mannish." "Mannish!" he said. "Not at all. I understand it took her all winter to color a meerschaum pipe."

Many of Mizner's lines have passed into the language. Some, like "Life's a tough proposition, and the first hundred years are the hardest," are passing out again after long and hard service. His rules "No opium-smoking in the elevators" and "Carry out your own dead," which he put into effect as manager of the Hotel Rand, in New York, in 1907, have become standard hotel practice. Among his philosophical maxims were "Be nice to people on your way up because you'll meet 'em on your way down," "Treat a whore like a lady and a lady like a whore," and "If you steal from one author, it's plagiarism; if you steal from many, it's research." H. L. Mencken, in his New Dictionary of Quotations, attributes to Mizner "I respect faith, but doubt is what gets you an education" and "A good listener is not only popular everywhere, but after a while he gets to know something." Mizner's comment on Hollywood, "It's a trip through a sewer in a glass-bottomed boat," was converted by Mayor Jimmy Walker into "A reformer is a guy who rides through a sewer in a glass-bottomed boat" and has since become a shopworn jewel of stump oratory. Two of Mizner's thirty-year-old lines have recently had revivals in the movies. A magistrate asked him if he was trying to show contempt of court. "No, I'm trying to conceal it," muttered Mizner. A friend argued that a certain Broadway producer "must have a head" to be so successful. "They put better heads on umbrellas," said Mizner.

"I may vomit," the smash line in "The Man Who Came to Dinner," is a Miznerism. Mizner was seated at his regular table at the Brown Derby in Hollywood, when a young stranger introduced himself as a novelist and said he had a big idea. The trouble with Hollywood, he said, was lack of literary conversation. He asked Mizner to join him in founding a club that would meet an evening or two a week for literary conversation. "Have I offended you?" asked the author, noticing the expression on Mizner's face. "Do you want me to leave?" "No, but you might move over a little," said Mizner, adding the statement that went so big on Broadway.

Among his miscellaneous lines are "You sparkle with larceny," "He'd steal a hot stove and come back for the smoke," "You're a mouse studying to be a rat," "Another pot of coffee, waiter, and bring it under your arm to keep it warm," "I've had better steaks than this for bad behavior," and "If you [a radio chatterer] don't get off the air, I'll stop breathing it."

Mizner usually avoided slang, although he had a few special words of his own, such as "croaker" for "physician," "heart trouble" for "cowardice," and "trap" for a "bank." He disliked puns, although a play on words was worth about $10,000 to him on one occasion. It made a jury laugh and saved him from a verdict for damages. After the Florida real-estate crash, a man had sued him to recover the purchase price of a barren plot, asserting that Mizner had falsely informed him that he could grow nuts on it. "Did you tell the plaintiff that he could grow nuts on the land?" Mizner was asked. "Oh, no," he replied. "I told him he could go nuts on it." He perpetrated a sort of physical pun once when playing poker with a man whose credit was not too good. The man threw his wallet on the table and said,

"I raise five hundred dollars." Mizner pulled off a shoe and threw it on the table. "If we're betting leather, I call," he said.

The earliest recorded example of Mizner wit belongs to the scientific school. He was in Nome, Alaska, in 1900. One of Mizner's close pals there was Willus Britt, who later managed Jimmy Britt, Stanley Ketchel, and other fighters. Willus was devoted to a lady known as Nellie, who was as notorious in the Arctic as Chicago May ever was in Chicago. One night, Willus ran out of the Northern Saloon and emptied his revolver at a stranger, who escaped in the darkness. Tradition, which always steals anecdotes from lesser men and pins them on the famous, erroneously states that Tex Rickard did the shooting. The best authorities, however, say it was Britt who fired at the stranger. Everybody wanted to know why he was shooting at the man. "He insulted Nellie!" shouted Britt. The shooting did not excite Mizner. The explanation did. "He *what?*" exclaimed Mizner. "He insulted Nellie," repeated Britt. "For God's sake, *how?*" inquired Mizner.

Howard Emmett Rogers, the playwright, was a friend of Mizner. Their acquaintance started with Mizner's quietly

raising a point of fact in the middle of a stormy scene. Rogers and
a man named Bert Sennigs had an apartment together over the
famous Jack's Restaurant, on Sixth Avenue, a couple of decades
ago. Under their agreement, each had the exclusive use of the

place on alternate evenings. On one of his nights, Rogers arrived with a party and found the door bolted on the inside. He pounded until it was opened. There was a wet sheet over the doorway and a strange odor in the apartment. Sennigs stood there with an opium pipe in his hand. On a couch, a famous Ziegfeld star lay asleep, with her head in the lap of a tall, large-headed stranger, later identified as Mizner. An anonymous fourth party lay asleep on the floor. Rogers, who was a little under medium height, raised himself on his tiptoes and howled. He showered abuse on his roommate. Sennigs tried to explain that he had got the nights of the week mixed up. Rogers shouted him down.

Mizner, taking no notice, went on preparing an opium pill for smoking. The ravings continued. Mizner finally looked up and asked, "How tall are you?"

The stranger's calm request for knowledge came so unexpectedly that the indignation of Rogers was sidetracked. He answered automatically, "Five foot seven and a half."

"Well," said Mizner, "you're the most unreasonable little five-foot-seven-and-a-half son of a bitch I ever saw."

Mizner had a vast first-hand criminal erudition, which he commercialized as a dramatist on Broadway and a screen writer in Hollywood. At various times during his life, he had been a miner, confidence man, ballad singer, medical lecturer, man of letters, general utility man in a segregated district, cardsharp, hotel man, songwriter, dealer in imitation masterpieces of art, prizefighter, prizefight manager, Florida promoter, and roulette-wheel fixer. He was an idol of low society and a pet of high. He knew women, as his brother Addison said, from the best homes and houses.

His formal underworld education began in his youth on the Barbary Coast in San Francisco, where he took up opium-smoking as an occasional pastime. After his years in the mining camps of Alaska, he continued his schooling in the New York Tenderloin, and got a final polishing in London, Paris, and the steamship lanes. He acquired the gold-rush psychology in Alaska; his idea of the good life was one bonanza after another. His greatest strike was a $7,500,000 widow whom he married in 1906, but he abandoned this rich claim because he lacked the patience to exploit it. After gaining and dissipating several minor fortunes, he won paper wealth during the Florida boom. He rejected an offer of $1,250,000 for his holdings; a little later the Florida crash left him penniless. After that, he became a Hollywood hack, with an interest in the Brown Derby on the side. "Turned traitor to vagrancy at fifty," he said.

Mizner was born in 1876. He was only the second most distinguished citizen of Benicia, the first being John C. Heenan, the Benicia Boy, heavyweight champion of America. Heenan's fight with Tom Sayers, at Farnborough, England, in 1860, is described by the Encyclopædia Britannica as "still the most celebrated prizefight of modern times."

Wilson Mizner was born in a house that had been shipped in knockdown condition around Cape Horn in the early gold-rush years. The Mizners being the great family of Benicia, Wilson was steeped in feelings of grandeur from childhood and always looked down on others from a towering height. He curried favor with nobody except suckers whom he was planning to fleece. Because he respected nothing and nobody, he was able to give his wit unlimited play. With all his raffishness, he had a superiority and independence of spirit, like that other disreputable aristocrat, Sir John Falstaff, who sharpened his wit on princes. A noncommercial comic, Mizner never pandered to public taste. Will Rogers, a good man who liked everybody and humored the entire population, wrote hundreds of thousands of words and is remembered for little except "All I know is what I read in the papers." Mizner, a bad man who despised nearly everybody and wrote almost nothing, put hundreds of lines into circulation. Mizner had other advantages in addition to contempt for the public. Humorous writers comment chiefly on topics and events that go out of date almost immediately; Mizner commented on human behavior, which does not become outmoded. Mizner specialized in exposing himself, so he had an ever-ready and vulnerable butt for his wit. He had one further advantage; using the oral medium, he could freely coin phrases for which rival wits, using the printed medium, would have gone to jail.

A large-headed, spindle-shanked boy during his Benicia days, Wilson was described by Addison as wearing a No. 7 collar and a No. 8 hat. Even at this period, he had a genius for getting into trouble with schoolteachers and the village authorities, but he always emerged triumphant because of the glorified status of his family. When he was thirteen, his privileged place in the world was recognized by international law when his father was appointed Minister to five Central American republics. The law of nations forbade the arrest of any member of the family for anything except murder. For the rest of his life, Mizner had a sort of subconscious belief that treaties had been entered into by the nations of the world authorizing him to commit anything except capital crimes. His only conviction—for running a gambling house in Mineola in 1919—came as a terrific shock because of his lifelong assumption that he was a man to whom the statutes didn't apply. Although sentence was suspended, he took the conviction to heart. He was so grateful to Al Smith for pardoning him and restoring his rights of citizenship that he named the Brown Derby in his honor.

The family returned to California after two years in Guatemala. Mizner's enjoyment of diplomatic immunity had given him too strong an I-do-as-I-please spirit for school discipline. After being expelled from softer institutions, he was sent to Santa Clara College, famous for changing young hellhounds into saints. Mizner caused a panic at Santa Clara by tying a steak to the rope of a fire gong after curfew, the alarm being sounded when the meat attracted the attention of the large dogs that roamed the campus at night to encourage students to stay in their dormitories. He was expelled for heating a cannon ball for several hours and then bowling it from a fire shovel along a corridor. He correctly forecast that the severest disciplinarian on the faculty would rush out and pick it up.

The elder Mizner died at about this time. For a while, Mizner enjoyed an allowance of $150 a month from the estate. He had already developed expensive tastes, and he made both ends meet

by gambling, borrowing
from his mother, and working at strange occupations.
He was always able, in a
pinch, to produce a gush
of tears and silver by singing old-home and inno-
cent-childhood songs in re-
treats on the Barbary Coast.
From time to time, he visited mining camps in Cal-
ifornia, Nevada, and Col-
orado, both as a prospector
and as a gambler or useful
man around a hot spot. He
boxed professionally a few
times. For a year or so, the
telegraph wire was his life-
line, but finally a request
for $100 brought from his
mother the reply "I didn't

get your telegram." This was intended to spur Wilson to feats of
industry, but, according to Addison, it caused him to become the
house guest of a girl named Belle.

When Wilson was about eighteen years old, he was hired
by Dr. Silas Slocum's travelling medicine show in the Northwest.
Having learned to speak Spanish fluently in Guatemala, he won
the respect of Dr. Slocum and the medicine-show audiences as
a Latin scholar. Years later, in telling this chapter of his life,
Mizner said that Dr. Slocum's best-seller, next to his combined
panacea and elixir, was a magic pill for expectant mothers that
insured that the contemplated child would be a boy. Dr. Slocum
kept careful records. He returned to the places where his pills
made a high score and avoided the places where they failed.

From 1897 to 1902, Mizner was on the Klondike River and
then in Nome. One season with the pick and shovel cut his
weight from 218 to 168 pounds. That was his last stretch of

hard physical work. For a time, he was scales clerk, weighing the gold dust with which miners paid for drinks and settled their gambling debts, at the famous establishment of Swiftwater Bill, who founded his fortune by cornering the egg market along the Klondike. Mizner also staged prizefights and dramas, making a particular hit with his presentation of "Uncle Tom's Cabin," with lavish Eskimo-dog effects. He devoted himself in the main, however, to poker.

The primary authority on the Klondike chapter of the life of Mizner is Sid Grauman, proprietor of the famous Egyptian and Chinese Theatres, in Hollywood. Going to the Klondike as a boy, Grauman sold newspapers from the States for a living—a dollar-fifty apiece in Dawson City and two dollars on the creeks, where deliveries were made by dog sled. The price was always paid in gold dust poured from a tomato can into scales, and as the miners made it a point of pride to give good measure, the newsboy made a little extra on each sale. He once took in $3,200 in three days.

In Nome, Grauman lived at McQueston's Hotel, which was operated by Mizner. The rate was two dollars a night for a stretch of canvas; stretches were hung three deep on the walls. The newsboy's attitude toward Mizner was one of profound hero worship, inspired partly by the fact that Mizner had the only private bedroom in McQueston's, that he had an individual pitcher and basin, and that he owned a private gold-monogrammed comb and brush. After becoming friends with his hero, Grauman won the privilege of using Mizner's comb and brush, the only ones in the Klondike that he would trust. Miners out of luck were employed as bedmakers. They were a fastidious set. They were ready to face the animal kingdom in the form of bears or wolves, but man after man resigned rather than cope with animated nature at McQueston's. Mizner solved the servant problem by inventing a method of making a bed with a walking stick, which enabled the bedmaker to remain at a distance. Mizner, who seldom spoke well of himself, used to be effusive in his own praise when he described this invention. He also boasted that he had the finest library in the Klondike, consisting of a table and a powerful kerosene lamp, which made it possible to read the finest seams.

Sometimes weeks passed before Grauman received a shipment of newspapers. The Spanish-American War was on and the Klondikers were crazy for news. Once, when a dog-sled shipment arrived, Mizner offered Grauman twenty-five dollars for the first paper, provided no others were sold for forty-five minutes. Grauman accepted, but regretted the bargain. Mizner filled an empty store with miners at fifty cents a head and read the news aloud to them. The newsboy stuck to his bargain, although he believed himself ruined. It turned out to be a good investment, however. Mizner's reading merely whetted the community's appetite for news and Grauman was soon sold out. Then Mizner gave him seventy-five dollars, half the proceeds of his show. According to Grauman, Wilson's purpose in giving the reading was to be the center of attention, to have hundreds of men hanging on his every word.

Mizner acted the part of big brother to the young newsboy. Once, when his papers were weeks overdue, Grauman was broke and hungry. Mizner invited him to a dinner of bear steaks at seven-fifty each. When they had finished, Grauman ducked out quickly at the suggestion of his host, who, it turned out, was also broke. Mizner casually asked the proprietor to charge it. He escaped with bruises and lacerations.

Grauman is a first-hand authority on the most romantic episode of Mizner's life. Wilson was in love with Nellie Lemoyne, a beautiful young woman, according to Grauman and others. Her nose had an attractive tilt, and because of this feature, she was called Nellie the Pig by miners, who had a limited stock of metaphors and used words for identification rather than as compliments. Nellie was courted by Mizner and Swiftwater Bill Gates, the only two men in the community who wore detachable collars. She was an honest working girl, earning a living by selling bits of chocolate the size of a finger end for a dollar apiece.

Whenever his papers were overdue, Grauman used to hear an imaginary dog sled coming up the road. He would hurry out into the cold to meet it, but he was apt to be disappointed scores of times before his papers actually arrived. On one occasion, the illusion of an approaching dog sled was so vivid that he sat down on a box outside and tried to peer into the distance through the Arctic night. As he waited, a man came out of the hotel. It was Mizner. Grauman was on the point of speaking, but stopped; Mizner was putting a black mask over his face, and the newsboy judged that it would be bad etiquette to interrupt. The mask adjusted, Mizner took a revolver out of his pocket and entered a restaurant. A few minutes later, he emerged with the cash register, threw it away without opening it, and ran. Grauman followed him to the Second Class Saloon, the most popular resort in Dawson City at the time and the only one that had a real mahogany bar. Mizner, having disposed of his mask, started singing "Sweet Alice, Ben Bolt." The place was soon shaking with sobs. Mizner was on his second or third encore when the hue and cry arrived from the scene of the holdup. Because of the build of the holdup man, Mizner was under suspicion. The miners crying their hearts out gave him an ironclad alibi.

Grauman knew it was bad manners to ask questions. He might have controlled his inquisitiveness if it hadn't been for the fact that it had obviously been a noncommercial holdup. He felt that he had to know why Mizner had disdained the contents of the cash register. He finally told Mizner that he had witnessed the holdup. Mizner was indignant. He assumed that the newsboy wished to be declared in. After being set right on this point, Mizner explained. He was in despair because Nellie the Pig preferred Swiftwater Bill to him. Finding that Nellie was out of chocolate, he wanted to give her some as a love token. The only chocolate in Dawson City was owned by the restaurant man; he refused to sell it, because he wanted to keep it for his regular customers. So Mizner held up the place. He failed, however, to get the chocolate, which had been locked up in the safe in order to reserve it for the chocolate-drinking clientele. Feeling that the case against him would be strong if it appeared that the robber was only in search of chocolate, Mizner carried out the cash register to confuse the trail.

In spite of this chivalrous crime, Mizner failed to win the heart of Nellie the Pig. Swiftwater Bill married her. He also, according to the histories of Addison Mizner and other Klondike authorities, married her two sisters. The literature is silent on whether the marriages ran consecutively or concurrently. Klondike custom sometimes followed Stevenson's definition of marriage as a friendship recognized by the police.

Chapter Five

THE KLONDIKE

DAMON RUNYON called Wilson Mizner the greatest man-about-town that any town ever had. He was referring to the period when Mizner was Broadway's leading wit and one of Broadway's successful playwrights and confidence men. But years before that Mizner had been the greatest man-about-town in Dawson City and Nome. He was the world's foremost authority on the hot side of the frozen north. Nobody was ever snugger and cozier than he was at sixty below zero. The star writers of the Arctic school—Robert W. Service, Jack London, Rex Beach, and others—raved about the snowscapes, the glittering stars, and the aurora borealis. Mizner liked the crackling wood stoves, flickering candles, and smoking kerosene lamps. The literary artists painted the lonely immensities of the great outdoors. Mizner mixed with the gang in stuffy interiors. "Flesh beats scenery," he said. The average Yukon literary artist found that the Arctic was God's Country, and then ducked out as quick as he could. Mizner found the place overrun with crooks, con men, fugitives from justice, cardsharps, adventuresses, and sporting ladies, and stayed there six years.

Like most men who make laughter the main object in life, Mizner was somewhat given to exaggeration. But while he liked

humorous exaggeration, he disapproved of solemn exaggeration. He had a lifelong contempt for Arctic fiction, with its supermen and superdogs, its abysmal brutes and exquisite ingénues. There may have been a touch of sour grapes in his attitude. Some of those who knew Mizner intimately believed that deep down inside he thought he could have been the chief of the entire literary mob if he had abandoned himself to the sad business of writing. Fifteen years after the death of Jack London, Mizner still got indignant at hearing him praised. London skipped through the Yukon in a season or two and had eighty-eight short stories and novels to show for it; Mizner was there for six years and had nothing but smoking-room anecdotes to show for it.

Mizner was a stern debunker of the Arctic literary tradition. Jack London had taught the world that the Yukon had some magic that turned ribbon clerks and ladies' tailors into ferocious primordial monsters. "The truth is," said Mizner, "that most of the fellows up there were the worst sissies on earth. I was in court when two hundred of them were robbed of their claims by a crooked judge and a set of thieving politicians. Did they string up the judge, as the forty-niners would have done? Did they tear the politicians limb from limb? No. They just sat there crying into their beards. Then they slunk back to their cabins and had to be treated with smelling salts."

The noblest characteristic of the land of ice and snow, according to the writers of the Northern Lights school, was the undying loyalty between pal and pal. "Nothing whatever to it," said Mizner. "I never knew the meaning of ingratitude until I had one of those Arctic pals. I had faith in that man. He made the first set of burglar's tools ever turned out in Alaska. I elected him chief of police. I paid his expenses, managed his campaign, organized a reception for him the day he took office, and pinned a gold star on his shirt, and the first man he arrested was me. At that time, there was only one typewriter in town. Somebody had stolen it and sold it to a butcher, who thought it was a cash register. Three friends of mine were in danger of being put away for life. We needed the typewriter to draw up the appeal, and in the emergency I borrowed it from the butcher shop when the butcher was out. My new chief arrested me. That is the comradeship of the North."

Another doctrine of the God's Country literature was that commercialism was unknown up there on the roof of the earth and that manhood was the only thing that counted. "On the contrary," said Mizner, "everything was on a sordid cash basis. For example, Jack McCloud was cleaned out in a poker game at Tex Rickard's Northern Saloon, in Nome. There was some gossip about the honesty of the game, and McCloud decided to kill Rickard. I carried his message—'Come out, and come out smoking'—to Tex. Tex grabbed his gun. Then he paused and reflected. He said, 'Tell Jack I can't afford it. Here I'm worth three hundred thousand dollars and he's broke. I won't stack up three hundred thousand dollars against nothing. It ain't business.' I went back and repeated the message to McCloud. He reflected a few moments and then nodded his head. 'Tex's right. It ain't business,' he said. Here was a wronged man with revenge in his heart, but the standards of commercialism were too strong for him. He went off to the mines with the idea of making a pile equal to Rickard's, so that he could shoot it out with him on business principles."

Mizner wouldn't even concede the minor literary point that men of the Yukon were marvellous marksmen. "I was in a saloon with a lot of those Yukon marksmen," he said. "They all agreed that there was no sport like bagging ptarmigan with a rifle at two hundred yards when you could see nothing but their eyes, their white feathers being invisible against the snow. They began to talk about throwing half dollars and quarters into the air and shooting them on the fly. One man won the undisputed championship of the saloon by telling how he tossed a dime into the air and barely grazed the rim, so that it would remain spinning in the air for a couple of hundred revolutions before it touched the ground. Just then a big Husky dog come in foaming at the mouth. Everybody began shooting at it. They hid behind the bar and made barricades of chairs and tables, took careful aim, and blazed away. The floor, walls, and ceiling were peppered with bullets. Every shot missed the dog by a mile. Finally, the bartender came out and killed it with one blow of his bung starter."

Mizner was twenty years old when he started for the Yukon Territory, in 1897. He left San Francisco with the fervent God-bless-yous, and don't-hurry-backs of his relatives. All they knew about the Yukon was that it was a remote and inaccessible region, and that no place could be too remote and inaccessible for Wilson. For years, he had brought only scandal and notoriety to his family. The Mizners were perhaps too grand and too genteel for their day and age. For three generations, they were State Department diplomats. The Mizner forebears had married themselves into a solid system of cousinships with the old Knickerbocker and Huguenot families of New York. Wilson's people had founded three California towns— Benicia, Colusa, and Vacaville. They had an aristocratic maxim that no gentleman works at anything except the dignified and honorable professions. Of Wilson's five older brothers, the first, Lansing, was a lawyer; the second, Edgar, was a diplomat and mining engineer; the third, William, was a physician; the fourth, Henry, was a clergyman; and the fifth, Addison, was an architect. Wilson was the most aristocratic of the lot. He abbreviated the family maxim to "No gentleman works." As a boy, he refused to study, because he regarded lessons as a form of work; he held, with Molière, that a gentleman knows everything without having to learn anything. His father was an old and sick man when he suddenly discovered that he had a fairly well-developed problem child on his hands.

At fourteen or fifteen, Wilson started running away from home. Necessity occasionally forced him to let down his standards and work, but he saved face by never working at any regular or respectable occupation. He became a singer on the Barbary Coast, a Chinatown guide, a lecturer for a travelling medicine show, a master of ceremonies for a trained bear, a faro dealer, a cardsharp, and an underworld handyman. He was arrested for vagrancy in Spokane at about the tenderest age that anybody had ever achieved vagrancy. The family regarded it as a heaven-sent opportunity when they were able to ship him to the Klondike. They would cheerfully have paid his fare to Tibet.

The family's opportunity to catapult Wilson into sub-zero oblivion came through his brother Edgar, the mining engineer, who took a post as representative in the Yukon Valley of the

Alaska Commercial Company. Activity had been increasing along the Yukon for years before the great gold strike, on the Klondike River, in 1896. Prospectors had been drifting in. The fur trade had come to have some importance. Anticipating a boom in the region, Alaska Commercial had bought up a series of trading posts, and Edgar was sent there to supervise the company's affairs. He induced Wilson to accompany him, and all San Francisco congratulated the family on its good luck. The two brothers started north when news of the Klondike bonanza was still believed to be a nonsensical rumor, but they soon learned that millions were actually being taken out of the old creek beds. Edgar wrote to San Francisco urging all other able-bodied Mizners to head for the Klondike and infinite riches. He sent Wilson to Skagway, Alaska, the chief gateway to the Klondike, to handle company business and prepare for the Mizner expedition to the gold fields.

By that time, Skagway was seething. Through the free-masonry of desert rats, news of the gold strike had been spread to prospectors all over the West. Skagway had become a roaring log-and-tent frontier town, with saloons, gambling joints, and a thriving red-light colony. Wilson had already received training from good underworld masters. At Skagway, he received a polishing and finishing from the greatest American professor of sharp practice, gentle larceny, and all-round crime—the celebrated Jefferson Randolph (Soapy) Smith, the real-life American version of the Man Who Would Be King. Soapy and Mizner were attracted to each other by the natural law that causes celebrities to gravitate into one another's society. Mizner travelled through life in a caravan of headliners—Soapy Smith, Swiftwater Bill Gates, Diamond Tooth Gertie, the Mit, the Half-Kid, the Scurvy Kid, and an assortment of Vanderbilts, du Ponts, Stotesburys, and Wideners; O. Henry, Paul Armstrong, George M. Cohan, Irving Berlin, Buffalo Bill; Tod Sloan, the king of jockeys; Frank Ward O'Malley, the king of reporters; A. Toxen Worm and Harry Reichenbach, the kings of press agents; Nat Goodwin, John McGraw, W. C. Fields, Gene Buck, Damon Runyon, Mickey Neilan, Bat Masterson, Tex Rickard;

Frankie Dwyer, the most popular crook on the steamship lanes; Swiftie Morgan, the quick thinker of Times Square; Tad Dorgan, Jimmy Swinnerton, Tom Powers, and other noted cartoonists; most of the stars of the stage, screen, and Tin Pan Alley; and most of the great prizefighters, beauties, showmen, first-nighters, gamblers, bunco steerers, fences, and international crooks of his time. Of all Mizner's idols and mentors, none had a greater influence on his life than Soapy.

Born in 1860, Soapy started out in life as a peanut boy with a small travelling circus. A circus is a little nation all by itself, and it probably implanted in Soapy his ambition to run a little nation of his own. At any rate, it taught him the shell-and-pea game and other methods of skinning suckers and getting ahead in the world. He got the name of Soapy in Denver, where, in the eighties, he used to drive up in a buggy to a busy street corner, set a tray of soap on a tripod, and start to sing ballads in a pleasing baritone. When he had a crowd, he would tell funny stories while he folded dollar bills around some of the cakes of soap and then wrapped them all in blue paper. He sold them for fifty cents a bar, many of the customers getting dollar bills with their purchases. Then he began wrapping up soap with twenty-dollar bills and auctioning the cakes off to the highest bidders, prices going to five dollars or more. Occasionally, with whoops of joy, a lucky customer would pull out a twenty-dollar bill. When the soap market was saturated, Soapy would auction off bottles of an all-curing elixir the same way. Now and then, a rumor would start that the twenty-dollar bills were either palmed or slipped to Soapy's confederates. Whenever trouble threatened, Soapy would sweep his merchandise into a suitcase, or "keister," leap into his buggy, and drive off at a rapid pace.

Soapy occasionally had trouble with the police. Mizner told how Soapy was once arrested in Chicago on a charge of operating with confederates and obtaining money under false pretenses. According to Mizner, the judge was confused. "I can't make head or tail out of this testimony," he exclaimed. "Let the defendant show me how it works, and let the police officers tell me how the law is violated." Soapy wrapped up several cakes of soap, first putting a fifty-dollar bill around one of them. "Now, Your Honor," said Soapy, "you give me twenty-five cents and choose one of these cakes." The judge handed over a quarter and chose the fifty-dollar cake. He shook his right fist at the police officers as his left folded up the bill and placed it in his vest pocket. "You!" he shouted. "You have been hounding an honest businessman for pursuing his lawful calling. His merchandising methods are obviously fair and honorable. Case dismissed."

Mizner studied the soap game under Soapy Smith in Skagway and practiced it occasionally in later life for amusement. In 1928, a Hollywood producer dragooned Mizner into going to Palm Springs, then a desert outpost, to write a motion picture. Mizner said that he had been kidnapped and that he couldn't write until he had restored his self-respect by trimming a few suckers. He went out in the street with a tray of soap, singing and shouting and waving twenty-dollar bills. Nobody paid the slightest attention to him. He was deeply wounded and felt that he was losing his talent. He comforted himself with the theory that Palm Springs people were all invalids and didn't have life enough in them to be suckers. He took revenge in a short story, "You're Dead," in which he stated that the entire population of Palm Springs was *in extremis*.

From the soap game, Smith rose to salted gold mines, banditry, and politics. His biographers, W. R. Collier and E. V. Westrate, say that he developed the finest set of confidence men this country has ever had. Soapy learned the king business from the ground up. He got his training in the science of government in Denver, Leadville, and other Colorado cities, where he and his gang got out the vote on election days and the testimony on trial days. He was a deft hand at the art of premature self-defense and had several notches in his revolver. From a political roustabout, he rose to be the political boss of Creede, Colorado, and later organized some small mining camps into his own vest-pocket kingdom. He even had poet laureates. Billy De Vere, the Tramp Poet, wrote the ballad "Jeff and Joe," in which he stated that Soapy never "throwed a friend." The chief troubadour of Soapy's court was Cy Warman, Poet of the Rockies, who is still remembered for his song "Sweet Marie" and his railroad ballads and stories.

Always looking for a new spot to establish a little monarchy, Soapy hurried north soon after the Klondike strike. Skagway was the ideal location for a new storybook kingdom. It was full of bewildered men with ready money concealed about their persons. Two tides of population—northbound gold-seekers and southbound gold-finders—were flowing through the bottleneck at Skagway, and Smith clipped them going and coming. When Mizner arrived in Skagway, Soapy had a saloon and gambling joint called Jeff's Place, which had become the seat of government. Mizner attracted attention almost immediately as one of Soapy's bright young men. Mizner admired Soapy's imagination and mental rapidity. Jefferson Randolph Smith certainly did have a gift for figuring out how to make any situation pay dividends. Most of the newcomers in Skagway wanted to get in touch with the home folks, so Soapy had a large sign saying "Telegraph Office" painted, and hung it on a log cabin. He charged five dollars for a telegram to anyplace. Within two or three hours, a five-dollar collect reply was always delivered to the sender. What the newcomers didn't know was that there was no telegraph line out of Skagway. Nearly every stranger was in dire need of information, so Soapy hung a sign saying "Information Office" on another cabin. His men imparted much information and they also acquired much information. The burglars and holdup men of Skagway became famous for clairvoyance in sensing where money was hidden. The San Francisco papers reported that there had been twelve holdups in Skagway in one night. James Wickersham, Alaska historian and federal judge, wrote that Soapy's gang had been unequalled anywhere since the palmy days of Virginia City, forty years earlier.

One of Mizner's stories throws light on Soapy's business methods. Skagway had a young clergyman who thundered against Soapy's rule. His church was a tent and he needed a log tabernacle for the winter. The tradition of the West was that bad men always have a soft spot in their hearts for the church, and the clergyman went to Soapy with his project. Mizner said that

Soapy instantly put his name down for a thousand dollars and handed over that amount in gold. With Soapy's prestige behind him, the young cleric collected thirty-six thousand dollars in one day. Unfortunately, he was held up that night and robbed of the entire amount. Here Mizner paused in his tale, and then added, "Thirty-six for one is pretty good odds."

After Mizner had left Skagway for the Klondike, an anti-Soapy faction arose in the form of a Committee of 101, which ordered "all sharks and bunco artists" to leave town. Soapy countered with a Committee of 303, which ordered the Committee of 101 to shut up. Soapy gave an impressive demonstration of power on the Fourth of July, 1898, when, riding a big white horse, he acted as grand marshal of the Independence Day parade. But four days later he was shot and killed in a clash between the Committee of 303 and the Committee of 101. Frank Reid, a 101 leader, was mortally wounded at the same time. Reid became the patron saint of Skagway. It was soon observed, however, that tourists neglected the grave of the law-and-order champion and worshipped at the shrine of the bandit. Then Soapy became the patron saint of Skagway. A section of the Pullen Museum, at Skagway, is now devoted to memorials of Soapy, including iron knuckles and a poker table with an almost invisible slit, called an "accommodator," through which he used to improve his hands. A life-size effigy of Soapy was installed as a perpetual passenger in Skagway's one streetcar. Nature, in one of her gruesome moods, had sculptured a Great Stone Skull in a cliff overhanging Skagway Bay. This was whitewashed, a famous gold tooth Soapy had was painted in, and a gigantic sign was painted on the cliff saying "Soapy Smith's Skull."

On a visit to Skagway after Soapy's death, Mizner found the place in a chaotic condition. Government had fallen into the hands of public officials and crime had fallen into the hands of amateurs. He was approached by two confidence men who had turned yeggs. They asked him to keep the sheriff out of mischief while they robbed a bank. Mizner got the sheriff into a poker game and kept him there until 3 A.M., when there was a terrific blast. Skagway, as Mizner told it, was reduced to a prairie. The yeggs had pulverized the bank, themselves, and much of Main Street, and the debris was scattered all over the landscape. "Those damned amateurs," said Mizner, "used two gallons of nitroglycerin to blow a safe that you could have kicked in with a pair of moccasins."

Thirty years later, when Mizner was a film writer, his greatest ambition was to do a picture on Soapy. A Hollywood magnate became enthusiastic and commissioned him to write a script. Mizner leaped into this project with one of his rare bursts of energy, but the picture was never made. The studio wanted the Skagway belles to be Sutton Place débutantes with Antoine coiffures and Paris boudoir armament; Mizner held out for two-fisted slammerkins with topknots and red flannel underwear.

It was in the middle of the glorious days of the bandit kingdom that Wilson resigned his post under Soapy to go to San Francisco to complete preparations for the Mizner expedition to the Klondike. Edgar had not succeeded in rounding up all the Mizner brothers. The doctor and the architect were interested, but the lawyer and the clergyman were not. Wilson had formerly been a singing partner of a dance-hall girl named Rena in the Crenmore, a wild all-night dive on Market Street, in San Francisco. He persuaded her that there was a great future for an artist of her type in the Klondike, and she went along. Four or five men not related to the Mizners joined the expedition. It had been Edgar's purpose to plant the various Mizners in strategic spots in the Yukon gold fields before the general population became excited over the Yukon strike. The Pacific Coast had been pretty well inoculated against gold fever. Tens of thousands of California families had thrown fortunes down ratholes in the hills, and the prevailing opinion at first was that the Klondike nuggets were the old, familiar gold bricks. But on July 14, 1897, the steamship Portland docked at San Francisco with a ton or so of yellow metal from the Yukon. Four days later, the steamship Excelsior docked at Seattle with a million dollars' worth of dust and nuggets. Men staggered ashore under the weight of tiny parcels. It was necessary to use both hands to struggle with a mooseskin "poke" the size of a lady's handbag. Nothing else struck the imagination so much as the grotesque attitudes into which strong men were bent by small bundles. This was the real stuff. This had no relation to those dreaded mining-stock certificates, those beautifully engraved invitations to the poorhouse. This was the filthy lucre, the vile trash itself. The whole civilized world was stirred, and gold-seekers started for the Yukon from six continents. Millions would have joined the rush except for one catch—it cost nearly a thousand dollars for a miner to equip himself. As it was, men rushed north by the tens of thousands, and the trail was filled with the Klondike-or-Bust procession before the Mizner expedition made a start.

The Mizners were an inventive clan, and the delay was caused by the perverse ingenuity of Wilson and his medical brother, Dr. William. They both regarded manual labor as the cruelest form of torture. They couldn't bear the idea of becoming galley slaves and rowing a boat five hundred miles down the Yukon. So they invented something new in the history of navigation—a flat-bottomed craft with sails and a pair of skates. They planned to go gliding down the waterway when it was frozen, making a winter sport, an ice carnival, out of a journey that caused untold suffering to other men. But there was a long wait while puzzled blacksmiths forged and sharpened the immense skates, weighing several hundred pounds. The invention made a crushing addition to the already massive collection of equipment that had to be carried over a ridge of mountains three thousand feet high before the watershed of the Yukon was reached. On Wilson's first visit to Skagway, the problem of getting freight over the mountains was child's play. All that anybody had to do was to hire Siwash Indians to carry it for nine cents a hundred pounds. But the Siwashes had grown worldly and were now charging thirty cents a hundred and upward. Prices sometimes went up to a dollar a hundred because of competition for their services. The Mizner budget was nearly exhausted, and it soon became apparent that the young gentlemen would have to be their own draft animals. On the lower half of the trail, they had a bit of luck. A man with a four-horse team became infatuated with Rena and hauled the freight over part of the distance for

love. From then on, the heavy work was largely done by brother
Addison, the architect, a cousin named Sam Taylor, and one or
two non-Mizners. Addison had the build and energy of a dray
horse. He took pride in struggling under huge burdens. He
thought he was shaming his brothers, but he didn't know them.
Wilson was a gentleman and a boulevardier even on the crags
and cliffs. He was six feet three, weighed over two hundred, and
was a powerful athlete. Dr. William had the makings of a circus
strong man; he could bend iron bars with his bare hands and
tear two packs of cards in half. But Wilson and William considered themselves the brains, not the brawn, of the expedition.
They wouldn't work, but they were willing to contribute strokes
of genius for the benefit of Addison and the other pack animals.
One day, when Addison paused in his labors, he found the two
mental giants working out the details of an invention to hoist
freight over the summit by means of hot-air balloons with enough
rudders to enable them to maneuver their way through adverse
winds.

The final half mile of the trail led to the noted Chilkoot
Pass. It zigzagged and wove up the almost sheer face of a cliff. A
host of Arctic writers have made this the most famous stretch of
mountain climbing in literature. Mt. Everest is nothing compared to it, as far as word painting is concerned. The fabled hero
of Chilkoot Pass was Klondike Mike, who carried a grand piano
over the pass and came back with a frozen judge. The authentic
hero was Jack Marchbank, of San Francisco, a one-legged man,
who climbed the pass on crutches, struck it rich, and died a multimillionaire in 1947. Some of the climbers carried bulky packs
with extraordinary nimbleness, but it was discovered that the
packs were stuffed with feathers. These were Soapy Smith's
men, who went along, disguised as miners, in order to introduce
the shell-and-pea and other games at resting places on the way
to the summit.

The Yukon is an odd river. It rises within eighteen miles of
the Pacific Ocean and, after meandering in a twenty-three-hun-
dred-mile horseshoe, empties into the Pacific. Standing on the
summit of Chilkoot Pass, the Mizners could see the ocean just

below them to the south; turning their heads, they could see Lake Bennett, the source of the Yukon, just below them to the north. Lake Bennett had already become the greatest amateur boatbuilding center in history. The shores were dotted with the tents of Klondikers who were chopping down trees for the jerry-built navy that carried more than twenty thousand men to Dawson City in 1898. The prevailing Klondiker craft was the "coffin," a long, open box big enough to bury a Cardiff giant in. Others looked like log cabins sawed off a foot above the ground. Now and then, a good shipwright or carpenter turned out a neat job, but this was an exception. Only green timber was available, and it sometimes shrank until a boat became a sieve before it was launched. When a boat proved unfloatable, the only thing to do was burn it up, to recover the precious nails, which were worth more than their weight in silver, and start all over.

The maddest man on the shores of Lake Bennett was Addison Mizner. His back still aching from the weight of the world's greatest pair of skates, he learned that the ice was covered with deep snow and that the whole idea of skating down to Dawson City had been preposterous. His ordinarily sweet temper was soured. Necessity now compelled Wilson and Dr. William to do some hard work, and their ordinarily lovely dispositions were spoiled, too. In addition to everything else, the journey would have to be delayed until the ice on the river had melted. The toughest of the boatbuilding chores was whipsawing long planks from spruce trees. After a tree had been chopped down and trimmed, it was placed on a scaffold six feet above the ground. One man stood under the scaffold, using both hands to drag the saw downward, while a second man stood on the scaffold and pulled the saw upward. For fifty years, the argument has been waged among Klondikers as to whether the high man or the low man had the worst of it. It was a backbreaking job for the top man to pull the saw upward; at each downstroke, the low man got his eyes full of sawdust. Nothing that happened on the Klondike trail caused hatreds more deadly than those between the high man and the low man. Partners became so enraged that they broke up on the spot. They sometimes nursed their wrath for weeks and at the bustup divided their equipment right through the center, breaking their only stove in half, sawing their boat in two, and slicing their tents through the middle. Addison and Wilson did the whipsawing for their party and tried to equalize their suffering by changing places forty times a day. The boat was finally finished. By sail and oar, it took the Mizner party through several hundred miles of rivers and lakes. They successfully shot the famous White Horse Rapids in it. Dr. William disappeared one day. He couldn't stand the company any longer and finished the journey overland with a man who had a dog team. A few days later, Wilson hit the overland trail with Rena. Addison stuck with the boat until it reached Dawson City.

Edgar had staked out mining properties for his three brothers, but Wilson and the Doctor were highly dissatisfied with them. They had expected to pick up nuggets like eggs at a hennery. They were prepared to stoop for them but not to dig. And even the digging wasn't the worst part of it. Klondike mining was essentially a wood-chopping business. It was necessary to cut down a small forest to work a claim. The subsoil of the Yukon was still in the grip of the Glacial Age. As much as a hundred feet of frozen gravel sometimes lay between the surface and bedrock. It took a big bonfire to soften a single foot of gravel so that it could be handled with pick and shovel. There were other terrible chores. The gravel was hoisted to the surface in buckets. When it was dumped out, it instantly refroze to the hardness of granite, and had to await the spring thaw to be washed for gold. The miners had to be lowered and hoisted by bucket. After months of labor, the yield of gold might not fill a tablespoon. It was all a matter of luck. On one claim, the miners might strike the course of an ancient stream where every rift and crevice in the bedrock was loaded with gold. An adjoining claim might be a total failure. The laborious operation bore no resemblance to the sure-thing game that Wilson and the Doctor had looked forward to. After a brief study of the situation, Dr. William went back to San Francisco. Addison worked a claim. Wilson stayed close to Dawson City and consoled himself with its spry indoor life.

Saloons, gambling hells, dance halls, sporting houses, and vaudeville shows were sprouting everywhere in town. Wilson became a faro dealer, and a professional singer again, and for a while was a cashier, or "weigher." A weigher was a rather distinguished creature who presided over large, shining brass scales into which gold dust was poured to pay for drinks, dance-hall tickets, poker chips, and other items. Mizner weighed at the famous Monte Carlo, which was operated by Swiftwater Bill Gates and Jack Smith. "I weighed a million and a half dollars' worth of gold dust and nuggets at Swiftwater Bill's," Wilson said in a newspaper interview in New York years later, "and never made a mistake that wasn't in favor of the house."

Paying in raw gold was a complicated transaction. The dust was first poured from the miner's poke into a small brass container called a "blower." From the blower, it was poured out until the scales balanced. The excess gold in the blower was then returned to the miner's poke. Nobody could cheat a careful and sober miner. The weighing transactions in the gambling hells were generally above suspicion. But weighing at the bars in the dance halls was different. A sourdough who was having a big night expected to be fleeced and was seldom disappointed. When the profession was very young, weighers let their fingernails grow long and cleaned them frequently. Some weighers kept their fingers wet with beer and would wipe off dust and small grains into their leather pockets. Mizner was a spiller. He had a thick piece of carpet under his scales. His aim was to enrich the carpet a little every time he manipulated the scales. Colgate Baker, who printed an interview with Mizner in the New York *Review* in 1911, quoted him as saying, "Once a week, I burned the carpet and never made less than twenty-five hundred dollars out of it." The figure seems high. Arctic reminiscences generally require more than the usual discounts. The carpet would have had to absorb about twelve pounds of metal to have been worth twenty-five hundred dollars at the then prevailing rates.

A clever battler named Young Jack McKernan, later known as Jack (Doc) Kearns, the manager of Jack Dempsey, learned the art of weighing from Mizner. Kearns, a pink-cheeked youngster, was fumbling with a pair of scales in Nome when Mizner took pity on him. "Come with me, my boy," said Mizner. Kearns went to Mizner's room with him. "Sit down, my boy," said Mizner. He got out a jug of syrup and plastered the boy's hair down with it. "Handle the stuff all you can. Keep running your fingers through your hair," said Mizner. The young Doc had a long mane. He ran his hands through it conscientiously as he worked at the scales. Between the syrup and the metal, his hair would gradually take on the consistency of peanut brittle. After every shampoo, the Doc had a pleasing addition to his pocket money. "Mizner was a wonder at the business," Kearns recalled. "He could make a pair of scales do anything."

Mizner's fattest pickings at Swiftwater's came in the spring. As the sun thawed the mounds of gravel that had been dug out in the winter, the gold was sluiced out. After a tough and lonesome winter, the miners came to town with gold burning holes in their pokes. Ordering drinks for girls at his table, a sourdough would often hand his poke to a waiter and let him superintend the transaction. The late Alexander Pantages, multimillionaire theatre owner, laid the foundation of his fortune with his pickings as a Klondike waiter. Happy sourdoughs slipped gold down girls' necks for the pleasure of seeing them wriggle. Dance-hall actresses complained that their ankles were black and blue from nuggets thrown at them by admiring audiences. There is testimony on record in the Dawson City court that an American

consul, tired of giving nuggets one at a time to girls at the Phoenix dance hall, emptied his poke by throwing handfuls of them into the air, shouting, "Take the whole cheese!"

It had been inevitable that Mizner, with his instinct for mingling with celebrities, would become connected with Swiftwater Bill. Swiftwater had already gained international notoriety. The Seattle *Post-Intelligencer* had paid him the compliment of printing a three-column obituary of him on a false rumor of his death. In 1897, in Seattle, Swiftwater had thrown nuggets out of his hotel window to crowds on the sidewalk and tipped bellboys to page him as King of the Klondike. A large part of his glory was founded on his nickname. The Klondike rechristened everybody, and Bill drew the grand prize in the lottery of nicknames. The word "Swiftwater" was a bugle note of adventure. Bill was accepted by the outside world as the daredevil pilot who laughed at danger as he steered treasure-laden arks and argosies through wild cataracts in the unexplored headwaters of the Yukon—the kind of man who would shoot between Scylla and Charybdis with no hands and make the descent into the Maelstrom for fun. The country had been suffering from a dearth of heroes since the Civil War, and Bill was hailed as a greater scout than Kit Carson, a cooler gambler than John Oakhurst, a bigger spender than Coal Oil Johnny. The *Klondike Nugget* said that Bill's hair flowed down his back like General Custer's and that his mustaches were so long that he could festoon them over his shoulders. He owned the first stiff-bosomed white shirt ever seen in Dawson City, and as he was unwilling to appear anywhere without it, he used to take to his bed for three days while it was being boiled. He once arrived in San Francisco wearing a Prince Albert, hip-length fur boots, or mukluks, and a massive chain of nuggets across his bosom. Robert Service said that Bill was the man who introduced the red necktie and yellow shoes with evening clothes.

Mizner is seldom mentioned in the early chronicles of the Yukon. After he became famous on Broadway, he began to figure more prominently in Arctic memoirs and annals, but he was slow to acquire Arctic renown. One reason may have been his nickname. Stirring nicknames were indispensable to Yukon celebrities. A man's Klondike title was generally an allusion to his appearance, habits, or business. It was an essential form of oral shorthand in a land where regular names were considered too formal and too hard to remember. The usual purpose of the alias was neither ridicule nor glorification but ready reference. Rex Beach had a partner with an Indian sweetheart who answered to the name of Short and Dirty. The Bible Kid was so entitled because of his habit of giving a Bible reading on a street corner so that he could take up a collection and get back into a poker game. The Hit-It-and-Take-It Kid got his handle from phrases he used in the game of twenty-one. D. E. Griffith, a sourdough historian, related that Waterfront Brown was a bill collector who used to frequent the docks on watch for debtors about to decamp, that Sparerib Jimmy was thin, that Jerkline Sam drove a ten-horse team, that Deep-Hole Johnson was the first to sink a hundred-foot shaft, and that Spieler Jim was a marathon conversationalist. Mizner got his nickname because of an ill-advised fit of industry. In spite of his hostility to physical effort, he would "stampede," like thousands of others, on rumors of a big gold discovery. The laziest of the Dawson loafers still dreamed of bonanzas with cantaloupe-sized nuggets and would lame themselves by long sprints over the thick Yukon moss, which resembled rubber sponge. Mizner limped back from one mid-winter chase with an empty poke and a front tooth missing. He had broken it off on a frozen doughnut. He was immediately nicknamed the Yellow Kid, after a pioneer comic-strip character who had met with a similar misfortune. There were no heroic or romantic possibilities in that title.

One day, when Addison was living in Dawson City, he sat down and wrote the truth about Wilson's Yukon escapades to their brother the Reverend Henry Mizner, then at Christ Church, in St. Louis. The clergyman replied that he had had prior knowledge of Wilson's prejudice in favor of disreputable women but expressed dismay at learning that Wilson could be "dishonest." "We must stick to him as long as we can—come what may," the clergyman's letter concluded. "Someday this may all be forgotten, horrible as it is now." The word "horrible" may have been the overemphasis of a saintly young churchman; exactly what scrape Wilson was in at that time is unknown. One tale that has come down through the years is that Wilson travelled about various Yukon camps as a faro dealer, that Rena appeared at his table in the guise of a stranger, and that Wilson slipped her such good cards that she broke the bank. It was said that the proprietor of one gambling house did not suspect Wilson but inferred that Rena was doing crooked work on her own, and that he hit her over the head with a small log. The windup of this story is that Wilson, in a moment of remorse, decided to reform, and that he punched a pine tree with all his might, in order to damage his right hand so that it would never again be able to slip an illegal card into a deck with the requisite dexterity. If Mizner did try to improve his character by cracking his knuckles, he failed. His right hand, which for one reason or another was badly gnarled, never lost its fraudulent agility. Earl Baldwin, a Hollywood writer and an intimate of Mizner's, heard the pine-tree incident from so many sources that he asked Mizner about it. "Now, Earl, why would I do a thing like that?" said Mizner. Earl was not entirely satisfied with the answer.

The stirring year in the Klondike was '98. By '99, the Chilkoot Pass had been rendered obsolete by a railroad from Skagway over the summit. The second crop of Klondikers was composed of holiday travellers, who arrived in comparative luxury by rail and steamer. Dawson City became semi-respectable and then respectable. The *Klondike Nugget* introduced a society column. The Northwest Mounted clamped down on characters who lacked visible means of support. On one occasion, Edgar Mizner saved Wilson from the Northwest Mounted's attention by giving him a share in a claim and appointing him foreman of a crew of miners. Wilson thought that the men were killing themselves by overwork. He first induced them to take it easy and then induced them to quit the pick and shovel and play poker with him. When Edgar visited the mine, it had ceased to function, and Wilson was fired.

Wilson became sick of British rule in the Yukon. It teemed

with jeopardy. Queen Victoria was always prying into his private affairs. In '99, he skipped to Nome, which had nothing but American law and very little of that. The town was in its infancy, and Wilson became one of the founding fathers of its underworld. Nome was Wilson's town. He was prince and pauper, bum and plutocrat, by turns, all during his stay there. He made a small fortune by fleecing suckers at card games and badger games; ran it into a big fortune by speculating in mining claims; and lost it all by mixing with heavyweight gamblers at Tex Rickard's Northern Saloon and Wyatt Earp's Dexter Bar. Broke, he was forced to work. He dealt faro, managed hotels, actresses, and prizefighters, and even did an occasional column for the Nome *Chronicle*. One night he was buying champagne for the house, and the next he was stealing coal to keep from freezing to death. He was the Grover Whalen of Nome when he was in clover. He greeted the steamers and serenaded the newly arrived leading ladies. He had the reputation of being able to borrow money from a lamppost and is said to have been the only man who ever hired the Nome brass band on credit. James Bain, who was known as Newsboy Red in Nome, recalled in 1947 that Mizner was the handsomest man in Nome and that he had had all the "parlor ladies in a daze." One of the most popular actresses to arrive in Nome asserted years later that Mizner had married her there, but he said he couldn't remember the incident. He was supposed to be the fashion plate of Nome. He used to go to San Francisco by steamer occasionally to replenish his wardrobe at the tailoring house of Bullock & Jones, which finally succeeded in collecting from him in New York years later, with the aid of a deputy sheriff.

One of Mizner's achievements in Nome was teaching the boxing racket to Jack Kearns. Kearns was an eager youngster, and in such a hurry to get rich that the first time he arrived at Nome, he didn't wait for a small boat to take him ashore from his steamer but jumped overboard into freezing water and swam to the beach. When he was baffled in his search for nuggets, he took to the indoor life. Mizner was then developing a small stable of prizefighters, and Kearns became one of them. Jack was too brainy for the mauling part of the game, and he was soon fired with the ambition to become a manager, like Mizner. In his last appearance on the tough side of the business, Kearns was matched against a bigger and better man. In order to equalize the thing, Kearns, according to his autobiography, wrapped strips of lead around his fists before he put on the gloves. The first blow astounded his opponent. Kearns was supposed to be a cream-puff hitter, but he had suddenly developed a pile-driving right and left. He raised lumps every time he landed, and in the first round the favorite was on the ropes. In the second round, Kearns was so arm-weary from throwing lead that he could hardly raise his fists, and he was soon on the floor for the count. From then on, he was in the intellectual side of the business. Mizner afterward took a certain pride in seeing his pupil grow into the smartest prizefight manager in the country and always regarded himself as the founder of the Mizner-Kearns-Dempsey dynasty.

The principal ambition of most of the men of the Arctic was to escape from the "ice trap." Mizner, however, never reached San Francisco without beginning at once to yearn for the wild life of Nome. Mizner had returned to San Francisco from Nome in 1900. Hearing, on his arrival there, of a new gold strike on the beaches at Nome, he immediately took a boat for the new diggings. At Nome, he devoted himself mainly to gambling. Addison Mizner arrived in Nome several months after his brother. He was gratified but a little puzzled at hearing Wilson casually referred to as "the bravest man in Nome." He was told on all sides of Wilson's reckless daring and his crazy disregard for his own safety. This reputation did not quite agree with Addison's mental picture of his brother; he knew that Wilson would fight desperately when the reasons seemed good and sufficient, but he could not conceive of him as a man who went around thoughtlessly wasting heroism.

Everybody told Addison how, as a member of a posse, Wilson, nonchalantly rolling a cigarette with one hand and holding a revolver in the other, had kicked in the door of a cabin to which three desperadoes, one of them wounded, had been traced.

The other members of the posse had hung back, regarding it as foolhardy to walk in on trapped bandits. They all expected to see Mizner filled with bullets. But he walked into the cabin uninjured and came out beckoning to the others with a lighted cigarette. They found the place empty. Fresh bloodstains showed that a wounded man had been there. Addison found Wilson uncommunicative on this subject, but he gradually learned the truth. The three bandits—the Mit, the Half-Kid, and Two-Tooth Mike—had been caught stealing gold from a sluice box and chased to the cabin after a running fight. They had escaped unseen from the cabin, however, and made their way to Mizner's hotel, where they begged him to conceal them. He hid them in his own room behind a burlap partition. A few minutes later, friends rushed in to tell him that a band of desperadoes had been cornered in the cabin; he then joined the posse and gave his memorable exhibition of intrepidity. Three days later, after things had quieted down, he helped smuggle the robbers to safety.

In April of 1902, after a visit to San Francisco, Wilson started north on the steamer Portland and nearly wound up his career in the neighborhood of the North Pole. The Portland was frozen in on May 7th and drifted for nearly two months, reaching a point farther north than any passenger ship had ever been before. A St. Louis paper, which took a special interest in the happening because the city was the home town of the Reverend Henry Mizner, printed a map that purported to show that Wilson and his companions had probably made a closer approach to the North Pole than the Duke of the Abruzzi's expedition, which then held the Farthest North record. Late in June, the ice broke up and the Portland reached Nome, after being sixty-eight days en route. Mizner had been the greatest single influence in keeping up the spirits of the passengers, according to Oom Paul Sutter, the Portland's steward. He had with him a big array of costumes for Nome theatricals, and he did his best to amuse the frightened passengers with amateur shows. Between shows, he wisecracked and clowned with great success. One of the tough days on the voyage was June 1st, when the horror-stricken passengers saw a ship upside down in the sky. This was taken at the time to be a hint of their fate, but the inverted vessel was later identified as the S.S. Nome City, seen in a mirage.

The scapegoat of the expedition was old Professor H. O. Blankenshrift, a doctor of astrology, mesmerism, and other reigning sciences of the time. The Professor's pretensions were that he could read the future like an open book. Naturally, he was badly discredited by his failure to discover the fate of the Portland in the stars. Moreover, when he tried to give exhibitions, his hypnotic eye completely failed to work on the scared passengers. By agreement, they all persecuted the poor old Professor. He became such a miserable outcast and underdog that his plight appealed to Mizner's streak of humanity. One day, the ice cracked and a patch of open water appeared beside the boat. Mizner dived into it, scrambled out on the ice, and screamed for help until he was hauled back up by ropes. As soon as he had got into warm clothes, he seized a revolver and ran about like a madman. "Where's Professor Blankenshrift?" he shouted. "The old devil hypnotized me. That water's forty below and he made me jump into it. I'll blow his head off." The poor old Professor went cowering to his bunk. Mizner gradually allowed himself to be talked out of his homicidal project. Blankenshrift was rehabilitated. Nobody doubted that he was a master of the black arts after what he had made Mizner do.

The Portland finally arrived at Nome at bright midnight on July 2nd. People by the thousands gathered on the beach, built welcoming bonfires, and put on their Fourth of July show two days ahead of time. They rowed out to the Portland in small boats with food and baskets of champagne. The celebration was one of the greatest in Nome history.

But Nome was not the place it had been. The Klondike had been prospected to death, and new gold strikes were a rarity. Nome was quieting down, and late in the summer Mizner took a boat back to San Francisco. He had finally had enough of the snow and ice, and he went to Honduras to run a banana plantation.

The Arctic achievement that Mizner was fondest of recalling in later years was his ten-thousand-dollar coup with a tomato can. He had gone to sleep after having had too much to drink. On awakening, he found that his revolver had been stolen. This was an ill-timed misfortune; a glance at his watch showed that he was already overdue at an engagement to play the part of a damaged husband in a badger game. Cursing his irresponsibility, he picked up a tomato can, stripped off the label, and hurried to the appointment. Crashing the door in with an experienced shoulder, he raged at the culprits and threatened to blow the entire triangle to heaven with the can, which, he gave the home-wrecking stranger to understand, was full of dynamite. The stranger purchased his life with a belt loaded with gold dust. When the heroine asked for her share, Mizner handed her the tomato can. She asked what good that would do her. "It just got me ten thousand dollars," said Mizner.

Chapter Six

A MANSION ON FIFTH AVENUE

WILSON MIZNER'S first New York headlines were the biggest. They came on February 2, 1906, three days after he secretly married Mrs. Mary Adelaide Yerkes, in her mansion at 864 Fifth Avenue. Mizner was twenty-nine years old, Mrs. Yerkes was eighty. He was penniless; she was reputed to be worth $7,500,000. The news got three-column headlines on the front pages of some of the papers.

Mrs. Yerkes had been a widow for exactly one month when she married Mizner. Her previous husband was Charles T. Yerkes, whose name is known today mainly because of the Yerkes Observatory, which he gave to the University of Chicago. At the time of his death, he was the celebrated Traction King. He built the Chicago "L" and part of the London Tube, and coined the golden text of city transportation, "It's the straphanger that pays the dividends." He was the hero of Theodore Dreiser's novels "The Titan" and "The Financier." He served a sentence for embezzlement in 1871 and boasted of wholesale bribing of city officials in Chicago. In spite of a Fifth Avenue mansion, an art collection, and a police record, Yerkes didn't penetrate beyond the outer defenses of New York society. As for Mrs. Yerkes, she, according to Mizner, couldn't get into the Haymarket, the least

exclusive night spot in New York, with a letter from the Pope.
A few years before the Traction King's death, he and his wife
had separated. She objected to his seraglio; he objected to her
drinking and making scenes in public. She once complained
loudly in a theatre that the Lady Teazle on the stage was not
really Lady Teazle, because she wore pink, whereas a painting
in the Yerkes collection showed that the real Lady Teazle wore
yellow. Mizner, a broadminded man in most respects, also complained of her tippling, and described her as "web-footed."

Mizner had moved into the Yerkes mansion months before
the death of the Traction King. The wedding was merely a rati-
fication of the status quo. Married at leisure, they repented in
haste. Addison Mizner hurried to the Yerkes mansion on hearing the news. He found Wilson in a bed that had once belonged
to the Mad King of Bavaria; it was on a dais with two green
velvet steps; gold cupids were putting an enamelled Goddess of
Night to sleep on the head of the bed and waking her up at the
foot. This was the late utility magnate's second-best bed; he
owned a costlier sleeping arrangement that had once belonged
to King Leopold of the Belgians. Propped up among pillows of
peach-colored satin, covered to the waist with point lace, the
bridegroom was wearing a gray woollen undershirt, the sleeves
of which had shrunk nearly to the elbow. He was holding a sack
of Bull Durham between his teeth and rolling a brown-paper
cigarette. Addison excitedly asked the reason for the marriage.
"The service is good here," said Wilson.

Addison disapproved of carrying the attachment to the point
of matrimony. He had introduced Wilson and Mrs. Yerkes at
the National Horse Show, where Addison was seated in a box
with Mrs. Yerkes and another glittering dowager. The purpose-
ful young architect had decided early in life that a talented but
penniless young man eager to rise in the world should attach
himself to glittering dowagers. In his early thirties, he had arrived at an arena box at the Horse Show through this policy. It
was against his will that Addison introduced Wilson to Mrs.
Yerkes. It was, in fact, against his will that he recognized Wilson
at all at the Horse Show. The brothers had last seen each other

REGINALD MARSH

in Alaska, about four years before. During those four years, Addison had polished himself up remarkably, and he feared that Wilson hadn't. When Wilson came in sight, the young architect winked, shook his head, and made signs with his hands. These were intended to convey that Addison didn't wish to acknowledge his brother at the moment. Wilson, however, ignored the signals and approached the box. Addison greeted him in a low voice but did not offer to introduce him. After an embarrassed moment or two, however, the architect asked Wilson where he was living. "In a house of ill fame on Forty-eighth Street," said Wilson. This statement was overheard by the ladies. They were charmed. The newcomer was immediately taken into their circle. Wilson, according to good authorities, had borrowed $10,000 from Mrs. Yerkes before sunup the following morning.

The glamorous misalliance was handsomely treated in the New York papers. The year 1906 was halfway between the Spanish-American War and the First World War. America had not yet learned that Europe existed. Washington was a secondary news center, even though Theodore Roosevelt was President. New Yorkers were almost exclusively concerned with the events of the village stretching from Yonkers to the sea. It was the golden age of local newspaper reporting, especially for morning newspapers, most of which had no early editions. There was no hurry. A reporter could keep on retouching his prose until 1 or 2 A.M. The stories of the Mizner-Yerkes case in the old newspaper files have a cuteness, and geniality, that went out of journalism in 1914, when local news lost its predominance.

The Mizner-Yerkes story was improved by the fact that the bridegroom vanished and the bride for three days denied the marriage. Reporters, however, found the Reverend Andrew Gillies, of St. Andrew Methodist Episcopal Church, who had officiated. He said that Mrs. Yerkes was conscious at the time; he added heatedly that he wouldn't have performed the ceremony unless both parties were conscious. The newspapers had difficulty in obtaining biographical material about the missing husband. All that was discovered at first was that he came from San Francisco and had spent some years in the Klondike and Nome.

Later dispatches from San Francisco said that he was interested in the turf. They related that in the course of a litigation over Lucky Baldwin's famous race horse Geraldine, Mizner stole her from a stable near San Francisco and rode her to Nevada in order to foil the California authorities. The New York *American* found an anonymous woman acquaintance of Mizner who said that he was "positively the most dashing young man in America," that he was "a belted knight transplanted directly from the age of chivalry," and that he was "an improved Robin Hood" and a combination of "a Sir Francis Drake and a Sir Richard Grenville."

A few days after the marriage, Mizner was found at the Hotel Astor. One newspaper account described him as a tall, large-headed young man wearing his hair long over his ears and parted far over on the left side. He had a tan topcoat with saucerlike pearl buttons, olive-green spats, and a cane. He confirmed the fact of the marriage and explained that he had absented himself from felicity for a few days because of important matters connected with his racing stable and his Alaskan and Mexican mining properties. The marriage, he asserted, was a most happy one. "Come and see," he said. With that he walked out of the hotel and hopped into an electric hansom. Reporters followed in horse-drawn cabs. On arrival, the long-legged bridegroom skipped up the steps three at a time, waving to the press to follow. Inside the residence, Mizner paused in the hall of statuary and gave a prolonged cry of "Coo-ee-ee!" The former Mrs. Yerkes appeared on a balcony in a lavender tea gown.

She readily owned up, saying she had been swept off her feet by a whirlwind courtship. She requested the press not to say that she was eighty years old, and the reporters, according to the *World*, "agreed on an average age of thirty-two." Mrs. Mizner then paid a tribute to the institution of matrimony, urging all her callers to marry without delay, after which she withdrew from the balcony on the plea of a slight headache. Mizner remained to answer questions. He was absent-minded during part of the interview, according to the *Sun*, which described him as "gazing reflectively at a priceless tapestry." The interview was personal at times. Hadn't Mizner, up to a few days earlier, been living with a fiery-tempered girl in a two-dollar hotel on Twenty-eighth Street? Mizner objected to the form of the question. Hadn't neighbors complained of wild revelling up to daybreak after the wedding? Not at all—or if so, the revelry must have been in the servants' quarters. Hadn't he sold a gambling joint in Nome for $200,000 and lost the $200,000 back to the new proprietor at one sitting? No! How did the Yerkes mansion compare with his shanty in Nome? It had it skinned a mile.

After other questions, Mizner showed the reporters around the gallery and lectured eloquently on the paintings, especially the Rembrandts. His favorite, however, according to the *Times*, was the painting "An Aged Dead Woman," by Balthasar Denner. It was so small that you had to look at it through a magnifying glass.

It was established that Mrs. Yerkes' wedding outfit had consisted of a black glitter gown and a Gainsborough hat with a white ostrich plume. In an exclusive interview with Violet Rogers, of the *Journal*, Mrs. Mizner said she had married Wilson because he sang songs beautifully and read like an angel.

The romance was on and off the rocks several times. The first quarrel, according to Mizner, was caused by anonymous letters, which poured in from the West and elsewhere. One charged that Mizner had killed a girl in Honolulu, a place he had never been. Others charged him with crimes of cunning and violence throughout a territory extending from the Arctic Circle to Mexico City.

The *Press* reported on June 16, 1906, that Mrs. Mizner had developed a disconcerting thrift. It added that Mizner complained that "she insisted that he tell her over and over again how much he loved her, and the constant demand that he reiterate the tale of his burning affection became monotonous to him." On one occasion, Mrs. Mizner patched up a quarrel by reënacting the big Camille scene. Mizner had left her after a financial argument. She waylaid him near an elevator in the Hotel Astor and pelted him with greenbacks. Describing this in after years, Mizner said, "The greatest humiliation I ever underwent was picking it up." He contradicted himself slightly in another version, saying, "I picked up eight thousand dollars before I realized I'd been insulted."

Because of Mizner's well-known acquisitiveness, it was assumed that he had bettered his condition substantially during his stay at the art-laden Yerkes mansion. It has been related by careless historians that he sang sentimental ballads to Mrs. Yerkes in an upstairs apartment while confederates substituted copies for originals of the old masters and walked out stiff-kneed because of the Corots and Van Dycks wrapped around their legs. But the fact is that Mizner was baffled at every turn by greedy little orphans. The Traction King had left a considerable part of his estate to selfish public institutions. Their representatives notified the widow, as soon as her romance with Mizner became known, that they would hold her personally responsible for every item in the collection. While it was not impossible to steal a painting or statue, it was practically impossible to dispose of it under these circumstances, and Mizner was always opposed to unnecessary risks. The executors never alleged that any of the art treasures had disappeared.

Mizner found that his bride had a prejudice amounting to a superstition against signing checks. A reliable witness on this point is Johnny Bray, a San Francisco sport, who was Mizner's confidential man at the time. Mrs. Yerkes' boudoir door had a wrought-iron lock of medieval workmanship, with an enormous keyhole. Through this, Bray maintained a vigil for more than an hour on one occasion while Mizner made eloquent confessions of love, blank check and fountain pen in hand. But Mrs. Mizner would not sign. She also kept a firm grip on her tiaras and lavalieres, and even on her brooches and rings. There were consolation prizes, however. The Traction King had had a mania for expensive studs, waistcoat buttons, cuff links, clasps, and necktie pins, especially snakes with emerald-and-ruby eyes. Seven weeks after the marriage, Mizner, who was then living temporarily at the Hotel Cadillac, reported to the police that he had been robbed of two snakes with emerald-and-ruby eyes and other necktie pins, three loose diamonds, and several pearl studs, the lot valued at $7,500. Even trinkets like these didn't come easy, according to intimates of Mizner. He was once reduced to dressing a Greenwich Village bartender in a white tie and red sash and introducing him as the Spanish Ambassador in order to take advantage of his wife's belief that it was a Fifth Avenue custom to present diamond cuff links to ambassadors who came to dine.

Mizner was reticent about the Yerkes adventure for many years. One of his few early references to it was made to his close friend Hype Igoe, the cartoonist and sportswriter. After sitting a long time with a faraway look on his face, Mizner exclaimed, apropos of nothing, "It's a damned unpleasant experience, Hype, to be stopped by two Pinkertons when you're walking out of your own house with a lard can full of jewels!"

In 1907, Mrs. Mizner obtained a divorce and the right to resume her former name. According to Addison Mizner, Wilson had nothing to show for the episode except an enamelled Russian spoon of modern design. The proof that he had gained no substantial amount was an item in San Francisco newspapers at about the same time, saying that he had gone to work there for Emile Brougière, who was one of the witnesses at his wedding. Brougière had a contract to remove debris after the San Francisco earthquake, and Mizner was in charge of two hundred of his carts. The newspaper story about his employment hurt Mizner's pride, as he had become the official ne'er-do-well and wastrel of the country. He quit the debris business after a few days and said in an interview in the San Francisco *Bulletin,* "Why should I work? I've committed no crime. Work is the poorest excuse for an occupation. I hate work like the Lord hates St. Louis."

Mizner returned to New York shortly after this and resumed living by his wits. He became a figure among the early-morning crowd at Jack's. He gained a reputation as a diplomat at Jack's because of an answer he gave when two gang leaders called him to their table and asked him to settle an argument. Both men were considered dangerous when disappointed. The argument was whether Lee or Grant was the greater general. "I don't know, gentlemen," said Mizner, "but they paid off on Grant."

An acquaintance picked up in Jack's became Mizner's backer in running the Hotel Rand, on West Forty-ninth Street. As a hotelkeeper, Mizner made such an impression that nearly twenty years afterward the Palm Beach correspondent of the *Morning Telegraph*, writing on March 10, 1926, of Mizner's Florida real-estate operations, recalled the Hotel Rand days in these words: "If a man named Butler or Francis subscribed himself 'Harrison' on the register, Mr. Mizner never gruffly called his attention to the error, but with the courtliness of the Old School affected not to notice it."

Mizner's bar at the Rand, designed by his brother Addison, was one of the fanciest in town. Mizner was once taken before a magistrate on a charge of throwing two guests into the fountain in the lobby for disputing their hotel bills. He asserted that the fountain would hold only one. "But I'm going to enlarge it," he added.

Karl Kitchen recorded in his column in the *Evening World* that Mizner used to shout "Keep the children away from the elevator!" from time to time in order to give the impression that it was a family hotel. Johnny Bray was the hotel manager. According to his conservative estimate, the guests were "eighty per cent keptees." Once, when Gene Buck and Mizner were walking along Forty-ninth Street, Mizner took him by the arm and led him across the street. Mizner explained that it was necessary to bypass the Rand. "Never walk in front of it," he said. "The girls throwing down keys to their friends will knock your brains out."

Mizner was arrested on the complaint of two guests, Edward W. Knight and Burton Verden, who said that he had beaten them up with what they judged to be brass knuckles. Mizner denied it. Friends of Mizner said that he always advised against brass knuckles, saying they harmed the user more than the victim. He advocated closing the fingers over a saltcellar or a handful of silver or pennies, asserting that the important thing was to fortify the fist by a grip on something solid. Mizner's own knuckles were badly broken and staved in. About a quarter of a century after the Hotel Rand days, James Cagney happened to notice the battered knuckles. He suggested that Mizner must have done a lot of fighting in his early days. "Oh, no," said Mizner. "I got those knocking down dames in the Klondike."

On October 8, 1907, the *Press* announced that Mizner had retired from the management of the Rand. The *Press* added, "The change in the management of the hotel was such an interesting topic that half the chorus girls missed their cues last night."

Mizner began writing for the stage. After turning out a couple of vaudeville acts, he wrote a full-length play, "The Only Law," in collaboration with George Bronson-Howard. It was produced at the Hackett Theatre on August 2, 1909. It concerned a broker named Bannister, who kept a chorus girl named Jean, who kept a gigolo named McAvoy. It was about the first unetherealized glimpse of the underworld that New York theatregoers had ever had.

The dramatic critics of 1909 were spiritual colleagues of Anthony Comstock. They hated, in the words of Dr. Henry Van Dyke, anything that was not "sweet and pure and of good report." It was clear from the start that Mizner would not get along well with these people. William Winter, dean of the evangelical critics, in his review of "The Only Law" in the *Tribune*, said, "The play, it will be seen, invited an audience to observe the proceedings of sluts, scoundrels, and boobies." Under the headline "NO GOOD END SERVED BY YEAR'S FIRST PLAY," Louis De Foe in the *World* called it a drama of "tenderloinized life," "a dishonor to the amusement profession," and "vulgar and reprehensible to the last degree." *Hampton's Magazine* said that the show pictured "one profession which has never until now been histrionically treated," but admitted that it had "reality and cleverness." The only strong champion of the play was Clayton Hamilton, who wrote in the *Forum* that it was "the best study of American underworld life yet written" and "the most sincere work of dramatic art" of the current season. The play had only a short run. It might have been a hit a decade or two later; today it would probably be regarded as a passé sermon.

The normal collaborators' hate between Mizner and Bronson-Howard was aggravated by romantic entanglements. Bronson-Howard took the typical revenge of the wronged literary man, writing Mizner up, under the name of Milton Lazard, in a novelette entitled "The Parasite," printed in the *Smart Set* in 1912. This fictionized biography charged that Mizner, besides cheating at cards, stealing pals' mistresses, riding a rail out of town after a Western escapade, and defrauding his own mother, was not funny. Mizner, he said, got his laughs by obvious tricks. Anybody who was willing to abandon his mind to such low devices could be at least as amusing as Mizner, according to Bronson-Howard, who continued:

He worked by formula, was amusing only in certain subjects. A detective couldn't catch a cold, couldn't find a third rail in the subway, couldn't locate a Saratoga trunk in a hotel bedroom, and so on, ad infinitum regarding the subject of detectives, a mere reversal of their astuteness. As for thieves, another class popularly supposed to be clever, a thief couldn't steal a bunch of grass from Central Park, or a handful of water out of the East River without getting an icicle down his back; or a swindler couldn't get a biscuit for a barrel of flour. Philanthropists wouldn't give the Lord a prayer, were closer than the next minute.

It was an ingenious fraud that Bronson-Howard charged Mizner with perpetrating on his mother. Mizner, according to Bronson-Howard, had a confederate send her a wire saying he was dead and requesting a modest sum to save him from burial in potter's field. Bronson-Howard pictured his old associate as a sort of Robin Hood of blackmail; Mizner, he asserted, sold a thousand dollars' worth of information to the victim of blackmailers, enabling him to turn the tables on his persecutors. The collaborator unfortunately gave no details of the alleged ride on the rail. This was probably an invention; a ride on the rail is the sort of honor Mizner would have boasted about for the rest of his life. The collaborator's physical description of Mizner was accurate:

He was like a giant Brownie—a huge head shaped like a coal scuttle, a heavy round stomach, and the thinnest legs and smallest of feet, which, in one more than 6 feet tall, made him something of a monstrosity.

Chapter Seven

GENTLE LARCENY

D AZIAN'S, INC., New York theatrical costumers for more than a century, received an uncommon order for merchandise in the spring of 1910. "Emil," said Wilson Mizner over the telephone to Emil Friedlander, then a young clerk, later chairman of the board of Dazian's, "hustle out to Woodlawn Inn with samples of that super-silk. Stanley Ketchel needs some shirts." Mizner's slightest wish had the urgency of a five-alarm fire to Friedlander. Mizner was the No. 1 sport, or man-about-town, in 1910. He was a glittering object, on display in all the leading Manhattan showcases, from the Haymarket to the Horse Show. A first-nighter and ringsider, he travelled about with startling exhibits like Diamond Jim Brady and Bet-a-Million Gates. He was a conspicuous figure at races, baseball games, and greenroom celebrations, in the company of mature birds of paradise like Lillian Russell or younger specimens like Grace Washburn, of the Winter Garden; Evelyn Nesbit, of the Thaw case; and a few of the breathtaking Mrs. Nat Goodwins and Mrs. Kid McCoys. Mizner was noted for his spectacular entrances. Hat-check girls being almost unknown at that time, he walked into restaurants wearing a made-to-order silk hat two inches higher than the norm. He was a little over six feet three, with a gigantic head and a large statesmanlike face; the caricatures of the time made him look like Woodrow Wilson. According to the Broadway sage Swiftie Morgan, Mizner had the highest collars in the world specially made for him, partly for the insolence of the thing and partly to conceal a frantically bobbing Adam's apple. He carried a white-handled, white-shafted cane three or four inches taller than any other known walking stick and wore an Inverness cape thrown back over his shoulders to show its white satin lining and a spacious white shirt front. The novelist Djuna Barnes, describing him in the *Morning Telegraph,* said that his fingernails were "ovals of opalescent opulence." He was as vertical as the savage ladies who carry baskets on their heads, and for a similar reason—his family explained his extraordinary physical rectitude by pointing out that as a gangling boy he had been compelled for years to balance a large head on a narrow neck. In spite of an air of intelligence, he looked like a young Gotrox, Astorbilt, or Millionbucks out of the pages of *Puck* or *Judge,* and that is exactly what Friedlander took him to be. After hearing from Mizner, Emil caught the next train and made the long, slow journey up to Woodlawn Inn, in the remote wilderness of the Bronx.

Mizner was in the midst of a strange interlude in a strange career. He had recently become the manager of the Michigan Assassin, Stanley Ketchel, middleweight champion of the world and, according to many ring experts, the greatest fighter of his weight since the bare-knuckle days. The new manager had chosen Woodlawn Inn as a training camp because of its remoteness and inaccessibility, but it rapidly became a branch of the Times Square Country Club. Mizner carried the glare of the Great White Way into the James Fenimore Cooper country, and the rustic training camp was filled with Manhattan celebrities. Mizner was managing a great drawing card. Handsome as a half-grown leopard, cute as a devil of two, young Ketchel threatened to become the biggest society fad since John L. Sullivan. Boxing was at a low ebb in 1910, but it became the fashion to make the pilgrimage out to the border of Westchester County to be with

Mizner and Ketchel. Mizner had the reputation of being the town's foremost wit, and his disciples considered it obligatory to open any conversation with "I was out with Wilson Mizner last night, and do you know what he said?" Addison Mizner, after becoming a famous Florida architect, asserted that he found it impossible to get near his brother in this period, because Wilson was always surrounded by a mob, some of them surreptitiously taking notes on his conversation for use in short stories or vaudeville dialogue. All through Wilson's life, the memorizers and middlemen of wit attached themselves to him like jobbers to a manufacturer. In 1910, Wilson was still supposed to possess bags of treasure salvaged from his marriage with Mrs. Yerkes—the sensational match between the Merry Widow and the Candy Kid, as the *Morning Telegraph* described it. Mizner had the double radiance of being a Klondiker and a Californian, although the California aura was becoming slightly moth-eaten. A little later, it disappeared entirely, and Mizner wrote his friend Sam Berger, the learned and philosophical San Francisco heavyweight, that if a man registered from anywhere in California, the hotel clerk automatically gave him drummers' rates and a room without a bath. Mizner blamed this on the Iowa invasion of the Far West and demanded to know why the California legislature, which had appropriated millions to keep out phylloxera, had not made equally large appropriations to keep out Iowans.

After being welcomed to Woodlawn Inn by Mizner, Friedlander laid his samples on a table. Ketchel came in accompanied by four beautiful chorus girls who were helping him train. The girls, all of them collectors' items, broke into cries of delight at the sight of the gorgeous silks. Every piece of goods looked like a small fortune, and the stuff was, in fact, almost prohibitively expensive even in that age of spenders. The material, too rich for the blood of this generation, has not been manufactured for years. The only fabric faintly suggesting it today is found on jockeys and "The Blue Boy." Back in 1910, it was specially woven for Dazian's, and sold to a few mad producers who staged musical extravaganzas on a damn-the-expense basis. The Dazian

silk was impregnated with gleaming metal. Under a dim illumination it glowed like hot iron, and in a strong light it became a
sunburst of color. Ketchel was wild about the samples. He led
off with an order for one set of shirts and tights in forest-fire red
and followed it up with a second order, in bonbon blue. Then
he had the girls select their favorite colors. Ketchel was shirt-
crazy, and so was Mizner. Some of the early caricatures of Mizner emphasize his gaudy haberdashery and show him wearing
the record-breaking high collars with vertical stripes. When
Ketchel knocked out a heavyweight named Tony Caponi in
Schenectady, Mizner and Ketchel spent the entire purse on
fancy shirts. The purpose in summoning Friedlander had been
to provide the fighter with a few dazzling garments to make an
appropriate flash as he entered the ring, but Ketchel kept on
ordering until he had a wardrobe for a small musical comedy and
colors to ride for seventeen racing stables.

Friedlander was happy at first. He felt that he was pioneer-
ing new territory. Dazian's had hitherto made costumes for the
theatrical profession only. The old champions Fitzsimmons and
Jeffries had each possessed one Dazian shirt but had worn them
only for stage appearances. As Friedlander was gleefully con-
gratulating himself, he suddenly experienced a slight chill. The
price of the shirts was fifty dollars apiece. The entire order, including tights and a few bathrobes, came to more than twenty-
four hundred dollars. Emil remembered that the theatrical-cos-
tuming business has two branches; the first is selling the goods,
and the second is collecting the money, and the second branch
requires far more brains than the first. He had shot up rapidly
in the Dazian organization because he was a bill-collecting wizard. He is still famous in the bad-debt annals of Broadway for
a couple of feats he had performed before the Ketchel episode.
Two celebrated theatrical magnates had rolled up huge bills at
Dazian's, had wiped them out by going through bankruptcy, and
had become rich again. Emil collected the outlawed obligations
in full by breaking the news to the magnates about an exotic
sensation called conscience and convincing them that they could
give their jaded nervous systems a completely new jingle by

merely making out checks in favor of Dazian's. With such
achievements to his credit, he decided, on his way back from
Woodlawn Inn, that he would look pretty silly if he allowed a
prizefighter to rustle in twenty-four hundred dollars' worth of
unpaid-for silks. The stuff had been ordered in Ketchel's name.
Friedlander would have had no misgivings if the order had
come directly from Mizner, who was one of the most solvent-
looking fellows he had ever seen. Further than that, Mizner was
a friend and next-door neighbor of Friedlander's. Mizner's address, like that of many other Broadway celebrities, was "Over
Dazian's," Dazian's being at 142 West Forty-fourth Street, a few
steps east of the Hotel Claridge. John Barrymore and others of the
Royal Family, Elsie Janis and her mother, and a long list of
other stars lived, at one time or another, "Over Dazian's." Wilson had a seventh-floor suite that has since been converted into
the office of the chairman of the board of Dazian's. In 1910,
Friedlander lived in a single room next to Mizner. It was not an
ideal location, for heartbroken quartets frequently sobbed out
old ballads around daybreak, and at times a burning-tannery
smell would seem to penetrate the walls. Mizner explained that
this was only the Campfire Boys commuting to the Orient, which
was his flowery way of describing an opium-smoking party. Feeling that Mizner was reliable, Friedlander went to him with the
problem of Ketchel's bill. Mizner whisked out a roll and peeled
off twenty-four hundred-dollar bills and some smaller ones. The
garments were delivered, and Mizner had the honor of managing the most expensively dressed fighter in history.

Managing Ketchel was a sideline with Mizner. Looked on
as a struggling young man of leisure, he was actually a responsible executive in a mysterious industry that he described as
"gentle larceny." He had a sixth sense, a kind of psychological
divining rod, for locating chumps with detachable bank rolls.
George Bush, a noted Broadway buccaneer, states that Mizner
was always known by his enthusiastic confederates as the
Champion, because of his unparalleled instinct for finding easy
marks and his accurate estimate of the amount of plunder that
could be taken from them without provoking a squawk to the

police. Djuna Barnes wrote that Wilson at street level could hear a ten-dollar bill fall on a plush carpet ten stories up. Captain Lefty James, of the Los Angeles Police Department, considered himself a leading authority on confidence games; after talking with Mizner, he said, "Nobody in America is qualified even to discuss the subject in that man's presence." Mixing in the gay and grand life was a business as well as a pleasure for Mizner, because it kept him in friendly communion with the rising generation of saps. The probabilities are that he used Ketchel as a wonderful piece of bait for attracting gilded imbeciles and taking over their quick assets. Mizner was nevertheless devoted to Ketchel, and he was still shedding honest tears over Ketchel's memory twenty years after the fighter's death. Mizner was originally a disinterested hanger-on in the Ketchel camp, and he rendered his greatest service to Ketchel on an honorary basis. Billy Papke had knocked out Ketchel in the twelfth round on September 7, 1908. The Ketchel adherents claimed that their man had fought in a daze, because Papke had stunned him with a sneak punch as they were shaking hands at the start of the fight. The two men were rematched. Mizner ostentatiously deserted Ketchel and enlisted under the banner of Papke. Ketchel was drinking and wenching himself into a dissipated wreck, according to Mizner, who said, "I'm through with that bum forever." Gaining a man's confidence was Mizner's vocation, and within a short time Papke believed that Wilson was the greatest pal any guy ever had. He wouldn't listen to anybody but his new chum. Mizner pointed out the folly of Papke's punishing himself with a hard training grind when he was to meet a sodden ruin like Ketchel. The Papke camp became a delightful scene of champagne parties attended by pretty girls, whom Mizner was always able to command in profusion. The return match was held on November 26, 1908, in San Francisco. Ketchel entered the ring in perfect condition. Papke was fat and couldn't coördinate well. The encounter became famous as the Cat and Mouse Fight. Ketchel could have knocked Papke out at any moment, but he preferred to make him suffer. Whenever he judged that Papke had had all the punishment he could absorb, Ketchel would slow up for a while and let him revive, in accordance with the old principle of the torture chamber. In the eleventh round, Papke became unconscious from general misery. From that time on, Ketchel worshipped Mizner. His manager was the famous Willus Britt. After Britt died, in 1909, Ketchel wouldn't hear of being managed by anybody but Mizner.

Mizner's connection with Ketchel was the climax of a sustained infatuation with the ring. He was probably the greatest unpaid sparring partner and training-camp hanger-on that the country ever produced. He boxed with a long dynasty of champions and contenders. Jack Johnson told Ashton Stevens, the Chicago drama critic, that Wilson could have amounted to something in the ring but for his pipestem legs. Mizner was an accomplished loafer, and the most important loafing in the world is done around training camps. He was not wholly platonic in his love of pugilism. He had good judgment in picking winners of unfixed bouts. Also, many of his best friends were miscreants, and he could usually make a killing with inside information on any fight with a preordained finish.

Wilson Mizner had become dedicated to the prize ring in childhood because he was born in Benicia. The cult hero of the place was the Benicia Boy, John C. Heenan, the best-known American fighter before Sullivan. When the Benicia Boy fought his celebrated fight with Tom Sayers, the British champion, at Farnborough, England, in 1860, Benicia was put on the map by a prizefighter as no other place has ever been, with the exception of Bendigo, Australia, a city of thirty thousand souls, which was named after the Great Bendigo. Wilson's five brothers, and all the other young men of his generation, wanted to be Benicia Boys. The windmill and tank house of the Mizner property was the Stillman's Gymnasium of Benicia. At least three of the Mizner brothers reflected credit on Heenan's memory. The oldest of the three, Edgar Ames Mizner, whipped twenty-six men in a Klondike barroom, according to the fraternal statistics of Addison. The San Francisco *Examiner* recorded the fact that Edgar beat up a mob of miners who attacked its Klondike corre-

Reginald Marsh

spondent, E. J. Livernash, in Dawson City. Addison, in spite of being an artist and a dude, tided himself over a financial crisis in Australia by becoming a professional heavyweight, and Wilson won fame as a rough-and-tumble fighter on the Barbary Coast.

Heenan had gone to California as a boy gold-seeker in 1852 and, after bad luck in the mines, made a living by swinging a thirty-two-pound sledge hammer for twelve hours a day in the Benicia shop of the Pacific Mail Steamship Company, which was the most important legal client of Lansing Bond Mizner, Wilson's father. Heenan earned the name of the Benicia Boy by whipping most of the amateur talent around San Francisco Bay and attracted national attention by knocking out a well-known Eastern professional named Gallagher, in a moonlight bout in Sacramento. After coming East in 1858, he was defeated by the American champion John C. Morrissey, but it was recognized that Heenan had made a great fight on one leg, the other having been badly damaged during training. Morrissey retired from the ring to enter New York politics and eventually became a state senator, leaving the Benicia Boy the undisputed heavyweight king.

Prizefighters were romantic heroes at that time because they were outlaws. The spectators were outlaws, too. There was a happy atmosphere of riot and revolution, of Shays' Rebellion and the Whiskey Insurrection, about the great encounters. Honors were showered on Heenan. He was painted, engraved, daguerreotyped, dramatized in the Bowery Theatre, biographied in the sporting press, appointed to a federal sinecure, and constituted a member of the Tweed Ring. As a matter of course, he married the supreme specimen of American womanhood—Adah Menken, the actress and poet, who was enshrined in verse by Swinburne and Rossetti, honored with attentions by Dickens and Mark Twain, made much of by Walt Whitman and Bret Harte, and taken as a mistress by the elder Dumas and Théophile Gautier. George Sand was the godmother of her child. Adah has a rightful place in history as the originator of the strip-tease act, according to Billy Rose, although the old photographs show her still mantled in silk and velvet clear up to the chin at the end of her sensational uncloaking scene in "Mazeppa."

It was the Heenan-Sayers fight that gave the Benicia Boy the fame that lasted long enough to influence the life of Wilson Mizner. No other fighter has ever been so thoroughly wrapped up in the American flag as was the Benicia Boy. America had been claiming to be one of the Great Powers, and Heenan was important evidence in favor of the claim. The British had almost a monopoly of the prize ring, and challenging the British champion was like challenging the British Navy. There was another reason for deep American anxiety over the showing the Benicia Boy would make. For more than a generation, British writers had reported America to be inhabited by a race of invalids. Some attributed American deterioration to tobacco chewing and overheated houses; Dickens blamed it on our drab existence and our table manners, particularly the habit of bolting one's food in order to be sure of getting one's share; the London *Times* took a larger view of the problem and suggested that the decrepitude of America had been brought about by geographical and climatic factors. Americans denied that this continent was one vast infirmary. The Heenan-Sayers fight had the status of a medical examination of the United States, and the patient naturally had a lively concern as to the outcome.

The battle took place in Farnborough, Hampshire, on April 17, 1860, in spite of determined efforts by the British police to stop it. The Benicia Boy complained that he had been "chased out of eight counties" in which he had sought to do his training. Sayers, disguised as a hostler, was smuggled to the arena in a dray for transporting horses. It was asserted that the Houses of Parliament were deserted for the fight, and historian R. J. Purcell states that Queen Victoria was reported to have commanded that tidings of the go be relayed to her forthwith. Heenan weighed about a hundred and eighty pounds. Sayers weighed only about a hundred and fifty, but he had knocked out many heavier men, including the Tipton Slasher. In the early rounds, Heenan scored knockdown after knockdown, but they were of minor importance, for it was the policy of Sayers to dive for the soft turf in order to avoid punishment. Sayers used his right elbow to ward off punches, and the tendons were so badly damaged by Heenan's bare knuckles that the Britisher's right arm was crippled by the sixth round. In the meantime, Heenan had so bruised his knuckles on Sayers' elbow and skull that his fists swelled up to twice their size, and he could land only puffball punches. The Benicia Boy was severely criticized afterward for having neglected to pickle his hands by steeping them properly in brine. At one point, the bobbies, or blues, broke into the ring and declared the fight at an end. The flash-men and the fancy, as British ring followers were called, wrung their hands in despair, but the American sports dragged the officers out of the ring and sat on them. Sayers' big weapon was a straight left. He almost completely closed both of his oppo-nent's eyes, and the half-blinded Benicia Boy knocked out two of Sayers' seconds and several spectators by mistake. Heenan's chance came when he got Sayers' neck on the rope and was about to strangle him, but some Britishers treacherously pulled out a ring post, causing the rope to fall to the ground. The spectators swarmed in and out of the ring during the next few rounds, and finally the blues, with the aid of volunteers, stopped the battle in the thirty-seventh round. The referee, who had disappeared some time earlier, was eventually located, and he said, "It's a draw." Both sides denounced the decision and charged dirty work. The war of words went on for more than thirty years in magazine articles and memoirs. One eyewitness, Lord Redesdale, stated in his autobiography that the rough Yankee element had invaded the ring to save Heenan and the bets they had placed on him; another eyewitness, Frederick Locker-Lampson, the British poet, stated in his autobiography that the rough British element had invaded the ring to save Sayers and the bets they had placed on him.

The literary and pictorial treatment of the fight made it the greatest of ring classics. No other slugging match has ever had such an extensive bibliography. Byron and Moore, Hazlitt and Thackeray had already made pugilism a high theme for prose and rhyme, and the contemporary British writers were on their mettle. *Punch* had a long poem on the fight; the London *Times* described it in a three-column word picture; other accounts say that Dickens was chagrined because previous engagements prevented him from covering it personally, but he assigned his best men, who wrote an animated account of it for his magazine, *All the Year Round*. The memoir writers hacked away at the story for decades. Gifted artists turned out engravings of the fight that today are art treasures, eagerly sought after by collectors—spirited color prints not only of the gladiators but also of the aristocracy and gentry clustered about the ring in their silk hats and beautifully tended whiskers. The saloons and stores of Benicia became museums of Heenan-Sayers art, and the boys of the town learned how to hold their dukes from the stirring old prints. A grammar-school classmate of Wilson's, Veola Kirkman, has told how Wilson, when he was eleven or twelve, drove her in a yellow-wheeled surrey with rubber tires and a fringed parasol to see the shrine—the crumbling adobe house where the Benicia Boy had once lived. The spot is now marked by a tablet.

Benicia had another association with the prize ring that stimulated Wilson's enthusiasm for boxing. In 1889, the home town was again put on the sporting map by the amphibious combat between James J. Corbett and Joe Choynski—the most picturesque land-and-sea action since the Texas cavalry captured the Mexican Navy in 1836. The Corbett-Choynski incident occurred practically in the bosom of the Mizner family. Jim Corbett, in his autobiography, "The Roar of the Crowd," wrote, "That night they put me on the train for the little country town called Benicia. From the station I was taken to the home of Wilson Mizner, the author of 'The Deep Purple' and other famous plays which later had long runs on Broadway." The Mizners were the great baronial family of Benicia. Elsie Robinson, who then lived in Benicia and wrote about it in her autobiography, "I Wanted Out!," asserts that the Mizners were the first people in California to have a modern indoor outhouse and that the red-letter event in Benicia social history was the brilliant function in honor of the improvement. The Mizner home was a social and sporting outpost of San Francisco, because it was practically in a duck marsh, near the quail and deer country, not far from a famous trotting-horse track, and in the vicinity of several important cockfighting arenas.

Prizefighting was still felonious and romantic in 1889. Corbett and Choynski were relentlessly pursued by posses before they were finally able to fight it out. Both men were products of the Olympic Club, of San Francisco, a famous nursery of athletes. Corbett, who was then twenty-three, was later known as Gentleman Jim and Pompadour Jim, but in 1889 he was called the Professor, because he held the chair of boxing at the Olympic Club. The Professor was still an amateur in 1889, although he could make nearly any professional look ridiculous. His pupils reported that to box with him was to participate in a fight between the past and the future; their punches always landed at points that he had vacated long before, and his antagonists looked as silly as men running after a streetcar. The Professor was reputed to have ten fists and a disappearing head. He loved his beautiful art and put on a show as graceful as Nijinsky's or Mordkin's. Ancient motion pictures show him pirouetting, fluttering, toe-dancing, darting, dematerializing, and occasionally smothering his opponents with showers of punches shaken out of an invisible pepperbox. According to the highly authoritative W. O. McGeehan, Corbett at the top of his form was the best of all modern heavyweights—a verdict that doesn't include Joe Louis, who came after McGeehan's time.

Corbett was apparently somewhat spoiled by hero-worshippers. Joe Choynski once told Will Irwin that it was an unwritten law of the Olympic Club that anybody who played handball, checkers, billiards, or any other game with the Professor had to lose to him in order to humor the young wizard. A faction grew up in the Olympic Club that regarded Corbett as too grand. This disgruntled element put forward a theory that Joe Choynski could lick Corbett any day of the week. Joe weighed only about a hundred and sixty pounds against Corbett's hundred and eighty, and Joe lacked science, but he was game and a slugger. Later in his career, he fought a twenty-round draw with

Jeffries and knocked out Jack Johnson. The Choynski faction rained insults on the Professor. Corbett's father had forbidden his son to turn professional, but he eventually became incensed and ordered him to beat Choynski for the honor of the family. Nat Fleischer, biographer of Corbett, states that a purse of twenty thousand dollars was raised by the sports of San Francisco, gate receipts being out of the question, since the law would have regarded the sale of tickets as something like charging admission to a train robbery. The twenty thousand dollars had to be returned to the subscribers, because the plotters weren't able to figure out a way of outwitting the authorities and holding the fight in private. Finally, a plan was worked out, and another purse raised. Sworn to secrecy, a couple of hundred San Franciscans crossed the Golden Gate on the morning of May 30, 1889, and made their way to a barn near Fairfax, in Marin County. But the news had leaked out, the barn was packed with local boys, and it took an hour for the sports to throw out the yokels. Meanwhile, the dusty roads leading to Fairfax were filled with vehicles, from dogcarts to hay wagons. The sun was almost hidden by dust, and the sheriff knew that it meant either a prizefight or a volcano. He was in a difficult position. Public sentiment was overwhelmingly in favor of the fight, but was likewise overwhelmingly in favor of removing any sheriff who permitted it. Following the traffic, the sheriff arrived during the sixth round and invaded the barn, where the spectators were hanging from the rafters and peering down a hay chute. At the cry of "The sheriff!," the stakeholders of side bets fled, California sheriffs being famous for the slogan "Confisticate the stakes and turn 'em loose." Corbett and Choynski switched from two-ounce to sixteen-ounce gloves and tried to convince the sheriff that they were holding Memorial Day exercises, but he threatened wholesale arrests and the broken-hearted sports made their way back to San Francisco.

Finding the fight impossible by land, the sports decided to hold it by sea. An enormous wheat barge was hired and secretly towed to an anchorage off Benicia. The location was chosen partly to cause jurisdictional confusion in the minds of sheriffs, as the barge lay near the boundary line between Solano and Contra Costa Counties. Two hundred oath-bound sports gathered at the San Francisco waterfront at 1 A.M. on June 5th and boarded the tugs Sea Queen and Richmond. It was planned to hold the fight at sunrise, in the hope of finishing it while the sheriffs were still in bed, but last-minute difficulties interfered with the schedule. Both tugs got stuck in the mud near Benicia, and the sports had to be transferred by rowboats. It was a dangerous scramble up the high sides of the barge. An extremely important politician named Phil Crimmins and a scarcely less important one named J. J. Kenny fell into the Bay and were nearly drowned. The deck of the barge was found to be full of cracks and splinters, and carpenters had to be called in to nail smooth boards over the arena. Paul Reveres began to carry the news along the shore, and the barge was soon surrounded by the whole sea power of Benicia—skiffs, rafts, scows, sailboats, and steam launches. The town boys tried to swarm up the sides of the barge. After all the trouble the San Francisco sports had had with the local plebeians at the Fairfax barn, they had come prepared to repel boarders. Wilson Mizner, according to some authorities, had the knuckles of one hand smashed with a boat hook as he tried to climb on the barge, and was forced to watch the fight from the rowboat in which he had arrived. The masts and yardarms of sailing ships at anchor near the barge were soon laden with fight fans. The event took place before the advent of the news camera, and the only picture that was printed on the day after the battle was a sort of child's drawing in the San Francisco *Chronicle* showing the barge with a two-story wheelhouse jammed to bursting with the ranking members of the hierarchy of sports, while the lesser ones stood on the deck. The two fighters were in the arena a little after 6 A.M. There was then a further delay; Choynski had forgotten to bring his gloves. A spectator furnished a pair of dogskin driving gloves, and after some argument these were accepted by both sides. Prizefighting was just emerging from its bare-knuckles stage, and the humane function of the glove was to protect the fist of the battler rather than the profile of his adversary. The bout finally got under way at about six-thirty. Corbett's eurythmic dancing and lightning jabs made Choynski look pathetic in the early rounds. But Corbett was too clever, too efficient. The wooden floor of the arena became slippery with Choynski gore, and the ballet-dancing Professor could no longer get a decent purchase on it with his toes. His greatness was in his toes; no other heavy-weight ever approached Corbett in footwork. The Professor was now unable to time his steps with his usual precision, and in the fourteenth round a powerful Choynski left caught him in the eye and staggered him. Historian Fleischer records that Corbett's brother Harry burst into tears and thought all was lost. But Choynski was too weak from loss of blood to follow up his advantage. All Corbett needed was a rest, while Choynski needed transfusions. In the twenty-seventh round, Choynski went down and stayed down. "JOE JABBED TO DEATH" was the San Francisco *Examiner's* headline. Some of his sympathizers blamed his defeat on the middleweight champion, Jack Dempsey (the Nonpareil, not the Manassa Mauler). The Nonpareil, a marvellous ring craftsman, had been hired by wealthy backers of Choynski to tutor him in the higher branches of boxing, and it was charged that Dempsey had spoiled Choynski as a slugger without making him a sensitive artist.

The Corbett-Choynski fight and the legend of the Benicia Boy were important influences in shaping the career of Wilson Mizner. The dream of his early life was to be a distinguished fighter or an illustrious sport. It was futile for his family to try to convince him that judges, senators, generals, and cotillion leaders were superior to leather-pushers and prize-ring followers. For generations, the Mizners and their in-laws had abounded in important people. Wilson's full name was Wilson Reynolds Mizner, the Reynolds coming from his great-great-uncle Sir Joshua. Two of Wilson's uncles were generals in the Regular Army. Brother Edgar was named after cousin Edgar Ames, a leading pork-packer and social potentate of St. Louis, who once lent his coach horses to the Prince of Wales. The family tree teemed with governors, senators, judges, and diplomats. Papa Mizner had been Minister Plenipotentiary to Central America.

Uncle Robert Semple had practically founded California with his bare hands. In view of Wilson's ancestry and his native brilliance, the Mizners expected big things of him, but one day they learned that he had run away in a red sweater and become the second of an obscure fighter named Kid Savage.

During the brake-beam tour of the Northwest in the Savage entourage, Wilson was stranded in the wide-open town of Spokane. For a time, he lived by his wits in the red-light district, where he was known as Little Willie, because, although only seventeen, he was already over six feet tall. He made his début on the professional stage as ringmaster of the Society Circus, at the roaring Louvre Café, but he was ruined by popularity, according to the Spokane *Spokesman-Review*, which stated that his every appearance caused such an outburst of cheering, whistling, shouting, and stamping that it became necessary to fire him so that the show could proceed. He was in such reduced circumstances, the account went on, that he had to borrow paper and an envelope and a stamp to write home for money. That was when Wilson was arrested for vagrancy. He was released in the custody of a lawyer hired by telegraph by the Mizner family. Telling about the case some years later, when Wilson had become front-page news, the lawyer said that Little Willie had been arrested without much justification and that the arresting officer was notorious for his literal interpretation of the vagrancy law and proud of his record as a "vagger." It was true that Wilson had no visible means of support and that even at seventeen he was a favorite of the she-meteors of nocturnal Spokane, but the lawyer said the young fellow was not wholly to blame, since his good looks and charming ways caused women of all social levels to go crazy over him at sight.

The only way for Wilson to foil the police was to get a steady job. There happened to be a vacancy in Dr. Slocum's Medicine Show, which was then holding a scientific seminar in Spokane, and one of the actors at the Louvre Café recommended Little Willie for the vacancy. "He learned to act with Daly's Stock Company in New York, and he can talk Latin," said the actor. "Let's hear him talk Latin," said Dr. Slocum. Wilson, who had lived in Guatemala during his father's plenipotentiary days, rattled off a string of Spanish oaths. "By God, he *can* talk Latin!" exclaimed Dr. Slocum, and he appointed Wilson professor of internal medicine and manager of the trained bear. Dr. Slocum had beautiful green, red, and yellow maps of the internal arrangements of the male and female anatomies. Standing on a platform, pounding the maps with a rattan stick, Wilson would describe how Dr. Slocum's medicine, in a grand steeplechase through the nerves, arteries, and vital organs, drove the devils of disease out of the human constitution. Whenever Mizner approached any part of the human geography that was considered to be in questionable taste, Dr. Slocum would ask him to express himself in the modest obscurity of a dead language, and Mizner would whack the embarrassing area with his rattan stick and swear frightfully in Spanish. Dr. Slocum outfitted his young colleague with a broad-brimmed felt hat, drilled him in "thee"s and "thou"s, and tried to make him a Quaker doctor, but he gave up the experiment because Wilson could never get the hang of radiating spiritual tranquillity.

In an interview in the New York *Press* of January 22, 1911, seventeen years after he had abandoned his practice, Mizner described Dr. Slocum's travelling medical center, which included a flea circus and Bianca the Beautiful, who did a fire dance with flaming, kerosene-soaked gauze while her husband, who had the pickpocket concession, played a portable organ under an iron umbrella. The interviewer tried to get a specimen of Mizner's medical eloquence but succeeded only in obtaining the following doubtful sample: "Do you experience a gnawing sensation after having abstained from food for several days? Do you feel an inclination to be tired after a walk of thirty miles? After a week or two of sleeplessness, do you suffer from falling eyelids? Are you conscious of a fluttering in the heart when passing millinery or delicatessen shops?" Lewis Wood, later of the Washington staff of the New York *Times*, who was a London correspondent when Mizner was director of Clifford Fischer's London show "Come Over Here," in 1913, once heard

Wilson describe his lecturing technique. The young professor started by showing glass jars containing historic tapeworms that had taken up residence in United States senators, heavyweight prizefighters, and revered theologians but had been dispossessed by dollar bottles of Dr. Slocum's Vermifuge. Now and then, Mizner would hold aloft a tremendous glass jar containing something that looked like a cross between the Loch Ness Monster and the Fabulous Dragon of Wantley, but he would put it aside without comment, in order to allow the suspense to rise. Finally, Bianca the Beautiful, a radiant little creature, would do her sensational arson dance. At the end, Mizner would again hold aloft the tremendous jar, and tell the tale of how this celebrated exhibit had once inhabited Bianca the Beautiful and had been summarily evicted by a single dollar bottle of Dr. Slocum's Vermifuge. Then the whole personnel of the medical academy would start selling the wonder-working remedy.

Mizner resigned from the medical fraternity after his activities had come to the attention of his uncle Eugene Semple, former Governor of Washington Territory. Semple telegraphed to the Mizner family, and they sent Addison into the Northwest to locate Wilson and bring him home. Addison found his younger brother managing Dr. Slocum's trained bear in sparring matches with dogs and gaining experience that was invaluable in his later career as manager of Kearns, Fitzsimmons, and Ketchel. The bear, chained to a stake in the middle of a small arena, was defeating all comers by slapping them over the ropes with right and left uppercuts. The story of the bear's last appearance under the management of Wilson has been widely circulated by Richard Barthelmess, Philip Boyer, Lytle Hull, Charles Speer, and dozens of others who had it from Addison. Their accounts differ in some details. The tale, however, was independently told by Wilson and Addison to Sam Morse, who was a friend of all six of the Mizner brothers. According to the Morse version, Wilson was comparatively rich from the bets he had won on the bear, but he agreed to go home with Addison after the bear had fought an important fight in a Montana town with a dog named Breen. Wilson said that Breen was being backed by a lot of sucker money and he wanted the chance to collect it. At the Montana town, the Breen following appeared so confident that Wilson became worried and demanded a look at the challenger. He and Addison were led to a dark stable, where they dimly made out a big, terrifically snarling animal. "He's a tough-looking hound," Wilson whispered to Addison, "but he won't last a minute with my bear." Wilson and Addison bet their last nickel on their entry. The gong sounded. The challenger charged into the ring. The bear roared and assumed its fighting pose. Instead of closing in, the two contestants paused, sniffed, and looked each other over. Suddenly, they seized each other with woofs of affection. Breen turned out to be an attractive young she-bear, and the champion couldn't be induced to lift a paw to her save in the way of kindness. At the end of three minutes, the stakeholders, despite Wilson's and Addison's protests, handed over the money to the backers of Breen. The brothers were completely cleaned out, but Addison had two tickets to San Francisco, and they took the next train home.

Chapter Eight

KETCHEL

WILSON MIZNER gave convincing evidence of his love of prizefighting in 1906, when, after marrying Charles T. Yerkes' widow, he turned one wing of the Yerkes mansion, on Fifth Avenue, into a training camp for prizefighters. Mizner was proud of his big brown home, with its Italian garden and two fine art galleries. He was highly pleased at being the successor of the man who had constructed the Chicago "L" and part of the London Tube. In one moment of enthusiasm, he exclaimed, "I own everything that runs on wheels in Chicago!," and in another he said, "I'm the only man who was ever accused of stealing a subway." It had taken Yerkes a lifetime of industry and rascality to build up this estate; Wilson sang himself into it in a few weeks. He had good looks and a wonderful line of conversation, but it was his singing of sad old ballads that made him irresistible to the widow.

Mizner was also proud of his neighbors. He was close enough to the Astors to run over with a plate of soup in case of illness. Thomas Fortune Ryan lived next door. Andy Carnegie was a few blocks up the Avenue. Mizner was now as close to the Fricks, Garys, Vanderbilts, Goelets, and Whitneys as he had

been in the Klondike to Diamond Tooth Gertie, the Scurvy
Kid, Nellie the Pig, Two-Toothed Mike, Deep-Hole Johnson,
and Jerkline Sam. Yerkes had fixed the house up very much
to the taste of Wilson Mizner. He had spent several million
dollars building the stately four-story edifice on the south corner of Fifth Avenue and Sixty-fourth Street. He had poured out
additional millions on carving, painting, gilding, and inlaying
the interior and had stocked it with art treasures selected with
considerable judgment. Prizefighters have seldom worked off
their surplus fat in more elegant surroundings.

Mizner said later that he had the shock and scare of his
life when he was running his palace as a training camp. Waking
late one morning with a hangover, he had walked to the great
Roman pool of gold-mounted green onyx that served him as
a bathtub. He was halfway down the marble stairs to the water
when he was petrified by the sight of the symbol of the Black
Hand on a tapestry. After his marriage, Mizner had received
sacks of begging letters, which were followed by sacks of threatening letters. He had scoffed at Black Hand letters, but in 1906
no man could scoff at the dread emblem in his own bathroom.
The Black Hand was then a busy organization, and bombs and
infernal machines were popping all over town. Mizner's first
thought was that some of his battalion of servants must be Black
Handers. Suddenly, however, to his immense relief, the explanation occurred to him. On the preceding day, one of the footmen
had, with some misgivings, ushered in a fighter named Kid
Broad, and Mizner had told the Kid to take a bath. As the Kid
was cautiously tiptoeing into the water, he steadied himself by
putting his hand on the tapestry.

The mansion was a marvellous playhouse for Mizner and
his sporting pals. Yerkes, who belonged to the old school of miscellaneous collectors, had picked up a vast variety of antique
hand bells, enamelled and jewelled with saints, heroes, and
landscapes, and Mizner could ring for his servants with any one
of a hundred little instruments of exquisite workmanship. Yerkes
had also been a collector of antique timepieces, and Mizner, a
perpetual adolescent, lost his mind over the Clock Room. The

clocks were silent when he became master of the mansion, and one of his first directions to his servants was to wind them all up and to bring in experts to deal with the recalcitrant ones. Every hour on the hour, the Clock Room was a pandemonium. A whole aviary of stuffed birds began to whistle and sing. Muscular men of cast metal stepped out of hidden doors and smote gongs with sledge hammers. A full orchestra of tiny musicians swung out on a turntable, slowly raised their bows, and then frantically sawed away at violin strings. Nineteenth-century railroad clocks clanged and whistled as locomotives emerged from one tunnel with a train of passenger coaches and disappeared into another. Steamships came out screeching, paddled under bridges, and cruised back into their cases. Peasants came forth and called their cows with melodious horns. Clocks pealed, tolled, and jingled, and rendered minuets from hidden music boxes. Roy L. McCardell, writer and inventor of a thousand advertising slogans, was a friend of Mizner's and a visitor at the mansion. He estimated the number of clocks at two thousand. The cream of the fun for Mizner was showing the room to friends with hangovers and seeing their nervous systems murdered when all the clocks let go at once. Mizner told McCardell that his first serious domestic strife arose over the clock

Reginald Marsh

situation. He came home sober one morning, went to bed a little after 3 A.M., and was roused at four by the shrieking of a cuckoo clock in his own room. He had ordered his servants to make every clock run, and they had taken him literally. He got up, cursing, and found the clock, high up on the wall and out of reach. He went to the Yerkes arsenal, on the fourth floor, returned to his room, and went to bed again. When the cuckoo screamed at 5 A.M., he lit the lights and gave it both barrels of one of the Yerkes shotguns. That, according to McCardell, started the bride wondering whether her new consort had the true Fifth Avenue spirit.

Mizner's honeymoon was still producing dividends when Willus Britt, one of the superior crazy men of San Francisco, arrived in New York. Mizner loved him like a brother. They had been pals and accomplices for years in Nome and San Francisco. Willus, who preceded Mizner in the dynasty of managers of Stanley Ketchel, was in 1906 managing his brother Jimmy Britt, a great lightweight, who was scheduled to fight at the old Madison Square Garden with Terrible Terry McGovern. Willus felt that the training camp in the Yerkes mansion lacked facilities for roadwork, and he took his brother to Coney Island. Mizner closed up his palatial gym and joined them there. This caused a certain amount of domestic friction. Mrs. Yerkes had been horrified by the publicity attending her marriage to Mizner, especially by the cartoons of Tom Powers and by reports that had reached her of the ribald ballads on the Mizner-Yerkes nuptials that were sung at Hammerstein's by Jack Norworth. Just as the notoriety was simmering down, the sporting pages broke out with accounts of Mizner's sparring with Sam Berger, the San Francisco heavyweight. Mizner was not a man to let a few millions stand between him and the fun of hanging around a training camp, and he became the new Coney Island sensation. He hired an infant prodigy called Groucho Marx to sing to Jimmy Britt in order to cure him of homesickness, and he helped Willus with the arrangements for the fight, which resulted in a victory for Jimmy Britt before ten thousand people. After the fight, the fighters were arrested on suspicion of fighting, but the case was dropped for lack of evidence. Mizner went home and made up with his lawfully wedded lady, but after several additional differences and reconciliations, he chucked the millions out the window forever, in the summer of 1906, by going to Goldfield, Nevada, to hang around the training camps of Joe Gans and Battling Nelson.

Mizner was thirty-three when he became the manager of Stanley Ketchel. At seventeen, he had managed the boxing black bear, and in the sixteen intervening years he had managed fighters in Dawson City and Nome and picked up great fistic experience in San Francisco. He had managed Bob Fitzsimmons and others on tours of the sagebrush opera houses, posting a money guarantee that all challengers would be disposed of in two rounds, and occasionally, it is said, saving the guarantee by tapping the challenger over the head with a mallet after he had been maneuvered into a suitable position against the backdrop. Bat Masterson, onetime free-shooting Western marshal and later sportswriter on the New York *Morning Telegraph*, has said that Mizner attracted much favorable attention as a gentleman sparring partner. Mizner, according to Bat, made such a showing against the great heavyweight Tom Sharkey that he *was implored by Sharkey's manager, Tim McGrath, to turn* professional, but Mizner was afraid of alienating his extremely respectable family. According to Bat, Mizner contemplated turning professional only once, and that was when a miner named Jack Munroe was matched with Jeffries for the heavyweight title. As Wilson made a practice of sampling the punches of all champions and contenders, he sparred with Munroe and found that he could handle him like a sack of potatoes. Thereupon, Mizner confided to intimates that he was going to take a shot at the heavyweight crown himself if Jeffries had any trouble with the miner. But when Munroe collapsed almost at sight of the champion, Mizner decided to cling to his amateur standing. Mizner was, in fact, a rather silly amateur in most matters. While he devoted much of his life to preying on suckers, he was himself the prize sucker of the era. He let everybody else cash in on his wit and brilliance. Short stories and theatrical dialogue were plundered from his conversation; he threw more anecdotes and epigrams into the public domain than any other man of his time. In similar fashion, he gave away his fistic science as an unpaid sparring partner and lavished it on the public in street fights and saloon brawls. Jack Hines, a globe-trotter and the author of "Minstrel of the Yukon," said he was present when Mizner took the revolvers out of the hands of two men who were blazing away at each other in a Nome saloon, and said, "You kids oughtn't to be allowed to play with these toys." One of the San Francisco weeklies commemorated a fracas at Spider Kelly's saloon in which Mizner fought against enormous odds until he was finally subdued by three civilians, a policeman with a nightstick, and a bartender with a bung starter named Dearest, in honor of Little Lord Fauntleroy's mother.

Tim McGrath wrote a letter to Mark Kelly, Los Angeles sports and screen writer, describing a battle in which Mizner knocked out longshoremen by platoons in a San Francisco barroom. Wilson, one of the leading dudes in town, wore a suit that was a declaration of war in a waterfront saloon. He started to sing "Sweet Alice, Ben Bolt," with which he had melted sourdough audiences in the Klondike and Alaska. There was a horselaugh. Mizner resented it, and in a moment everybody was punching. Mizner was, luckily, accompanied not only by McGrath but also by the savage middleweight Mysterious Billy Smith, so called because in his early days in the ring he kept disappearing and changing his name. He was famous for biting off a chunk of the ear of the Barbados Demon, Joe Walcott, and for biting a chunk off the index finger of his manager, who had taken the liberty of shaking it at him. McGrath wrote that in the end only one of the longshoremen was on his feet. Mizner was punching away at this man, and the man was paying no attention. Poor Mizner was in despair, believing he had lost his wallop, until Mysterious Billy Smith shouted, "Leave him alone, Wilson! I knocked him out five minutes ago!" Billy's punch had wedged the man between two pieces of furniture, so he couldn't fall.

Mizner was arrested several times in New York for rough-and-tumble fighting, twice becoming the hero of spectacular

trials that resulted in acquittals. One complainant asserted that
he thought Mizner had hit him with a pile driver; another
penned a challenge to Mizner in blood. Wilson's physical condition deteriorated in his early thirties, but he was still able to
throw one terrific punch. If his one punch landed, it would
finish an average opponent; if it missed, Mizner was through.
Old-time acquaintances of his say that when Mizner saw that
war was inevitable, he would arrange for friends to interfere and
stop the brawl after his one punch. In an interview in San Francisco, in his riper days, Mizner delivered a sermon against striking one's fellow-man with one's fist. "If you do," he said, "he
goes out to the washbasin and is soon almost as good as new.
But you go to the emergency hospital with two awkward doctors
trying to get your broken knuckles back in place. Then you are
out for two months. Always hit a man with a bottle—a ketchup
bottle preferred, for when that breaks, he thinks he's bleeding
to death." Mizner was loyal to this principle in the latter part of
his life. Once, a year or two before his death, when he was dining in a Los Angeles restaurant with Cecil Beaton, Irving Berlin,
and Anita Loos, some people at another table started to heckle
Berlin. Fat and decrepit though he was, Mizner went into action
with bottle, glasses, and crockery, driving out not only the
hecklers but the peaceful patrons of the restaurant. "How are
you, Cecil?" Berlin asked after it was all over. "I am gray," said
Beaton.

Mizner was introduced to Ketchel by Willus Britt in a hotel
room in San Francisco, and Ketchel opened the conversation
by cursing Mizner hysterically for throwing his hat on the bed—
the worst kind of bad luck. After this poor start, Mizner and
Ketchel got on wonderfully. They had much in common. Both
of them were ordinarily brimming over with high spirits, and
neither of them cared much about anything, although they were
both rank sentimentalists, always ready to cry over a sad story
or a sad song. The main difference between them was that
Mizner was a sophisticated child of nature and Ketchel was an
unsophisticated one. Ketchel had been a bouncer in the underworld of Butte, and Mizner had been an executive in the under-

world of Nome, and each was tinged with the red-light philosophy of life. Ketchel had a thirst for knowledge, and Mizner had a passion for imparting it. Whenever he could get his clutches on an untaught intellect, he tried to inspire it with a love of literature by reciting poetry. Irving Berlin was the most eminent of Mizner's pupils. Catching Berlin just after his singing-waiter days, when his mind was still a blank sheet of paper as far as general culture was concerned, Mizner sought to create an appetite for literature in the young genius by reciting Kipling's "If" and Wallace Irwin's "Chinatown Ballads" to him. Ketchel delighted in hearing Mizner declaim verses and read O. Henry stories. The middleweight champ was stunned by Mizner's recitation of the Langdon Smith classic that starts "When you were a tadpole and I was a fish, In the Palaeozoic time" and follows the romance of two lovers from one geological age to another, until they wind up in Delmonico's. Ketchel had a thousand questions about the tadpole and the fish, and Mizner, a pedagogue at heart, took immense pleasure in wedging the whole theory of evolution into the fighter's untutored head. Ketchel became silent and thoughtful. He declined an invitation to see the town that night with Mizner and Britt. When they rolled in at 5 A.M., Ketchel was sitting up with his eyes glued on a bowl of goldfish. "That evolution is all the bunk!" he shouted angrily. "I've been watching those fish nine hours and they haven't changed a bit." Mizner had to talk fast; one thing Ketchel couldn't bear was to have anybody cross him. He was a creature of emotions, and he could be a lamb or a devil, according to which emotion happened to be stirred up.

One night, Mizner, Britt, and a famous newspaper artist took Ketchel to meet the chatelaine and maids of honor of one of New York's gaudiest establishments. They received a wild welcome. Corks popped, and eyes sparkled with love and larceny. Suddenly it was discovered that Ketchel was missing. There was a quick search, and he was found in the entrance hall weeping and wailing. On the wall was the picture entitled "Lost in the Storm," showing a sheep in a blizzard. "Oh, the poor little thing!" Ketchel sobbed again and again. A few days later, he opened fire with a Colt .44 through the door of his bedroom at Woodlawn Inn and put a bullet through the leg of one of his best friends, Peter (Pete the Goat) Stone, a night-club owner, who had persisted in knocking at the door to get him up for his roadwork. In the ring, Ketchel was handicapped at times by his humanity. He was loath to hurt any opponent he regarded as a nice fellow. Edward Dean Sullivan, author of "The Fabulous Wilson Mizner," stated that Ketchel, in order to overcome the disadvantage of his good humor, would say to himself in the middle of a round, "That son of a bitch insulted your mother," and filial piety would then turn him into "an example of tumultuous ferocity"—to borrow Philadelphia Jack O'Brien's description of him.

Ketchel had emerged from obscurity on July 4, 1907, when he fought a twenty-round draw at Marysville, California, with Joe Thomas, claimant of the middleweight championship. In the next two years, Ketchel knocked out middleweights and heavyweights in great abundance. He was being managed by a San Francisco photographer named Joe Coffman, who was said to hypnotize him, keep him locked in a bedroom, and impound his clothes every night to prevent other managers from stealing him. In 1908, Willus Britt climbed up a fire escape and stole Ketchel in a bathrobe, according to W. O. McGeehan, the famous sports columnist. Britt was regarded as the smartest manager in the country. A few years earlier, he had been considered rattle-brained. He had once tried to borrow five hundred dollars from James W. Coffroth, the San Francisco sporting czar, for a business trip to New York. Noticing that he was dressed in evening trousers but no coat, Coffroth loaned him a hundred freshly minted pennies, which Willus took for five-dollar gold pieces. Overwhelming Coffroth with gratitude, Britt caught the next train East in his shirtsleeves, with his rouleau of one-cent pieces, and a few weeks later came home comparatively wealthy. Coffroth was greatly impressed, named a saloon the Willus, in Britt's honor, and went into business with him. Willus was credited with inventing the Native Son decision, according to which any Californian, if alive at the end of a prizefight, was automatically victorious over any nonresident. After mopping up the Western territory with Ketchel, Britt decided to take him East. W. O. McGeehan, who was then living in San Francisco, called on Britt and Ketchel shortly before they left California and was surprised to find Ketchel wearing a Phi Beta Kappa key. Britt said that he had procured it at Abe Attell's pawnshop and that he intended to present Ketchel in New York as a young fellow fighting his way through college. Coffroth disapproved of the idea because Ketchel said "dese," "dem," and "dose." Britt said that New Yorkers would never know the difference, but Coffroth had the key stolen, and Britt decided to take Ketchel to New York as a cowboy in high-heeled boots, spurs, chaps, and a sombrero.

Mizner became involved in the management of Ketchel as an unpaid specialist on the political and graft setup in New York. Prizefighting was as illegal as cockfighting or bullfighting. The referees never named a winner, since the fighters were not supposed to seek victory but to coöperate like dancing partners. Any person who "instigated a contention" was liable to a five-hundred-dollar fine or a year in jail; the same penalties were incurred by persons who "published a challenge" or who "trained or assisted a fighter to train." Like streetwalking and gambling, however, prizefighting was generally tolerated upon the payment of protection money. In his ignorance of New York, Britt found himself paying protection to the wrong parasites, and he called Mizner in to teach him the difference between the responsible tapeworms and the frauds. Fights were at that time put on by "athletic clubs," which were organized the way speakeasies were later. Every new arrival was scrutinized by sentinels; anybody who looked like a reformer or stool pigeon was barred. There was no public sale of tickets. Only duly elected club members were admitted. The payment of two dollars at any saloon near the arena made any man a duly elected club member and provided him with a card calling for a good seat; one dollar made him a junior member, with a card entitling him to a bad seat. According to the late Bob Davis, every card was issued in the name of John Smith, in order to simplify the clerical work. Club

meetings usually started with a speech bawling out members for
being derelict in attendance at previous meetings and threatening drastic action under the bylaws.

In spite of the punctual payment of graft, fights were raided
whenever the authorities were seized with a fit of law and order,
and elaborate precautions were considered necessary to prove
that the entertainment consisted strictly of amateur sparring exhibitions of, for, and by club members. The principal arenas
were an old dance hall and an old stable, Madison Square Garden having become too ladylike for fistic programs. The legal
niceties of boxing were like those of drinking in the prohibition
era. Soft punches were innocent, like soft drinks under the Volstead Act. But a hard blow was like hard liquor and instantly
transformed all present into criminals. The only thing that saved
the boxing game in those dark days was club loyalty. It was impossible to find a clubman who had seen a violation of the law.
On one occasion, a Headquarters detective tried to stop a fight
in the stable. He was thrown down a twenty-foot hay chute. The
incident was invisible to fifteen hundred clubmen, including
about a hundred policemen, all honorary members. But at best
the boxing situation was precarious. Newspapers joined the re-
formers in demanding the suppression of the sport. The New
York *Globe* asserted that the so-called "sparring matches" were
gory encounters, denoting a low state of civilization, and charged
that "the brutalized spectators howl with delight at a knockout."
A bill was offered in Congress making it a crime to mail a picture of a fighter and cancelling the postal rights of newspapers
that printed news of fights. It was dangerous for a pugilist to
admit that he was a pugilist; it placed him outside the law, in
danger of being "vagged," or jugged as a vagabond. Ketchel and
Mizner were once arrested on a charge of speeding. When
Ketchel appeared in court, he was asked his occupation. "Physical instructor," he said. In view of the general situation, Britt
felt that he couldn't have too much unpaid advice. He wouldn't
trust anybody but Californians, and Mizner became his chief
adviser. Britt and Mizner called in Hype Igoe, who was himself
of Native Son origin, as an additional consultant.

One of Britt's peculiarities was that although he constantly solicited advice, he seldom took it. After collecting the best opinions available, he would leave all important decisions to a pack of playing cards. He had studied under celebrated fortune-tellers, and he always carried in his pocket a deck of cards, which he used as an artificial brain. Whenever he had to make a decision, he would select a card and take a surreptitious look at it. If the card was lucky, he would say "Yes;" if unlucky, "No;" if dubious, "We'll cross that bridge when we come to it." One day, Mizner stole Britt's little god of fifty-two opinions and substituted a deck consisting entirely of queens of spades. Every time Britt peered into the future, the lady of disaster glared at him. He went all to pieces, spent a week in bed under a doctor's care, and thereafter meekly accepted the suggestions of Mizner and Igoe.

Ketchel's most spectacular fight in New York was his ten-round battle with Philadelphia Jack O'Brien. Nobody knows who won it. O'Brien, the light-heavyweight champion, was one of the cleverest fighters alive—a jigging, feinting, shuttling, side-stepping, jabbing artist. For seven rounds, he played Ketchel like a snare drum. But his style required incessant motion and, beginning to tire in the eighth round, he spent the rest of the fight trying to save himself. Ketchel landed one of his authentic knock-out punches in the closing seconds of the last round. As the referee was counting "six," the gong sounded. O'Brien was unconscious for half an hour. Referees' decisions being forbidden by law, there was only the "newspaper decision," which was mixed, some writers declaring for Jack, since he had won the majority of rounds and was way ahead on points, while others maintained that no man could win a fight in a coma. Some weeks later, in Philadelphia, Ketchel knocked O'Brien out in three rounds. The contemporary accounts credit O'Brien with great gameness under a savage battering, but O'Brien told a different story to Leo McClatchy and other Washington correspondents nearly twenty years later, when he was in the capital in quest of publicity for Philadelphia Jack's Gymnasium for Business Men, in New York. The newspapers had revealed that President Coolidge was taking off weight by riding a mechanical horse, and O'Brien had memorized a speech to the President in which he offered to come to Washington three times a week and fight the President into condition in the White House basement—free. But when he was presented to the President, Jack turned pale, trembled, and couldn't say a word. He tried afterward to salvage a little publicity by telling the correspondents the nature of his mission, and he threw in the story of his life, including the statement that he had taken a dive in the third round of his second fight with Ketchel. Ketchel's backers, he said, were willing to pay for a quick knockout, believing that it would convince the public that Ketchel was a genuine White Hope, with a real chance of delivering the great Caucasian race from its bondage to Jack Johnson, the colored champion.

Nineteen hundred and nine was the big year of the White Hopes. The barrooms were the chief intellectual centers of the country at the time, and it was their despairing conviction that the long career of the fair-skinned peoples had ended with the defeat of Tommy Burns by Jack Johnson in 1908. The gymnasiums were full of clumsy giants training to save our pasty-faced civilization. Ketchel was the best bet of the disinherited albino, although he weighed only a hundred and fifty-five pounds, while Johnson weighed over two hundred. This discrepancy was minimized by the use of crooked scales, which built Ketchel up to a hundred and seventy and cut Johnson down to a hundred and ninety-five. The fight between Ketchel and Johnson was held in Colma, California, on October 16, 1909, and the high tide of Ketchel's career came in the twelfth round, when he knocked Johnson down. Low tide came an instant later, when Johnson knocked him out. The orthodox analysis of this contest was that Johnson had agreed to "carry" Ketchel, or handle him carefully, but that Ketchel attempted to double-cross him. According to Marty Forkins, manager of the late Bill Robinson, the only agreement was that the men were to fight gently for ten rounds in order to let the motion pictures run for a decent length, and that after ten rounds it was each man for himself. Tiv Krelling, a photographer at the fight, says that both the knockdown and the knockout were faked in order to give a box-office climax to the fight pictures. The greatest of living ring chroniclers, Dumb Dan Morgan—nicknamed Dumb by the cartoonist Tad Dorgan because he once talked seven and a half hours without pausing for punctuation—was told by Johnson that Ketchel hit him honestly and hurt him badly. Johnson said that he had a few seconds of intense meditation when he was sitting on the canvas; he felt that his situation was distinctly awkward and that the only course to pursue was to put all he had into one tremendous punch. This was a critical resolution for Johnson to take, since he was preëminently a defensive fighter. A great defensive fighter hates to turn loose his best wallop at an undamaged adversary; it spoils his defensive arrangements, for if the punch misses, he is likely to find himself a wide-open target for a counterpunch. But Johnson didn't miss. His final punch not only flattened Ketchel but knocked out his two upper front teeth, sensational relics that Willus carried in his vest pocket and displayed to spellbound crowds in San Francisco barrooms.

Willus Britt died shortly after the Johnson-Ketchel fight, and Mizner became the full-fledged manager of Ketchel. In his first few months under the Mizner banner, the middleweight champion added little to his reputation. Wurra Wurra McLaughlin, sporting editor of the New York *World*, wrote that Ketchel had ruined himself by "hitting the hop." Ketchel refused to leave a bar in Johnstown, Pennsylvania, to keep a contract to spar in the local opera house, and he was chased out of town by a posse. Mizner pledged the appearance of Ketchel at another exhibition there, but he couldn't find his fighter in time. He eventually located Ketchel lying in bed smoking opium with a blonde and a brunette. Mizner was later asked how he met this crisis. "What the hell could I do?" said Mizner. "I said, 'Move over.'"

Ketchel was a fighter who often took his training seriously, and, in spite of his wild life, he would at times work furiously at Woodlawn Inn, or at New Dorp, S. I., to get himself back into condition. His most famous fight under Mizner's manage-

ment was a six-round, no-decision battle with Sam Langford, the
Boston Tar Baby, in Philadelphia, on April 27, 1910. According
to the accounts, it was a savage affair in which each man gave
and received terrific punishment. The *Morning Telegraph* said
that Ketchel looked like the loser at the end of the fifth round
but that he earned a draw by pounding Langford ferociously in
the sixth. The New York *Press* also called it a draw. The *Morning* and *Evening World* reported that Ketchel had won by a
wide margin. His share of the receipts was nine thousand dollars, the largest sum he ever collected for a fight in the East. In
retrospect, it was the Battle of the Legends. Ketchel and Langford are two of the great heroes of prize-ring folklore. As a whim,
Ketchel is said to have knocked out six heavyweights in Butte
one afternoon and, while half stupefied with opium, to have
knocked out four heavyweights by mistake at a charity benefit
in New York. Damon Runyon wrote, "It has been my observa-
tion that the memory of Ketchel prejudiced the judgment of
everyone who was ever associated with him. They can never see
any other fighter." There is an ever-growing flood of reminiscences about Ketchel in the sporting pages and the gladiatorial
magazines. Ketchel's ghost is the biggest contemporary ring figure, next to Joe Louis. Langford is not the swaggering demigod
that Ketchel is, but the old-time experts generally rated him
above Ketchel. Dumb Dan Morgan, for example, claims that no
fighter, with the exception of Jeffries, could have held his own
with Langford in an unfixed combat. Langford was short and
weighed only a hundred and sixty-five pounds, but he had long,
powerful arms, and staggering statistics are presented as to the
number of ribs he broke with his left to the body. Jack Johnson
is said to have fled three continents to avoid risking his title
against Langford. Veteran fight fans tell of one of Langford's
exploits that parallels Babe Ruth's alleged feat of pointing his
bat toward the centerfield bleachers and then driving a ball to
the spot indicated. Langford, they say, once fought a White
Hope whose manager had proclaimed him to be the coming
champion of the world. Skillfully maneuvering the White Hope
along the ropes, Langford knocked him into the manager's lap,

shouting, "Here comes your champion!" It is asserted that Langford, when he was old and almost totally blind, knocked men out by ear, getting the range of his opponent's jaw by calculations based on the sound of the opponent's feet shuffling on the canvas.

Many of the thirty-third-degree experts of 1910 refused to make the trip from New York to Philadelphia to see the Ketchel-Langford bout. They were convinced that Ketchel wouldn't enter the ring with Langford unless the fight was fixed. The newspapers said it was a glorious and evenly matched contest, but many of the experts were skeptical, and some of them are skeptical to this day. One of the Langford idolizers happened to be Mizner's lawyer. He asked his client for inside information. "Why, the fight was written like a play," said Mizner. "We had it surge to and fro like a melodrama. First, Ketchel in dire distress, then Langford, then Ketchel, and so on. It's the old, old plot." Mizner told his lawyer that he would have had Ketchel win the newspaper decision had he not feared an outcry from the Langford fans that might hurt the fight business, so he arranged to have Philadelphia newspaper opinion add up to a draw. Mizner stated further that, in order to make sure that the scenario was enacted as written, Langford was authoritatively informed that he would not receive a cent of his five-thousand-dollar share of the purse if he knocked Ketchel out.

Ketchel was matched to put on a similar six-act melodrama, ending in a draw, with Willie Lewis, a dashing middleweight. Both fighters gave their word of honor that they wouldn't try for a knockout. The day before the fight, Willie's manager went into a church and lit several candles before the statue of a saint —a common practice of pious fighters and managers. Dumb Dan Morgan, who accompanied Lewis's manager to the church, was aware of the gentlemen's agreement for a draw and was surprised to hear his companion utter a petition for a victory for Willie Lewis and then drop twenty-five cents in the contribution box. As the fight got under way, Ketchel began to swing with studied inaccuracy at his opponent. Willie, however, picked a nice opening and hit Ketchel with all his power, and followed

the blow up with a try for a knockout. Ketchel barely managed
to weather the storm. At the end of the round, instead of sitting
on his stool and being fussed over by his seconds, Ketchel stood
up on it and fixed his eye on Willie with an eloquent and re-
proachful stare. In the second round, Willie kept running away,
but Ketchel caught up with him and summarily knocked him
out. "You are the smartest manager in the business," said Dumb
Dan Morgan to Willie's manager. "You tried to get the world's
middleweight championship for two bits." "I would've if that
saint had stood up," replied Willie's manager.

In New York, on June 10, 1910, Ketchel fought his last
fight, his opponent being Jim Smith, a mediocre heavyweight.
Reporting the Ketchel-Smith fight, the *Morning Telegraph* said,
"Wilson Mizner was on deck, of course, bossing the fight in the
champion's corner. He was dressed as though for a party instead
of a fight and did not soil his immaculate attire by swinging a
towel or dashing water with a sponge." The *Telegraph* added
that Mizner's face showed signs of anxiety under its icy gambler's mask. Ketchel failed to exhibit his old power. He nearly
exhausted himself before he succeeded in dropping Smith in the
fifth round. The general opinion of the fight critics was that
Ketchel was no longer the old Michigan Assassin. Bat Masterson said that Ketchel had been ruined by dancing masters and
tailors. He also remarked that with his own eyes he had seen
Ketchel leading a grand march at Hot Springs, Arkansas, and
that he had a wardrobe of beautiful clothes that would sap any
fighter's vitality.

Ketchel was still deeply concerned over the destiny of the
white race. Its last Hope was the former champion Jim Jeffries,
who after six years of retirement was matched to fight Johnson
in Reno on July 4, 1910. Ketchel and Mizner went to Reno late
in June. They were realistic enough to see that Jeffries was in
no condition to save the white race, and they were philosophers
enough to bet their shirts on Johnson, but Ketchel brooded and
brooded. Shortly before the fight, he came to Mizner with a
statesmanlike project. Just before the bout, the attending celebrities would be introduced to the spectators and would shake

hands with the fighters. Ketchel proposed that, instead of shaking hands with Jeffries, he clip him on the chin. One punch, he said, would knock him cold. This would save the honor of the unpigmented, since a Caucasian wallop would have finished the career of Jeffries. "But think of our dough!" said Mizner. "Look at the money we stand to win when Johnson beats him!" It took an hour's arguing to convince Ketchel that he ought to let the white race take care of itself.

In August, 1910, Mizner arranged for Ketchel to fight Bill Lang, an Australian heavyweight, in New York. At the last minute, Mizner cancelled the match, saying that Ketchel had a boil and a sore foot. Charles I. Meegan charged on the front page of the *Telegraph* that the bout had been shelved because Hugh McIntosh, manager of Lang, refused to post a five-thousand-dollar guarantee that Lang wouldn't knock Ketchel out. Mizner treated the Meegan charges with haughty silence. He had his defenders among the insiders in the fight game. Most of them knew that Ketchel was on the downgrade when Mizner became his manager and that "knockout insurance" was necessary to prolong the colorful battler's career.

In September, 1910, Ketchel went to a farm near Springfield, Missouri, to live the simple life for a while. A dispatch from Springfield to the New York *Sun* said that his doctor had told him that he could not last out the year at the pace he was travelling. Ketchel had been living at the Bartholdi Hotel, in New York; the *Morning Telegraph* said that his bill for his last two weeks there had been five hundred and ninety-three dollars—whirlwind spending at a time when highballs were ten cents apiece. Ketchel was only twenty-four and hoped to get back into fighting trim. By then, Mizner's first successful play, "The Deep Purple," had opened in Chicago and he had lost interest in the prize ring. According to Bat Masterson, Mizner planned a stage career for Ketchel and was working on a vaudeville monologue for him. Out in Missouri, the middleweight champion behaved like a model boy at first, but there was a woman on the farm. Dispatches bluntly described her as ugly, but she possessed the irresistible magic of propinquity. She was known as Goldie

Hurtz, and one morning Mr. Hurtz, a farmhand, shot and killed
Ketchel with a .22 rifle. It looked for a time as if Hurtz would
be saved by the plea that he only did what any honest farmhand
would do under the circumstances. But it turned out that the
honest farmhand was really a dishonest barber named Walter
Dipley, a city slicker hiding out from the Kansas City police.
The unwritten-law defense collapsed when it was found that
Mr. and Mrs. Hurtz had never been married. Tried as accomplices in the crime, they were both convicted and sent up for
long terms.

Chapter Nine

THE DEEP PURPLE

NINETEEN HUNDRED AND ELEVEN was Wilson Mizner's big year. He had suddenly become important and legitimate. He was a successful Broadway playwright. "We were lunching at Shanley's, and the Beau Brummell of Nome and Broadway was magnificent in every way," wrote Colgate Baker in a full-page story about Mizner in the New York *Review.* "The headwaiter bowed lower than I had ever seen him bow before. Even the chef came up from the kitchen to pay his respects. Ah! It is something to be the author of the dramatic sensation of the hour." Mizner was not only a box-office success, he was also the center of an intellectual disturbance. His play, "The Deep Purple," written in collaboration with Paul Armstrong, was a landmark in American culture—the first effective drama about modern city-bred criminals. It was the pioneer get-together of Broadway and Sing Sing, and it started a trend in public taste in bad men, leading audiences to favor metropolitan scalawags over Western outlaws with seventeen notches on their cannons. Conservative critics were outraged by "The Deep Purple." The conservative critics were theological authorities in disguise. They looked on Broadway as a theological seminary and were scandalized when Mizner invaded the campus with his highly specialized rogues.

The professional criminal was not a complete stranger to the stage. He had occasionally appeared as a stylized figure, like Vice or Iniquity, in the old morality plays. But the Mizner scamps were carefully and lovingly painted from life, and he was furiously reprimanded for presenting them as human beings rather than mere symbols of sin. He had defenders, but he was taking a hard pounding when "Oliver Twist" unexpectedly came to his rescue. The old Victorian thriller became the chief exhibit in justification of "The Deep Purple." Bill Sikes and the Artful Dodger were held to be the literary godfathers of Frisco Kate and Pop Clark. Montgomery Phister, a prominent drama writer of the period, did an essay on the parallels between Mizner and Dickens, giving Mizner credit for higher literary integrity because he had actually joined the criminal classes, while Dickens had only read about them. Mizner, making common cause with Dickens, defended that great novelist against the charge of having undermined public morals. "Every church deacon in the country has revelled in the school for crime in 'Oliver Twist,'" he said in an interview in the New York *Press*, "but I have never yet met a safecracker who read it."

"The Deep Purple" caused New York critics to differ more widely than usual. The *Sun* called it stupid and vulgar; the *Evening Sun* called it great. Charles Darnton, of the *Evening World*, said it was the best crook play since "Deacon Brodie;" Louis V. De Foe, of the *Morning World*, classed it with "Nellie, the Beautiful Cloak Model." The *Times* deplored it; the *Herald* said it was no play to take your grandmother to; the *Press* said it "knocked the spots out of all the Arsène Lupins, Jimmy Valentines, and Raffleses." Percy Hammond, then of the Chicago *Tribune*, said it was the greatest melodrama since "Sweeney Todd." Mizner was ruffled by only one of his hostile critics, and that was the man on the *Sun*, who was anonymous. "If that fellow can criticize a play," said Mizner, "I can make a watch that will give milk."

The storm centered on Mizner rather than Armstrong because it was assumed that Mizner had furnished the underworld stuff and his collaborator the theatrical craftsmanship. Mizner's new role as a successful playwright made a startling change in his standing in the community. Previously a dubious character, he was now, at the age of thirty-four, an illustrious literary man. Tales of his earlier knaveries and rogueries only added to his prestige. He "sparkled with larceny," as he said; he had the sinister lustre of Chaliapin, who used to paint himself with phosphorus when he played Mephistopheles. Crook drama was the rage, and Mizner was its prophet. As the only first-hand crime authority among the playwrights, he was proud of his preëminence. In an interview in the *Press,* he said, "I know more about crime than any other man who still owns a controlling interest in his own liberty." Ashton Stevens pointed out in an interview with Mizner that he couldn't have spent all his life tilting at the penal code, since Stevens himself had seen the card of a rubber corporation that read, "WILSON MIZNER, PRESIDENT." Mizner confessed that he had once been a rubber magnate but said he had retired when a prospect turned out to be a rubber expert. "He let me talk for an hour," Mizner said, "and then he turned on me and said, 'Mr. Mizner, it is perfectly clear that you don't know whether they gather rubber with a stepladder or a diving bell.'" But after getting out of rubber, Mizner continued to be the president or chairman of the board of some of the prettiest oil, steel, and aluminum companies ever printed. He was one of America's greatest captains of industry to anybody who believed in lithography. Stevens couldn't understand why anybody would abandon big business for the stage. "What lured you into playwriting, Mr. Mizner?" he inquired. "Stringent vagrancy laws," said Mizner.

"The Deep Purple" was based on the now archaic "badger game"—the time-honored device of decoying a victim to a lady's apartment, where her confederate breaks in, shouts "You hound!," waves a six-shooter, and collects spot-cash damages for alienation of affections. It was understood on Broadway that Mizner had been a badger-game specialist in his Alaska days. Having achieved a long, vivid past before he was old enough to vote, he had started reminiscing in his early twenties, and Mizner stories were already in general circulation. The New York *Review* slyly remarked, "Mr. Armstrong's taking into partnership of Mr. Mizner upon the exploitation of a topic so delicate and so technical may be accounted for upon various theories, none of which need of necessity find exploitation in this paragraph." Colgate Baker bluntly asked Mizner where he had learned the "badger" technique. "You must remember that I once kept a theatrical hotel," said Mizner.

This was a reference to the Hotel Rand, the Times Square caravansary that Mizner had run for a few months in 1907 and that had added considerably to his knowledge of crime. Old inhabitants of Times Square still look back on the Rand as the most lurid oasis in the town's nocturnal history. Mizner operated it as he had earlier operated the Hotel McQueston (which he called the Hotel No Questions), in Nome, and the Rand stands out in Manhattan folklore as the Paul Bunyan of shady hotels. The only mid-Victorian touch at the Rand was a set of gongs that rang on all the floors at 3 A.M. to notify guests that it was time to go back to their own rooms, if they were so disposed. Guests were forbidden to play their pianos before 5 P.M., so that they would not awaken their fellow-guests. There was a big welcome for everybody at the Rand, its hospitable slogan being "Get off at any floor and walk in any door." Besides the world-famous rules "No opium-smoking in the elevators" and "Guests must carry out their own dead," Mizner made, or so he claimed, another important contribution to American hotel practice—a net at the third floor to catch falling bodies. He asserted that he had problems at the Rand that no other hotel man had ever faced. Tired of shivering on the fire escapes while their girls entertained customers within, the pimps held a meeting and demanded steam-heated fire escapes. Mizner's greatest trial occurred when his brother the Reverend Henry Watson Mizner, a High Episcopalian clergyman from St. Louis, came to New York to visit him. Wilson rushed to an employment agency and hired several mothers to sit in the lobby with their little ones in order to give the illusion of a family hotel. Ashton Stevens dropped in to see

Mizner during another crisis at the Rand. Practically every room in New York had been taken by a great Christian Endeavor convention, and the Rand found itself infiltrated with practicing Christians, some of whom are probably still scandalizing their parishes with the tales of what went on in Mizner's uninhibited hostelry.

Before operating the Rand, Mizner, as the husband of the former Mrs. Yerkes, had operated the Charles Tyson Yerkes mansion on Fifth Avenue. This caused some people to consider him a great authority on society as well as on "gentle larceny," confidence games, and other brainy felonies. It was rumored that he was about to write a drama about high life. "No," said Mizner. "People are tired of high life. The average person sees all the royalty he wants in a deck of cards." Nothing ever happened on Fifth Avenue, he added, because seventeen butlers stood between you and first-hand contact with the world. "If you were shipwrecked with all of society on a desert island for three years," he concluded, "you wouldn't have enough material for a ten-minute sketch."

According to the good old custom, the new celebrity automatically became a journalistic authority on everything. Mizner's views were sought and obtained on a great variety of subjects. He censured the Taft administration for treating all successful men as criminals. He was concerned about the corruption of the judiciary. At one time, he said, he had looked on all judges as saints. "Today," he said, "I would bribe one with a peanut, and my only fear would be that he would hold out for a walnut." The big question in all these interviews was how to achieve success in life. "Impudence" was the secret, according to Mizner. He illustrated the thesis with the story of the judge who said, "You're charged with petty larceny," to which the defendant replied, "What other kind of larceny is open to a poor man?" "Now," Mizner would continue, "you take that very same man and give him a little more gall and a new fountain pen, and he could split Wall Street up the back." The next question was usually why crime plays were so popular. "Because everybody is dodging laws," Mizner said. One reporter, alarmed at Mizner's cynical attitude, asked him to comment seriously on the hypothetical case of an eager young man just starting out in life, full of ideals and firmly believing in honesty, integrity, and human goodness. "What would you do with him?" asked the reporter. "Give him a bath," said Mizner.

By the time Mizner became a hit playwright, he had had a desultory connection with the stage as performer, writer, and stage-door Johnny for many years. His first dramatic dialogue was, according to his own account, a skit written for the Cyranose Sisters, a vaudeville team that played Nome. The scene was laid in a grocery store. One character asked, "Have you any coffee in the bean?" The other replied, "No, this is the ground floor." The poor reception accorded this act retarded Mizner's writing career for years. Billy Huson, a veteran vaudeville performer who struggled along the Trail of '98 with a section of the first piano to arrive in Dawson City, stated that Mizner gained some reputation in the Far North as a songwriter, one of his compositions being "The Ruby Sands of Nome." Jim Tully implicated Mizner in the authorship of "Frankie and Johnnie," and one legend has it that he composed that classic in collaboration with George Hart, a Reno singer and piano player, but this is not the fact, according to Hart. Not having a copy of the music of "Frankie and Johnnie," Wilson, with the assistance of a snake charmer, was helping Hart pick out the tune when a python glided across the piano. Wilson thought he was seeing things and would have to give up drinking. Then a voice from the next room called, "Agnes got out!" Mizner was a piano-playing professor on the Barbary Coast of San Francisco and in other red-light districts when he was in his teens. For a while, he toured the West Coast singing pathetic ballads to accompany magic-lantern slides. The old "illustrated-song" artists were hired for practically nothing by the cheaper vaudeville houses and were considered the lowest form of life in the entertainment world—fathoms below acrobats and swingers of illuminated Indian clubs. Mizner always claimed that he had no shame, but he apparently never confided to his Broadway and Palm Beach pals that he had once sung illustrated songs. The fact came out in a letter written by a Fresno man to Mark Kelly, a Los Angeles sportswriter, who had done a column about Mizner. "Is this man Mizner," demanded the Fresno man, "the six-fingered thief who came to Fresno under the name of Gerard Salvini, the Golden-Throated Thrush?" The writer said that the Thrush had attempted to elope with a Fresno girl without being aware of the fact that she was the daughter of a high Fresno official, and that he missed a prison cell only by fast footwork. The letter enclosed an old vaudeville program with a picture of the singer, who was unmistakably Wilson Mizner around the age of twenty. On being shown the documentary evidence, Mizner confessed that he was the golden-throated Salvini and added, "I didn't think there was another man alive who knew about that." People in Nome believed that Mizner had a grand-opera voice, according to Jack Hines, author of "Minstrel on the Yukon," who wrote of a New Year's party at which Diamond Jim Wilson, owner of the Anvil Saloon and head of the Nome Fire Department, raised his glass and asked everybody to drink the health of Wilson Mizner, "the best damn songbird in Alaska." Diamond Jim dropped dead of apoplexy as he drank; Mizner and two or three others opened his safe and divided his jewels and gold among them, probating, administering, settling, and distributing the estate in about ten minutes. A. J. Cody, former United States Marshal of Nome, a personal friend but official enemy of Mizner, who was under suspicion of several major crimes, once said that the famous old light-opera star Henry Clay Barnabee went crazy over Mizner's voice and begged him to train for the operatic stage. Mizner's great opportunity for stardom came, according to Walter Moore, theatrical-printing executive, from George M. Cohan, who wanted Mizner to play J. Rufus Wallingford in "Get-Rich-Quick Wallingford." Because of Mizner's physique and his aura of romantic nefariousness, Cohan, Moore said, pleaded with him by the hour, exclaiming more than once, "Wilson, you've got to take the part. You *are* J. Rufus Wallingford." But Mizner was appalled at the thought of killing the sweet of the evening by regular appearances on the stage.

"ALIAS"
JIMMY
VALENTINE

WILSON MIZNER

THEATRE

Many years before he won success as a playwright, Mizner had had vague literary ambitions. Edward Dean Sullivan, author of "The Fabulous Wilson Mizner," quoted him as saying that he was trying to write even during his turbulent domesticity in the Yerkes mansion. Mizner travelled with a literary set in New York and was a close friend of O. Henry. One of his prized possessions was a nine-page O. Henry letter addressed to "Wilson Montagu Mizner" in London at a time when Mizner was engaged in taking ancient American burlesque gags and adapting them for the Cockney audiences at the London Circus. Pretending to be Mignonette Le Clair, the widow of the burlesque king who owned the copyright on the stolen gags, O. Henry wrote demanding royalties and threatening to expose some of the unsavory chapters of Mizner's career in Alaska and San Francisco. The letter said that the exposé would not be a "knock" in Mizner's New York set but would hurt him with the British aristocracy, which Mizner was then said to be worming his way into. O. Henry offered to sell Mizner all the late burlesque king's copyrighted material, including the give-me-two-tens-for-a-five joke and the hold-this-baby-for-a-minute joke, as well as two sets match-scratching whiskers, one red nose that lights up by electricity, one pair funny pants with red flannel patch on prat, one laughable bald-headed wig with wart that explodes. "With the above funny stuff," O. Henry concluded, "you may be able to stay in London several years."

Other literary friends were always urging Mizner to write his stories instead of telling them over highballs. On one occasion, Sam Berger, the erudite heavyweight, got pencils and paper for Mizner and mounted guard while he wrote, but a cute voice over the telephone interrupted in the middle of the first paragraph, and Mizner disappeared for two weeks. Now and then, Mizner became excited about collaborating with somebody, but usually nothing whatever came of it. At one time, he talked of a literary partnership with Louis Joseph Vance, author of "The Brass Bowl" and other best-sellers, but he lost his enthusiasm before writing a word. Next to Paul Armstrong, the man most successful at getting work out of Mizner was George Bronson-

Howard. He bullied Mizner into dictating "Three Saved," a short story that *Collier's* bought for two hundred and fifty dollars and published. The statement has been printed that Mizner wrote the story to win a bet from Paul Armstrong, who contended that it had become impossible to sell any magazine a story containing the battered old phrase "God's Country" in the title. Mizner is said to have won the bet, although "God's Country" did not appear in the title or anywhere else in the story when it was published. *Collier's* was very enthusiastic and wanted all the stuff he could write. At lunch with the editors, he outlined stories until they begged him to stop, as he was threatening to write the whole magazine for years to come. A typical nonwriting writer, Mizner executed none of these projected masterpieces. Bronson-Howard succeeded, however, in getting him to dictate a second short story, entitled "An Eye for Business," and Francis J. Timmey transcribed some of Mizner's conversation into a tale published as "The Harmony Kid." Mizner told Agnes Smith, an interviewer for the *Morning Telegraph,* that he gave up magazine fiction because of an experience with an editor. In a short story, Mizner explained, he had had one character say to another, "I'm going to pick some wild flowers, and when I've tamed them, I'm going to give them to you." "What does that mean?" asked the editor. "It's an expression of contempt," said Mizner. "But," said the editor, "you can't tame wild flowers."

Before he attempted a full-fledged drama, Mizner wrote several sketches. He made his Eastern début as a writer for the stage in an Asbury Park vaudeville house on June 5, 1907, with a one-act play entitled "A Loyal Deception"—"a tenderly sentimental love story of sacrifice and loyalty [that] combines an original and wholesome plot with a fine drawing of character," said the review in the *Morning Telegraph.* "The Three Thieves" was another Mizner sketch. It apparently never hit Broadway, but old newspaper paragraphs tell of Mizner's being arrested for exceeding the speed limit while hurrying to Yonkers in his automobile to catch the opening of it there. Appearing as a witness in a John Doe inquiry into gambling in New York, Mizner mentioned the sketch "Ships That Pass in the Night" as among his stage triumphs. According to Ben Piazza, the Hollywood executive, this was one of the most brilliant sketches ever written. Mizner's first full-length play was "The Only Law," on which he collaborated with Bronson-Howard.

At every stage of his career, Mizner was associated with hair-raising people. Bronson-Howard was probably the most blood-curdling of them all. He was New York's literary bad man, the Billy the Kid of the typewriter. He shot up the town with paper bullets. He blazed away at his enemies in his column in the *Morning Telegraph*, in essays, skits, and plays, in short stories, novelettes, and serials. His best writings were the by-products of vendettas. His grudge novel "God's Man," an attack on Magistrate Joseph Corrigan, was praised by Henry L. Mencken. He worked off the accumulated grievances of years in "Snobs," his most successful play. Sooner or later, Bronson-Howard tore apart all his old pals, lady friends, and business associates. The feud he eventually had with Mizner was the greatest eye-gouging in the dark and bloody history of collaboration.

Starting at the age of fourteen as a clerk in the Weather Bureau in Washington, Bronson-Howard shifted about in the federal service, winding up in the Philippine Constabulary. He had little schooling, but he had a great ambition to be a man of letters and devoted all his spare time to reading and writing. After breaking into journalism in the Philippines, he returned to this country and found work on a paper in Baltimore, where he became acquainted with Mencken, who was just emerging from the cub-reporter stage. Following another trip to the Orient, as a correspondent in the Russo-Japanese War, he began to write adventure fiction at half a cent a word. He firmly believed that there was nothing so glorious as a writer, and he became a sensational dude in order to do justice to his position in the Republic of Letters. Percy Hammond wrote that, as a timid Middle Westerner, he found himself overawed by the size, shape, and glitter of Bronson-Howard's silk hat. Bronson-Howard told Mencken that he devoted half an hour every morning to studying his collection of neckties before selecting the one perfect pattern for that particular day. He once printed an attack on Mizner's sartorial illiteracy. Mizner had jeered at an English barrister who wore his handkerchief in his coat sleeve; this proved, Bronson-Howard claimed, that Mizner was ignorant of the fact that the swellest tailors made the swellest pants without pockets. In 1907, Bronson-Howard became a sort of hero of an early type of comic strip. His married life was the subject of numerous animated drawings by Tom Powers and others who did comic sketches to illustrate funny news stories. With the help of his literary eminence, Bronson-Howard had won a Virginia belle, but she walked out during the honeymoon and made a career of touring the country warning American girlhood against marrying a literary man. She charged that her literary man pounded out twenty thousand words a day during their honeymoon, repulsed her with the exclamation "I got to make a deadline!," went to bed at night with his shoes on, started to dress in the morning by putting his hat on, used her beauty lotions, and always addressed her as "Thing." One of Bronson-Howard's oddities was suddenly becoming related to important people. Without warning, he became Howard Fitzalan, a cousin of the Duke of Norfolk. Originally, his name had been George Howard; he changed it to Bronson-Howard to establish kinship with Bronson Howard, the famous author of the Civil War play "Shenandoah." The real, and aged, Bronson Howard was fearfully chagrined by the general assumption that Bronson-Howard was an error of his youth.

Mizner and Bronson-Howard were an ill-assorted pair, Mizner being passionately dedicated to a life of ease, while Bronson-Howard suffered from an industry neurosis. "He appalls me by his power of work," said Mizner in the *Dramatic Mirror*. "He spills words by the gallon. Phrases ooze out of every pore. I have seen him write twenty thousand words at a sitting, get dissatisfied with them, tear them up, and start all over again." Bronson-Howard turned out serials on Yorke Norroy, of the Secret Service, and other dashing characters who became standbys in the pulps. He was a mainstay of *Popular* and other action magazines. At the same time he was writing a drama column for the

Morning Telegraph, he wrote heavyweight essays for serious publications. In spite of being one of America's greatest manufacturers of claptrap, Bronson-Howard coolly bracketed himself with Mencken and George Jean Nathan as a crusader for integrity and realism in American letters. The one thing Mizner

hated above all else was literary vanity, and that was a thing Bronson-Howard abounded in. Their feud originated in the fact that Bronson-Howard felt that magazine writing called for magnificent mental endowment, whereas Mizner contended that it was a low, grovelling occupation for plodding dullards. "Anybody who can write home for money can write for the magazines," Mizner told Bronson-Howard. Their rows broke into the newspapers from time to time. "Bronson-Howard thinks," Mizner told a *Review* reporter, "that if you stuck a knife in him, he would bleed pure English. Except for his use of the written cleverness of other men, he couldn't write a letter to his tailor." The friendship between the two men continued for years, in spite of episodes that would have parted Eeko and Iko or Chang and Eng. One day, Bronson-Howard rushed into Rector's with what sounded like a just complaint against Mizner. The two men had had a falling out, and Mizner had chased Bronson-Howard out of the brownstone house on Forty-fourth Street he and Mizner occupied. Then Mizner told him to come back and get his trunk. Bronson-Howard drove up in a hack, walked up the steps, and rang the bell. There was a terrific crash. His trunk, dropped by Mizner from the third-story window, hit the front porch and broke into pieces, hurling the peacock wardrobe in all directions.

The original bond between Mizner and Bronson-Howard was their taste for the opium pipe. A third party at their "campfire" was a literary critic who wore a monocle and Oriental robes, put in his spare time catching the Encyclopædia Britannica in errors, and later became one of the top murder-mystery writers in the country. The old belief was that hitting the pipe was bad for the chuckleheaded multitude but excellent for Tiffany intellects like those of Mizner, Bronson-Howard, and the man with the monocle. This tradition was supported by the examples of Coleridge, Rossetti, Crabbe, and other inspired hopheads; De Quincey had exclaimed, "O just, subtile, and mighty opium!;" Baudelaire had glorified the paradises of opium and hashish. Sherlock Holmes was a more recent testimonial to the affinity between genius and dope. Opium-smoking is bad for the nerves, however, and it was responsible for some of Bronson-Howard's worst literary efforts. Mizner, Bronson-Howard, and the monocled encyclopedia-hater adopted a young Argentinian beauty called Teddie Gerard, who is said to have been the "chef" or "cooker" in charge of the complicated chore of heating, bubbling, and stirring opium pills to prepare them for smoking. According to eminent Broadway chroniclers, the three men coached the girl, corrected her diction, cultivated her personality, and started her on a stage career. The three Pygmalions were left at the post. Their protégée soared to greatness on Broadway, became La Belle Théodora in Paris and Teddie the Great in London, and compiled a list of adorers that included a Russian grand duke, a Hungarian prince, a couple of titled Britishers, a New York real-estate baron, and the heir of one of America's large fortunes. Bronson-Howard was distracted when she first showed signs of forsaking the little poppy-steeped home on Forty-fourth Street. Later on, he sat down to his avenging typewriter and wrote the customary invective against her, but at the moment he contented himself with merely stealing back a diamond ring he had given her and threatening her life with a bowie knife that had an eight-inch blade. At this time, Miss Gerard was a big hit in the Broadway musical comedy "Havana." Bronson-Howard was arrested at the stage door and taken before Magistrate Joseph Corrigan. An extremely smart audience turned out for the preliminary hearing. The *Morning Telegraph* said that Miss Gerard appeared at the morning session "in a black evening gown with rooster plumes in it and a ten-thousand-dollar diamond necklace with a heart-shaped pendant" and that she was "one of the most dazzling creatures that ever brightened the gloomy old courtroom with her hesitating and pouting complaint." She became so tangled up in her story that the diamond-ring charge had to be dropped, but Magistrate Corrigan held Bronson-Howard anyway, for carrying a deadly weapon. He was bailed out by Mizner, who put up a twenty-five-thousand-dollar house he owned on Eighty-fourth Street as security. Bronson-Howard considered that Corrigan had been impertinent to him. When he wrote the novel "God's Man" to square accounts with the disrespectful Magistrate, he christened his villain Cornigan and on one page spelled it "Corrigan" to make sure that nobody would misunderstand. The Magistrate, a man of spotless reputation, sued the publisher for two hundred thousand dollars. Several witnesses told of hearing Bronson-Howard say he had written the book to get even with the judge. One testified that the writer had refreshed his inspiration by smoking opium. "You mustn't say 'opium,'" interposed Justice Goff, who presided at the trial. "That's a conclusion. Say he was smoking 'a substance.'" The witness then described how Bronson-Howard manipulated "a substance" over an alcohol lamp, inhaled the smoke from a bamboo pipe with a porcelain bowl, and soon began to look funny. The jury returned a verdict of thirty-five thousand dollars in favor of Corrigan, but a higher court reversed it on a technicality, and the case was never retried. After his release on bail on the deadly-weapon charge, Bronson-Howard fled to Europe. He remained there until the excitement was over, then reappeared on Broadway as Fitzalan, the Duke's cousin. The authorities forgot to try him or to demand the forfeit of Mizner's twenty-five-thousand-dollar house.

"The Only Law" was the chief product of the friendship of Mizner and Bronson-Howard. When it was produced in New York, in 1909, the *Dramatic News* called it "the most daring play since 'The Narrow Path' went to smash after a single performance." "The Only Law" was ahead of its time in several ways. Its nearest approach to a hero was the gigolo, and he failed to live up to gigolo standards. Virtue was not only not triumphant but not even favorably mentioned, and on top of all that a successful Wall Street man, instead of being the villain, as required by all the canons of art, was the sole respectable character in the play. "The Only Law" was ahead of its time in another respect. Mizner wrote entirely by ear, and, in spite of an overdeveloped taste for wisecracks, he anticipated Ring Lardner and John O'Hara in his fidelity to spoken English and his disdain for book English. His press agent said that "all Broadway is talking the new language;" the fact was, however, that Broadway needed reëducation to understand Mizner. The *Morning Telegraph* said that the dialogue was "slang of the richest and rarest type;" the *Dramatic Mirror* said it was unintelligible to the ordinary man. The title came from the line "Being on the square with a pal is the only law we know," which was uttered by the heroine when she began to suspect that her gigolo had feet of clay. Conservative critics were dissatisfied with the moral, which was that a bad girl, if she plays her cards right, can marry a model boy from Wall Street. "The Only Law" closed after a few performances. It was originally billed as a play "By Wilson Mizner and George Bronson-Howard." Mizner claimed that every line in it was his and that his collaborator had merely typed it. Bronson-Howard later revived it in Chicago as "The Double-Cross," and advertised it as a play "By George Bronson-Howard and Wilson Mizner." Mizner, then in London, cabled Percy Hammond, who was reviewing it in Chicago, "The position of my name was stolen outright by George Bronson-Howard. Please say so." Hammond reported that, except for some vivid phrases, the play was "awful offal" and that it mattered little who got the lion's share of the glory.

Bronson-Howard now sat down to his fire-eating typewriter and did the novelette on Mizner entitled "The Parasite." It was a brilliant bit of grudge literature, but in some respects it was the testimony of a reluctant witness in Mizner's favor. It used to be considered obligatory for a novelist to explain any odd character by giving him an odd heredity, and Mizner was explained rather handsomely as the illegitimate descendant of "a Rabelaisian-Villonesque poet." He was presented as a confidential adviser and Dutch uncle to "the field mice," Bronson-Howard's name for the minor characters of Times Square. In general, however, Mizner was pictured as a bad egg and, still worse, a bad dresser. Jimmy Johnston, the prizefighter manager, said that Bronson-Howard was amazed to find that a coolness had sprung up between him and his old pal merely because he had written that Mizner had defrauded his mother and been tarred and feathered in a Western community. Johnston had lunch at the Claridge with Mizner a short time after "The Parasite" was published, and Bronson-Howard came in. His face lighted up at the sight of Mizner, and he hurried toward him with outstretched hand. Describing the incident long afterward, Johnston said that, despite his forty years in and around the prize ring, he was still able to blush at the memory of the language Mizner used on that occasion. Bronson-Howard walked away slowly, shaking his head from side to side, hopelessly mystified by Mizner's attitude.

Chapter Ten

SEA SERPENTS

IT WAS IMPOSSIBLE for Wilson Mizner to exist without a lot of ears around him, and he didn't particularly care whom they belonged to. He was usually able to provide himself with a small senate of eager listeners, and at Palm Beach, in the twenties, he invented a curious device to keep it from adjourning. He had a sprinkler placed on top of his favorite speakeasy. A secret signal to a waiter caused the sprinkler to be turned on when his audience showed signs of breaking up after lunch. As the speakeasy was windowless, Mizner was generally able to convince at least newer members of his little parliament that a heavy rain had started and that they might as well stay put until it was over. His invention sometimes enabled him to talk an extra two hours.

A Yorick born a few centuries too late, Mizner considered nothing important except setting a table on a roar. He looked on the world as the human burlesque show and looked on all experience as raw material to be worked up into gags and anecdotes. He studied himself like an introspective novelist, alert for the conversational possibilities in his own reactions to any situation. Falstaff used the same technique when he paused in the midst of fleecing Justice Shallow to soliloquize on the fun he would have telling about it later. Mizner had rather austere standards. He hated drummers' jokes. He regarded anecdotes strictly as illustration and would as soon waste time shaving an egg as telling a story that threw no light on the subject of the conversation. A smutty yarn left him as unenthusiastic as it would have left Queen Victoria, although their responses were different. Mizner's enormous face would spring open like that of a hippo and he would let loose a terrifying false laugh when anybody told him the latest one about the farmer's daughter. Nearly all his comedy came from his own experience and imagination. He was an amateur at heart. He loved applause more than money, although he talked himself into a Fifth Avenue mansion, a Times Square hotel, and Florida millions. In his early cardsharping period, the chief part of his equipment was conversation. He had, as he explained in his comparatively respectable later days, an extremely difficult method of arranging a poker deck so that the suckers would receive very fine hands and he would receive a slightly better one. It required prolonged shuffling, and he had to talk in the most fascinating manner to prevent attention from wandering to the fact that he was taking a confoundedly long time. It was absolutely indispensable for him to laugh the boys out of their senses. He had to pour on the comedy until the chump at his left was in such a stupid state of suggestibility that he would automatically cut the cards as Mizner desired. Years of rigorous practical training were behind Mizner's mature conversational flights.

Mizner had millions of dollars' worth of comedy in his system, but it couldn't be marketed in the ordinary way. If an unlimited stock of similes and an instinct for the pulverizing, obliterating phrase were all that a writer needed, Mizner should have been the premier literary artist of his time, but his brain always seemed to go numb when he took pen in hand. He needed hysterical merriment, faces distorted with laughter, to warm up his inspiration. He felt like a professional mourner in the tomblike silence that surrounded him when he tried to write. He discovered, too, that there were some mean little stumbling blocks to putting words on paper. As a conversationalist, he could change the subject whenever a better one showed up. As a writer, he was supposed to stick to the subject or to struggle agonizingly over transitions in order to fool the reader when he changed it. As a raconteur, he could use a gesture in place of a sentence; he could, according to the old, old recipe, convey a libel in a frown and wink a reputation down, but he was unable to acquire the knack of translating conversational tricks into literary tricks. He occasionally wrote a good sentence, but he never learned enough about literary welding and steam fitting to write a good paragraph. He was puzzled. He had a low opinion of writers as a class, and couldn't understand how they were able to outscribble a celebrated wit, raconteur, and epigrammatic philosopher like himself.

Mizner's troubles multiplied when he undertook a complex literary task like writing a play. He needed a collaborator, and a good one. His literary partner had to be a Lost and Found Department for Mizner's mislaid ideas, a Missing Persons Bureau for Mizner's wandering characters. Mizner was lucky when he was chosen as a collaborator by Paul Armstrong, because Armstrong was the ablest dramatic technician of his time. Mencken, in his "Newspaper Days," calls Armstrong the King of Broadway and estimates that his royalties were greater than those reaped by any of his contemporaries or predecessors. Mizner's contribution to the Mizner-Armstrong merger was conversation, and that was not too easy to get out of him, because he began to regard conversation with Armstrong as work. In newspaper interviews, Armstrong explained their method of collaboration. He said that the first step was to find Mizner. That might take weeks. Then came a period devoted to "argument, supplication, threat, and entreaty," to induce him to get down to business. Armstrong was more conceited about his coffee-making than about his playwriting. He didn't claim to be the greatest American playwright; he said that William Gillette, author of "Secret Service," "Held by the Enemy," and "Sherlock Holmes," was entitled to that designation. "But," he said, "Paul Armstrong is our greatest coffee-maker." Nothing in the world, he asserted, except Paul Armstrong coffee could get Mizner up in the morning. Mizner's nocturnal ways were indicated by contemporary newspapers, which quoted him as saying, "I always get up at night, when everything is twice as high," and "Be sure it's light, then go to bed." Armstrong would break into his collaborator's apartment at an early hour, make a pot of coffee, and put some life into him. Mizner would then, according to Armstrong, buckle down to a strenuous morning's conversation on any subject that would take their minds off the play they were working on. Progress on their first joint enterprise, "The Deep Purple," written in 1910, was slow until Armstrong got Mizner away from the temptations of Broadway and held him a prisoner in a hotel in Baltimore. There, Mizner, rolling his own cigarettes, conversed at a rate of one act for every three sacks of Bull Durham.

In preparation for their second play, "The Greyhound," written in 1911, Armstrong took Mizner on a transatlantic voyage. "The Greyhound" was a melodrama about ocean-going crooks—"sea serpents," "deep-sea fishermen," or "pearl divers," as they used to be called. Mizner had a scholarly grasp of this subject. He knew international low life as Henry James knew international high life. For years, he had been practically a commuter from New York to London and Paris, and had made a total of thirty transatlantic round trips. He had dabbled in the theatre in London, and he called himself "the father of free lunch in Paris," because, with the help of some international characters, including the Broadway Polonius Swiftie Morgan and the colored heavyweight Sam McVey, he induced the proprietor of Ciro's to give away lobster, goose liver, caviar, ham, and anchovies in order to lure an American clientele to his place. Mizner was also something of a sea serpent or deep-sea fisherman himself. He said he was always able to win the confidence of strangers by warning them against strangers. He knew every twist of fraud and larceny on the high seas, but Armstrong didn't, and Armstrong insisted on the trip so that Mizner could brief him on background and atmosphere for their drama of deviltry on the steamship lanes.

Mizner usually won when he played games of chance, by

land or by sea, but he never claimed to be a really great card-sharp. He was, however, a supreme artist at taking a lot of people thrown together by chance and quickly converting them into one big, happy family. His power to produce mirth in a small or moderate-sized group of people is said to have been un-equalled. On the first night out, he would have the whole ship's population of prospective suckers bellowing. His function was to deprive them of their reason with Mizner gags; once the brain was completely abstracted, it was time for the cardsharps, dice wizards, and con men to go to work. Mizner, his mission accom-plished, might then disport himself as he pleased for the rest of the trip. If his crooked friends prospered, they would make a suitable recognition of his contribution to the success of the voyage. One of the few survivors of the happy days on the high seas is Swiftie Morgan, who had a special talent for breaking down the reserve of upper-class Englishmen. Being small and wiry, Swiftie was introduced as the coming wonder of the American turf. Great jockeys were irresistible to British swells. According to Swiftie, Mizner seldom joined the big card games, but he would sometimes amuse himself by playing bankers-and-brokers. He would start it as a sort of solitaire, dividing a pack of cards into several small stacks. He would scratch his head, mutter to himself, and then finally pick up the cards and examine them with little exclamations of joy or chagrin. If anybody asked ques-tions, he would explain that he was trying to guess the number of high cards in each pile. He would never invite another man to join in a game, but he would never churlishly reject the sug-gestion if it came from a likely-looking prospect. Swiftie says that Mizner relieved the Pittsburgh steel baron William E. Corey of fifteen thousand dollars at this pastime. Corey didn't know that Mizner always took the precaution of bending the high cards lengthwise and the low cards crosswise before he started to amuse himself. The curvature was microscopic, and would never catch the eye of an unsuspecting opponent, but Mizner could tell by a glance at the side of a pile how many high cards it contained. He also earned considerable sums by winning ship's pools with enlightened guesses as to the distance that would be covered by the ship in each twenty-four-hour period. Because of the generally high calibre of ships' officers, the steamship pool is usually regarded as an unfixable form of gambling, but, so

Swiftie says, one transatlantic steward with a private pipeline to the bridge of his ship retired a millionaire merely by selling inside tips on whether an even or odd number of miles would be covered in a given day, much of the betting being on "odd or even." The gifted steward never purported to foresee the total mileage on a given day, but Mizner and two confederates drew the lucky number three times in succession. It all started with a ship's officer who was practically a clotheshorse for medals. His chest, as Mizner described it, was ablaze with chafing dishes. Mizner couldn't believe that an honest heart beat beneath a whole showcaseful of jewelry. Standing outside the cabin of the glittering officer, Mizner mentioned to a confederate the number he had drawn in the pool for the next twenty-four hours, and added in a loud voice, "You know what I would do to show my gratitude if I won? I'd stick a thousand dollars under the right officer's pillow." Somehow or other, the day's run came out exactly right for Mizner, and a thousand dollars of his winnings turned up under the medal collector's pillow. There were two more conversations outside the cabin and two more miraculous strokes of luck for Mizner and his confederate. The fourth time they approached the cabin, however, a hoarse voice growled through the door, "Get out of here, you bastards. I'm four hundred miles off my course now."

When Mizner started to work on "The Greyhound," he patterned his hero after Frankie Dwyer, an ace of salt-water crooks. Although not given to hero worship, Mizner had an unbounded admiration for Frankie, who was almost perfect in the major branches of crime—raking in ill-gotten gains over a long period and baffling attempts to prosecute. Although arrested on innumerable occasions, under many names, he died in 1929 without a single conviction against him. Fair-haired, blue-eyed, and handsome, he had an irresistible smile. The New York police had him dead to rights on one occasion, but they were forced to release him because the victim's indignation melted away at one beautiful smile from Dwyer. Mizner imitated Dwyer in some respects. It was against the ethics of high-class oceanographers like Dwyer to speak to strangers, but they were free to respond when a stranger started the conversation. Dwyer was always studying ways to make it easy for strangers to break the ice. He had one invaluable method of cuing in a stranger—rattling dice in his hand in an absent-minded way, dropping one near the stranger, walking away rapidly, then coming back a few minutes later and peering anxiously at the carpet. Venerable authorities say that Charles M. Schwab once returned the missing dice with a hearty laugh and wound up losing seventy thousand dollars to Frankie in a crap game. Mizner was infatuated with the "lost-dice" gambit, and used it extensively. In his almost blameless later years, he practiced it for sport, hooking strangers merely to convince himself that he hadn't lost his genius. In his predatory days on the ocean, he suffered one of his greatest defeats in an effort to imitate Dwyer. He lost a spotted cube three or four times within plain sight of an Englishman. There was no response. Mizner continued to dribble dice at the Englishman all day long, but without making a dent in the man's reserve. A friend of both men happened along and introduced them. The Britisher took a great liking to Mizner and was soon bleating wildly at his jokes. Mizner kept on losing dice at his new pal, but he always had to pick them up himself. Finally, in deep disgust, he dropped one into his companion's tea. Nothing happened for several minutes. Suddenly the Englishman screamed, "Steward, my sugar has specks in it!"

Looking around for a villain for "The Greyhound," Mizner selected William A. Pinkerton, who had been Frankie Dwyer's nemesis for years. He had finally queered many of Dwyer's best schemes and would have landed him in jail except for the traditional unwillingness of suckers to have their misfortunes aired in the newspapers. Frankie took a rather humorous revenge on his persecutor. In the files of the Pinkerton National Detective Agency, in New York, is a message from Scotland Yard informing the agency that Frankie was attempting to establish credit with suckers by representing himself as one of the oldest and closest friends of William A. Pinkerton. After holding an international fencing match with the famous detective for twenty years, Frankie was able to talk about Bill Pinkerton in a familiar and convincing way. In addition to Dwyer and Pinkerton, Mizner did a full-length portrait of Deep-Sea Kitty, an interesting seafaring lady. He also dragged in one of his old Yukon pals, the Scurvy Kid, but he changed the designation to the Pale-Faced Kid when the original Scurvy Kid showed up in New

York and threatened to start shooting if his good name was
dragged into a Broadway melodrama. Paul Armstrong was delighted with the gallery of international felons that Mizner
painted for him, but he double-crossed his collaborator by turning the moral values inside out. To his partner's great disgust,
Armstrong made Pinkerton the hero and Dwyer the villain.
"The Greyhound" was practically a manual for teaching suckers
how to take care of themselves. The play didn't hurt Dwyer,
however, as he had already given up his marine career, following some deplorable scenes on the Mauretania in June of 1908.
Dwyer was playing bridge with three suckers named Eric Thornton, F. C. Pirkis, and R. L. McLeay when Thornton got suspicious and threw a brandy-and-water in Dwyer's face. Dwyer and
a couple of confederates pounced on the three men and there
was a free-for-all fight in the smoking room. Later, the fight
was finished outside, where Dwyer, showing a remarkable mastery of *savate,* kicked his three opponents into the scuppers.
Twenty passengers signed a petition to the captain of the Mauretania, asking him to provide them with a little peace. Sensational
accounts of the affair were carried in all the New York papers,
most of them quoting the words of Vernon H. Brown, the New
York agent of the Cunard Line: "Any passenger that plays cards
with a stranger ought to have a nurse." Dwyer was held in jail
in New York for a few days. Nobody made a charge against
him, but the incident destroyed the usefulness of the ocean, and
Frankie operated on dry land thereafter. For a while, he was an
English nobleman with a monocle. One Pinkerton report tells
how Frankie was ejected from a New York race track for passing bogus ten-pound bank notes on the bookmakers. It was one
of Frankie's famous "safety-first" rackets; the bookies couldn't
prosecute without confessing their own illegal operations. Frankie
wound up selling phony oil stock and running a fake medical
institute.

Mizner had to accept the change in program when Armstrong decided to make a hero out of the honest man and a
villain out of the charming rascal. Mizner had no voice in the
matter. Armstrong was the senior partner in the writing team,

and it was understood that he could construct the play as he thought best. He and Mizner got along pretty well for a couple of temperamental and fantastic characters. There was no jealousy or rivalry between them. Armstrong was a distinguished playboy himself, but he was realistic enough to know that he couldn't play in the same league with Mizner. Nobody else approached Mizner's standing as the town wit and cutup. Damon Runyon called him "the Alcalde of the Roaring Forties" and "the wisest guy between the Battery and Spuyten Duyvil;" Irvin S. Cobb classed him as a wit with Mr. Dooley and the attorney Joseph H. Choate; the columnist Karl K. Kitchen called him the greatest wit on this side of the Atlantic; the *Morning Telegraph* dubbed him the "Rapier of Broadway;" the New York *Review* rarely referred to him as anything but "the peerless boulevardier;" Mizner's hostile friend and collaborator George Bronson-Howard described him as "the night key of Broadway." Armstrong was a celebrity of a different type. He was contentious, litigious, and pugilistic. He denounced producers, actors, critics, newspapers, and the public in curtain speeches, interviews, stage dialogue, and magazine articles. A columnist on the *Morning Telegraph* said that Armstrong had boasted that by simply doubling up his fist he had converted a critic from an unfavorable to a favorable opinion of one of his plays. Percy Hammond wrote that Armstrong "merely looked upon a 'juvenile' in 'The Greyhound' and the young man straightway went from the theatre back to the ribbon counter in Alpena, Mich." James Young, a star in Shakespearean tragedies and college-boy comedies, recovered damages of three thousand dollars from Armstrong, the testimony showing that, besides punching Young, Armstrong had called him Corse Payton, who was universally known as the world's best bad actor, and had then apologized to Payton. A Mirror candy-store clerk sued Armstrong for applying five thousand dollars' worth of language to him, and a Chicago *Tribune* reporter sued him for ten thousand dollars' worth.

For every man he punched or cursed, however, Armstrong cut ten people dead. During much of the time when George Tyler was producing Armstrong hits, Armstrong wasn't talking to him. In Tyler's life story, written in collaboration with J. C. Furnas, Tyler said that his feelings weren't hurt by the Armstrong silent treatment, because it happened to everybody, but it made producing quite a chore, especially in the case of "Going Some." Armstrong and Rex Beach wrote this play in a room at the New York Athletic Club, where they took their lunch in tin boxes and put in a regular ten-hour day, but at the end of the collaboration Armstrong wasn't talking to Rex Beach, either. When the first Armstrong-Mizner play, "The Deep Purple," opened in New York, Armstrong wasn't talking to Tyler; Hugh Ford, who was the director; or a dozen others connected with the show. Somebody asked George M. Cohan why Armstrong hadn't made his usual curtain speech opening night. "Paul wasn't talking to the audience," said Cohan. When "The Deep Purple" was produced in Chicago, Tyler hired private policemen to keep Armstrong away from the theatre and got out an injunction against him. Armstrong planned a violent countersuit, which he described in a wire to Mizner, who was in New York. "ARE YOU WITH ME?" asked Armstrong. "I AM WITH YOU IF YOU WIN," wired back Mizner. Armstrong once sued Tyler for twenty-three cents, claiming that a royalty check was short that amount. Armstrong carried the art of making enemies to the point of writing a letter demanding a retraction when the *Morning Telegraph* referred to him as a member of the Lambs Club. He may have taken the idea from Mizner, who, when he was blackballed by the Friars Club, distributed hundreds of engraved business cards with "WILSON MIZNER" in the usual position and "BLACK-BALLED BY THE FRIARS CLUB" in the corner generally used for vaunting and self-advertisement.

Armstrong fought with everybody, from vaudeville-house managers to the greatest of the theatrical magnates. He had an epic struggle with the Keith-Albee company over a door that figured in one of his one-act plays. Armstrong wanted a solid wooden door that could be slammed resoundingly against a solid wooden frame, but the manager insisted that it wasn't possible to provide anything better than a lathe-and-paper portal. "I want a door that goes 'bang' and they give me one that goes 'phuuf,' " said Armstrong. The controversy was taken to J. J. Murdock, the Keith-Albee general manager, who said, "Give Paul what he wants," and ever since then stage doors have banged like cannons. Charles Frohman had the greatest reputation of all the producers of Armstrong's day, but Armstrong abused him savagely in newspaper interviews. The playwright claimed to have discovered that Frohman had been a butcher in early life, and he referred to him as the Butcher. Frohman directed the career of Maude Adams, the super-superlative star of the time. So awe-inspiring was she that a *Times* critic, on receiving a thank-you note from her, is said to have fainted. Frohman always wanted her to appear in boys' or men's attire, as in "Peter Pan" and "The Jesters," in order to underline the contrast between the elfin etherealness of Miss Adams and the obtrusive femininity of her rivals. In spite of his love of melodramatic obviousness and wallop, Armstrong was eager to turn out a play for the quaint and lovely Frohman star. "I'm just bughouse to write a play for Maude," he said, if the *Morning Telegraph* quoted him correctly. The *Morning Telegraph* added that Armstrong wanted to turn the enchanting little sprite into a sex-mad home-wrecker. Frohman had made the statement that Armstrong was the best writer of dialogue in America, and he agreed to hear an outline of the proposed play. Armstrong said that when he was halfway through, Frohman interrupted, exclaiming, "Oh, Paul, if you will only write a play where Maude can appear in men's evening clothes in the second act, I'll pay you any price for it."

Armstrong was as theatrical as any of his characters. He had large, dark, dramatic eyes, thick, crescent-shaped black eyebrows, and a handsome, ruddy face, with mustache, whiskers, and beard effects that varied according to the play he was writing. Working on a thriller about blooded horses and blooded families in the South, he wore the mustache and goatee of a hot-headed Confederate colonel; turning to a Western, he cultivated a set of black Buffalo Bill whiskers; turning to crime, he wore an up-to-date villain mustache and tiny con-man chin whiskers. Charles W. Collins, the Chicago columnist, writing of Armstrong in the *Green Book Magazine*, said that he "makes you think of gentleman-buccaneers, soldiers of fortune, duellists out of 'The Three Musketeers,' Cagliostro, and Baron Chevrial at forty." Ashton Stevens said that Armstrong appeared in real life made up as a "heavy" but that two or three strokes of a razor would turn him into a cherub. Armstrong affected a slightly ecclesiastical touch—an enormous amethyst ring of the type that is sometimes worn by bishops and *monsignori*. Even his drinks were melodramatic symbols of the knock-down-and-drag-out combat between good and evil. He usually consumed either an almost black potation or a snow-white one. The dark drink was Amer Picon sweetened with a little grenadine and mixed with soda. He called the white one the Milk of the Wild Cow—just gin and milk. He was not usually a heavy drinker, but he was a sensitive one, and a small quantity of the Milk of the Wild Cow was sometimes enough to make him feel abused, aggrieved, wronged, and insulted. In his physical encounters, Armstrong always acted in the spirit of a Christian martyr socking the lions.

There was a good deal of kindness and good nature in Armstrong, and his truculence was probably the result of years of struggle and disappointment before he gained recognition. He never apologized for himself, but in newspaper interviews he placed some emphasis on the fact that he was born at Kidder, Missouri. In his boyhood, he and his parents moved to Saginaw, Michigan, where, after a sketchy education, he went to work on a steamboat. Armstrong claimed that the Saginaw River ran through the toughest region in the world and that he developed his philosophy of combat there. He became a competent street fighter, and even after he was famous he boxed regularly in gymnasiums, so that the big bullies would find him in the pink when they insulted him. He was purser on a steamboat running between Saginaw and Chicago during the World's Fair in 1893, and he later became a Great Lakes captain. This chapter in his biography was under suspicion at one time, according to H. L. Mencken, because Armstrong suffered almost continuously from seasickness when he made the trip to Europe with Mizner to get local color for "The Greyhound," but Armstrong had a Great Lakes master's license to corroborate his claim. The ambition to

write took possession of him early in life, and he was scribbling
short stories before he left Saginaw. Every one was rejected, so
he decided to tackle literature from the journalistic angle. An
episode in Armstrong's career as a reporter on the Buffalo *Express*
became the plot of "The Cub Reporter," a short story by Rex
Beach. A woman had been found dead under sensational circumstances, and her identity was a mystery. After the police and
first-line reporters had failed to clear up the case, Armstrong
was assigned to it. He had two clues—a key and a mitten. By
methodically visiting baggage rooms, he found a trunk that
opened with his key. In the trunk was the other mitten. Armstrong went back to the *Express* office with an enormous scoop.
Shortly thereafter, he was fired for incompetence by his city
editor, Samuel G. Blythe, eventually a star of the *Saturday Evening Post.* "Sam'll be remembered only as the man who fired Paul
Armstrong," predicted Armstrong.

When, later, Armstrong was looking for a job in Chicago,
he happened to read some "goldbug" literature put out by Senator Mark Hanna's Sound Money League in the campaign
against Bryan's free-silver heresy. The "goldbug" propaganda
consisted of economics and statistics utterly unintelligible to the
average reader. Armstrong, who was a great natural actor, put
on a big scene in his effort to prove that the Republicans should
use old-fashioned blood-and-thunder stuff to expose the silver
horror. He was hired for fifty dollars a week, and Hanna was
so pleased by his work that he kept the young man on the payroll a year after his job had been abolished. Armstrong used his
salary to support himself while writing his first play, "Just a Day
Dream," but although he received encouragement from Joseph
Jefferson, he couldn't find a producer who would take a chance
on it. Returning to newspaper work, he became Right Cross,
prizefight chronicler on the New York *Journal.* He was soon
famous. He knew his stuff well enough to make thirty-seven
hundred dollars by betting on Jeffries, who was generally conceded very little chance to beat the great Bob Fitzsimmons when
they met in 1899. One line written by Right Cross about the

Jeffries-Sharkey fight at Coney Island in 1899 is sometimes quoted today: "Sharkey kept coming in like the surf."

Armstrong decided to put on "Just a Day Dream" himself. He used most of his savings and the money collected on bets to back it. The play opened in Boston and failed immediately. His other early efforts met similar fates. His mishaps in the theatre greatly entertained the *Journal* staff, and life in the office became rather painful to him. Even the office boys were in stitches at the thought of a prizefight reporter attempting to write a play. For years, Armstrong never walked past two people in conversation without believing that he could detect muffled laughter. The New York police were the first to recognize his talent. They gave tremendous applause to a sketch he wrote for a police benefit, and from then on Armstrong always treated his stage cops as sympathetically as his plots permitted. After saving up four thousand dollars, Armstrong got a leave of absence from the *Journal* in 1902 and opened his newest play, "St. Ann," in Baltimore, in the midst of strenuous backstage activity. He knocked out the leading man in a dispute over the leading lady. Armstrong's face and whiskers were covered with dirt, and he nearly suffered worse damage when a sandbag whizzed past him, after being launched at him from on high by a stagehand who had enlisted under the leading man's banner. Some members of the cast quit in terror because of the cursing and fighting, the ingénue ran off with the press agent, and quick substitutions had to be made at the last minute to enable "St. Ann" to open. In spite of being borrowed from Sardou, Pinero, Augustus Thomas, and other good sources, the play flopped badly. One of its by-products was a lifelong friendship between Armstrong and Mencken. Armstrong liked the lively way in which Mencken, then a young reporter on the Baltimore *Herald,* wrote up the turbulent offstage action.

The reigning American playwright of that era was Clyde Fitch. His mincing personality outraged the grizzly-bear masculinity of Armstrong. Armstrong undertook to destroy Fitch by satirizing him in a play, "The Superstition of Sue." To make doubly sure of laughing Fitch out of the theatre, Armstrong modelled "The Superstition of Sue" after Charles Hale Hoyt's "A Texas Steer," which was then putting people into hospitals with internal injuries from wild hilarity. The humor of "The Superstition of Sue" arose from a long series of odd coincidences that frustrated the hero's attempt at suicide. Armstrong succeeded in interesting the producer Al Woods. Al and Mrs. Woods went to Armstrong's apartment to hear the play. Two friends happened to drop in to see Armstrong, and they consented to remain for the reading. Mr. and Mrs. Woods sat with frozen faces through the first act, but the two friends howled with glee. During the second act, Mrs. Woods joined the strangers in their ungovernable merriment, and she was weak from laughter at the end of the reading. Al never cracked a smile during the entire four acts, but he believed in democracy and the score was three to one against him, so he produced "Sue" on Broadway. The general opinion of it was summed up by the *Sun,* which called it "the drizzliest drivel." It closed in a week, in spite of vehement protests from the author, who pointed out that the nightly receipts had risen steadily from a low of twenty-three dollars to a high of forty-seven. Armstrong was now the author of a Broadway flop, and it was the turning point of his career. "Have a failure on Broadway," he advised young playwrights in later years, "and then all the producers will be interested in you." His first great hit was "The Heir to the Hoorah," in 1905, but that success, instead of soothing his uneven temperament, became the torment of his life. The play bore so much resemblance to "The Transmogrification of Dan," a short story sold for eighty-five dollars to *Smart Set* by H. J. W. Dam, that Armstrong was a target for plagiarism suits until the end of his life, and, in fact, for six years thereafter. He made a countercharge to the effect that the short story had been stolen from his play, in a Baltimore restaurant where he had talked too freely about his idea for it. One jury held that twenty-three thousand dollars' worth of damages had been done to Dam's eighty-five-dollar tale. Sixteen years of litigation left the issue in doubt, Armstrong stealing the play from Dam in some courts and Dam stealing the short story from Armstrong in others.

Armstrong's next hit was "Salomy Jane," which was produced by George Tyler as a vehicle for Eleanor Robson. Armstrong wrote it in a week. He always did his best work, according to Tyler, at the highest possible speed. He became known as the Hair-Trigger Playwright, as well as Strong-Arm and the Apostle of the Punch. "Salomy Jane" nearly resulted in another plagiarism suit. It had been taken from the Bret Harte story of the same name. Armstrong thought that he was perfectly safe in helping himself to a classic, and he was astounded to learn not only that the story was copyrighted but that Bret Harte had heirs who were alive and animated. An out-of-court settlement was promptly negotiated.

Armstrong was at the height of his career when he announced that he had formed a partnership with Mizner. The new playwriting firm was a mystery to some people. It seemed odd that the most successful American dramatist should team up with a man who had only a few vaudeville skits and one full-length failure to his credit. Armstrong's motives were mixed, but friendship was undoubtedly a factor. Fundamentally a big-hearted fellow, Armstrong was one of the many people who wanted to "make something of Wilson." Hundreds of people believed that Mizner had great talent, were concerned over the way he was wasting his life, and kept saying to him, "Oh, you must write." Armstrong was the only one with the ability and resolution to carry through the project of "making something of Wilson." He was ready to go to great lengths to help a friend. He had not become a successful writer of melodrama by accident. Nature had crammed him with the primary emotions. He was as quick with sobs and tears as with swings and hooks. Mencken, who heard him read scenes from his plays, has said that he never saw another actor of such emotional power and pathos. Among producers, Armstrong had the name of being "a dangerous play-reader." He could take the driest of scripts and turn it into such an emotional debauch that the tearful magnate would sign a contract on the spot, in the belief that he was about to produce the Niobe of the theatre. Rex Beach described, in a letter to Frank Case, of the Algonquin, an occasion on which Armstrong was nearly mobbed by wild Tammany women. The playwright had been asked to give a gold watch to the best-dressed lady at a Tammany district-club dance. For a while, he solemnly studied some very fancy creations. Suddenly he began to sniffle. A down-and-out-looking girl in a miracle of bad needlework and wrong color had entered his field of vision. The one spot of dowdiness in all that class went straight to Armstrong's great celluloid valentine of a heart. He handed the watch to the needy-looking girl and then made an exit before the general indignation could catch up with him. In spite of his occasional bursts of savagery, Armstrong inspired deep affection in many people. David Burton, a Broadway and Hollywood director, who played the juvenile lead in "The Greyhound," said that there was a theory among the young actors that Armstrong would do anything for you if you caught him in the right mood.

It was partly a sudden infatuation with crime that led Armstrong to adopt Mizner as a collaborator. Armstrong was a man of violent infatuations, and he usually contracted a major passion for any subject that he was writing about. It went beyond his changing the style of his whiskers to fit the play he was working on. When he was doing mint-julep drama, he fell in love with Southern belles, wore broad-brimmed Confederate-colonel hats, bought an old Southern manor named Acton, near Annapolis, and even mixed a little Dixie dialect in his conversation. Writing horse drama, he bought a stock farm at Holmdel, New Jersey, and was photographed with his arms around the necks of race horses he had purchased from Homer Davenport, the famous cartoonist. Writing Westerns, he turned his broad-brimmed hat up in front and down behind and worked the tall crown into a caved-in pyramid, in Deadwood-sheriff fashion. During a spell of illness, he happened to look into the Bible and he almost turned into an Old Testament character. "What a book, Henry!" he exclaimed to Mencken. "It's *full* of plots!" Dipping into American history, he planned a great motion-picture epic of Washington's march from Newburgh to Yorktown to bottle up Cornwallis. Had he lived, Armstrong would, in Mencken's opinion, have become the first writer of movie supercolossals. The infatuation with crime that led to the Armstrong-Mizner collaboration started when Armstrong wrote his safecracking masterpiece, "Alias Jimmy Valentine," in 1909. He got an unparalleled crush on the felonious life. He induced judges to parole old offenders in his custody, so that he could always have hardened criminals near him. One of them wormed his way into the box office of a theatre where an Armstrong play was on the boards and ran away with three thousand dollars of the receipts. Another, James Brown, alias Daniel Mason, had been convicted of throwing a brick through the plate-glass window of a store and looting it. Armstrong borrowed him from Judge Otto A. Rosalsky and gave him a small part in the Armstrong drama "A Romance of the Underworld." After some months of acting, James Brown, alias Daniel Mason, threw another brick through another plate-glass window, stole a ninety-eight-cent suitcase, and waited for the police to pick him up. "PREFERS PRISON TO APPEARING IN ARMSTRONG PLAY," said a headline in the *Morning Telegraph,* over a story that quoted Brown as saying that he felt free as a bird in his prison cell after his life in the theatre. Armstrong was so crime-smitten that he wrote "Alias Jimmy Valentine" in Warden John J. Fallon's office, in the Tombs. He proudly unveiled his new crook vocabulary in a Sunday page interview in the *Times,* letting the world in on the fact that the "big house" meant Sing Sing, that "stir" was prison, that a "rattler" was a freight car, and that a "short rattler," or "short," was a streetcar. Columnists of the period said that Armstrong had obtained the authentic lingo in "Alias Jimmy Valentine" from Wilson Mizner and from Captain William J. Peabody and Lieutenant Val O'Farrell, of the New York Police Department. The natural law of celebrities, which wrests honors from waning headliners and gives them to rising ones, has almost succeeded in stealing the authorship of "Alias Jimmy Valentine" from Armstrong. Edward Dean Sullivan, in "The Fabulous Wilson Mizner," makes Mizner the half author of "Alias Jimmy Valentine." Wilson's brother Addison, in "The Many Mizners," leaves Armstrong out completely and makes Wilson the sole author of the play. It is certain, however, that Mizner had nothing to do with the play beyond possibly acting as a consultant on underworld phraseology.

Another reason for the formation of the Armstrong-Mizner team was that Armstrong could not depend entirely on his own dramatic resources, and since he felt he needed a collaborator, he decided that he might as well have an entertaining companion like Mizner. Armstrong was a master mechanic in working with other men's brains. "Alias Jimmy Valentine" is an illustration of how various talents contributed to an Armstrong success. The Broadway star H. B. Warner happened to read O. Henry's "A Retrieved Reformation," the story of a reformed burglar who betrays himself by getting out his burglar's tools and opening a bank vault in which the little niece of his fiancée is accidentally locked and is in danger of smothering. The matinée idol could see himself starring in that scene, and he took the matter up with George Tyler. Tyler did his best to incite O. Henry to dramatize the story, and advanced him several hundred dollars. This investment bringing no results, Tyler offered him five hundred dollars for the dramatic rights. O. Henry leaped at this as a most generous proposal, and emphasized his gratitude by telling Tyler to help himself to any other O. Henry story, free of charge. When Armstrong was getting enormous royalties from several "Alias Jimmy Valentine" companies, O. Henry still insisted that the story wasn't worth a cent more than five hundred dollars and that it was a stage hit only because of the work of "a truly great dramatist." Armstrong had help on this play from others besides O. Henry. Percy Hammond said that the evidence was conclusive that "Alias Jimmy Valentine" was largely borrowed from "The Ticket-of-Leave Man," an English hit of the middle nineteenth century by Tom Taylor, editor of *Punch*. The literary heredity of the play was complicated by the further discovery that "The Ticket-of-Leave Man" had been adapted from "Le Retour de Melun," by Edouard Brisbarre and Eugène Nus. One of Armstrong's last plays, "The Escape," was based on a conversation with Mencken about sin. Mencken was not against it. With his customary refusal to accept the orthodox point of view, Mencken found certain cultural advantages in the life of shame. Starting with the novel idea that the underworld could be a sort of Sorbonne, Armstrong wrote his one elaborate excursion into sociology.

The first Mizner-Armstrong play, "The Deep Purple," was a great hit and a big money-maker. Mizner called his new occupation "telling lies at two dollars a head." Armstrong told Ashton Stevens that Mizner didn't believe that you could legally make so much money so easily and that he didn't cash his royalty checks for several weeks for fear of a trap. The second Mizner-Armstrong play, "The Greyhound," was strong in character, incident, and comedy but lacked the melodramatic wallop of its predecessor. The authors told too much in advance, so the climaxes were twice-told tales. The multi-scene technique was just becoming popular in the theatre. Armstrong, in spite of seasickness, had conceived one of his passionate enthusiasms for the ocean liner, and he chopped the dramatic action up into many scenes in order to show the audience all over the ship. The actors were continually confused. The curtain had to be rung down one evening because David Burton miscounted the scenes, his mental processes being a little upset by the fact that he had a date after the show with a Winter Garden chorus girl. He was getting ready to leave the theatre when there was a pounding on his dressing-room door and loud cries for him to go on in the final scene. The stage manager made a curtain speech, saying that there would be a slight delay because Mr. Burton had met with an accident. After he had his stage clothes and makeup back on, he appeared, affecting a limp and an expression of agony. The audience, thinking that the old trouper spirit had triumphed over a broken leg, gave him the greatest ovation of his career.

Another trouble with "The Greyhound" was that it had been rashly cast. A young actress, charming and lovely in light scenes, failed in the big, emotional climaxes. One day, it was reported backstage that Mizner was pale, shaken, and unnerved. He was talking to himself and looked as if he had seen a ghost. He kept muttering "What next?" Later, it was explained that somebody had carried a tale to him to the effect that the disappointing emotional actress was a good girl in private life. Mizner had been sure that some untoward factor was preventing "The Greyhound" from being a sensational hit, and he believed that all was now revealed. He was very polite to the young actress and never let her know of the imputation against her. He blamed the leading man as an accessory, and was furious with Armstrong, who had cast the show. But the various misfortunes of "The Greyhound" were soon overshadowed by a real disaster. The play had been running in New York for several weeks when the Titanic hit an iceberg and sank, on April 15, 1912. People were too horror-stricken by that tragedy to endure a play about an ocean liner. Box-office receipts, which had been running upward of twelve thousand dollars a week, fell to five thousand, and the play soon folded.

After "The Greyhound," Mizner and Armstrong broke up their writing partnership. They had had only minor feuds. Armstrong had given the silent treatment to his collaborator for a few weeks because Mizner complained that Armstrong used long words when he might as well have used short ones, and used pure English when vulgarity would have served. The splitup came partly because Armstrong was worn out by the task of finding Mizner and inducing him to talk, and partly because Mizner was dissatisfied with the division of the spoils. In view of his proved money-making talents, Armstrong received two-thirds of the royalties and Mizner one-third, and he wouldn't agree that his partner was entitled to a higher percentage.

Mizner and Armstrong were brought together again a few months later by their old friend A. Toxen Worm, the most brilliant theatrical press agent of the era. He was a Danish-American of immense girth; his full name was Conrad Henrik Aage Toxen Worm, and he was generally called Tox, the Great Dane, or Tanbark Worm. The *Morning Telegraph* said that he was known among his overshadowed rivals in the publicity field as Anti-Toxin Worms. He was a *bon vivant* of aristocratic manners, having had a touch of high life in his youth, when he played with the heirs apparent who later became Kaiser Wilhelm II, Czar Nicholas II, George V of England, Haakon VII of Norway, and Christian X of Denmark. Toxen was a village boy in Charlottenlund, where the five little princes spent their summers, and he was called in with other village boys to be chased and mauled by young potentates in the game of soldiers-and-robbers. After a boyhood with five future monarchs, Toxen was naturally a little majestic. The name A. Toxen Worm was inscribed in press-agent history forever on January 20, 1902, when he carpeted a section of Forty-second Street with tanbark because Mrs. Patrick Campbell was sensitive to sound. Horse-drawn trucks with iron tires rattled over the cobblestones of Times Square at that time, and Mrs. Pat asserted that the street-cars seemed to crash right into her dressing room in Hammer-stein's Republic Theatre. The tempestuous star, who was ap-pearing in repertory, endured the racket until she started to pre-sent "Beyond Human Power," a Björnson play that called for muttering, whispering, and long silences. Then she gave signs of losing her mind. In 1902, when national heroes were tossing on a bed of pain or great public funerals were being held, it was a routine thing to hush the street noises by laying tanbark on the cobblestones. Acting on that idea, Tox telephoned to a tannery supply house, in Newark, and ordered truckloads of tanbark to be laid outside the theatre. When the police, street-cleaners, and re-porters came, demanding an explanation, they were told, "Mrs. Pat Campbell has to have quiet." After several conferences, the police and Commissioner John M. Woodbury, of the Street Cleaning Department, agreed to let the tanbark stay. But three days later, Borough President Jacob A. Cantor, of Manhattan, ordered it removed. Newspapers that thoroughly hated press-agent stunts and free advertising had to print the story or cheat their readers of the talk of the town. The *Morning Telegraph* described the tanbark as "papyrus leaves" that would carry the name of A. Toxen Worm down the ages, and the tanbark inci-dent is still considered the most inspired of all press-agent stunts except the milk baths Florenz Ziegfeld, Jr., provided for Anna Held.

Toxen became Mizner's closest friend and the leader of those who wanted to "make something of Wilson." He contended that a shorthand-writing Boswell ought to be kept at Mizner's elbow to record his talk for posterity. Toxen thought that the collaboration with Armstrong was the greatest thing that had ever happened to Mizner, and he had furthered it every way he could. He had crossed the Atlantic with Mizner and Armstrong when they went in quest of atmosphere for "The Greyhound." On August 31, 1912, Toxen gave a dinner at Rector's to celebrate the reunion of the collaborators, and on the spot they laid plans to write "The Pirate," which was to be a vehicle for the idol Lou Tellegen, an import from Holland. Before work could be started on "The Pirate," however, Mizner had a severe attack of appendicitis. He had a wild terror of croakers and sawbones, and it was not until his life was in imminent danger that he would consent to an operation. He drew up a will naming Toxen Worm as executor, and instructed him, "Have my coffin fit well around the shoulders." Mizner was such a Broadway institution that his operation, which took place on September 20th, made the front page of several New York newspapers. The *Press* quoted Addison Mizner to the effect that Wilson's first words on coming out of the anesthetic were "So this is America." In a letter to Frank Ward O'Malley, of the *Sun*, Mizner subsequently told of a painful preliminary dispute he had had with the hospital's "booking agent" over where the remains were to be sent. He said that, wheeled into the operating room, he still clung to the one last hope that the joint would be raided, and that he would have fought against the chloroform except that it was against his principles ever to interfere with the dealer. The *Morning Telegraph*, announcing that Mizner was out of danger, said, "He will never leave this world while there is anything left in it." Mizner made a quick recovery, but he used the operation as an excuse for avoiding conversational story conferences with Armstrong. Much as he loved conversation, he hated work more, and by now he definitely identified conversation with Armstrong as work. Mizner went to Europe to escape from Armstrong. That was the last of the firm of Armstrong and Mizner.

Chapter Eleven

A MATTER OF PHILOSOPHY

WILSON MIZNER was fond of moralizing. When younger men came to him for advice, he told them that the great rule of life was "Never gamble except with a little the best of it."

He was at times content with a very small advantage. In the Klondike, he had trouble with the Northwest Mounted because he had five deuces in a deck, the minutest possible degree of dishonesty. His approach to any topic was a calculation of odds. Writhing with agony from an attack of appendicitis, he was told that he was to be operated on by a surgeon who had performed eighteen successful appendectomies in a row. Mizner handed a roll of bills to his pal Lew Lipton, of Broadway and Hollywood, saying, "See what odds you can get that I don't break his run."

He preferred odds of 100 to 0 in his favor and often made arrangements that insured those odds. He was also ready to accept odds of 51 to 49 in his favor, and he would rather gamble honestly than not at all. When he became a celebrity in New York in 1906, through his marriage to the wealthy Mrs. Yerkes, a news dispatch from San Francisco gave an idea of his range and versatility as a gamester. A ferryboat had stopped in San Francisco Bay at the cry of "Man overboard!" A lifeboat was lowered and the sailors found Mizner treading water, a stopwatch in his hand. He had a bet on the length of time necessary for his rescue. He was walking across Times Square once with Honest John Kelly, the famous gambler and referee, when a street-

car knocked over a fish wagon. A lobster and a crab landed side by side on the pavement and started for the streetcar tracks. "A hundred on the lobster," said Mizner, but Kelly wouldn't bet.

Mizner won a good deal by betting on Jess Willard to beat Jack Johnson in their bout in Havana in 1915. By a simple device, he had convinced himself that the fight was fixed. A few days before the bout, he cabled, "WHAT SHALL I DO?" to Jack Johnson. Johnson and Mizner were close friends. Mizner reasoned that if the fight was on the level, Johnson would cable enthusiastically about his chances of winning, and that if it was a fake, Johnson would not reply at all. After two days without word from the black champion, Mizner bet everything he had on Willard.

Mizner won $10,000 on a big race in England by characteristic foresight. On the day of the race, Mizner, who was living at the Hotel Claridge, at Forty-fourth and Broadway, had a late breakfast in his apartment with a New York businessman who was famous for his eagerness to back his judgment on any subject that came up. The two men began to deplore the fact that they had failed to bet on the race. Mizner offered to put up $200 just to increase their interest in the event. His guest snorted at such a picayune sum, and said, "Let's make it ten thousand." Mizner said he didn't have that much; his guest insisted on trusting him for it. Mizner sipped highballs, talked, and studied the entries for a long time. Finally, he chose the horse listed in the newspapers as No. 7. An hour or two later, they went downstairs. The evening papers were out with the news that No. 7 had won. Mizner had picked No. 7 advisedly. Across the court from his room, he had a confederate whose telephone was connected with a poolroom. When the confederate got the news that the horse had won, he went to his window and held up five fingers of one hand and two of the other. Mizner then made the bet on No. 7.

He won a roll of bills at Atlantic City once by a game that was halfway between a lucrative practical joke and a crooked gamble. He and some other sports were lounging along the boardwalk betting on anything in which they could find an element of chance, such as which of two sunbathers would be the first to go into the water or which of two swimmers would be the first to come out of it. One of the party noticed a pair of gigantic feet sticking out of a window on the first floor of a boardwalk hotel. The owner of the feet was out of sight, apparently lying back in a chair. Mizner and his friends began to guess how tall the man was, from the evidence of his feet. Finally, they backed their guesses with money. Most of the bettors placed the man's height at well over six feet. Mizner made the lowest estimate. With a curious disregard of the principles of human symmetry, he guessed five feet one. When the money was up, they called on the man in the hotel room. He was a dwarf, four feet six inches tall, with No. 11 shoes. Mizner had brought him from New York and planted him there, figuring he could probably win a few bets on the man's paradoxical physique.

Mizner once employed a practical joke for the purpose of giving Nat Goodwin, the famous comedian, a lesson in ethics. Goodwin had pleaded to be allowed to be Mizner's confederate in a crooked card game. The comedian didn't want ill-gotten money, but he craved experience. Mizner explained that he was playing on the level at the time because all his fellow-players were as sophisticated as he was. Goodwin, a hero-worshipper, would not believe that Mizner would stoop to honesty under any circumstances. He continued to plead for a chance to help swindle somebody, and Mizner finally gave in. He promised to bump Goodwin's knee under the table at the point when the crooked work started. After the game had been going for three or four hours, Mizner bumped him and then handed over a new deck for Nat to deal. The actor dealt the first three cards but failed to get the fourth off the deck. He struggled furiously with the fourth card. Finally, he noticed that everybody was grinning at him. In order to instruct the actor in the principle of honor among thieves, Mizner had driven a nail through forty-nine cards, leaving only the three top cards loose.

On another occasion, Mizner used a practical joke to remind a young woman friend that he had given her a warning. He had advised her not to spend a weekend with some people with whom he had quarrelled. He had insisted that she would be bored; she had insisted she wouldn't. During her visit, a present arrived for her. It was a bulky object, fussily beribboned. She started to unwrap it in the presence of her hostess. Finding Mizner's card in it, however, she hurriedly introduced another topic of conversation and then carried the gift to her room. It was an enormous pie. A rope ladder and a file were concealed in it.

Whether he was playing on the level or had a little the best of things, Mizner was a pretty consistent winner at gambling. But even when he was taking large pots and enjoying considerable royalties from Broadway hits, he succeeded in living up to his revenue. At some periods of his career, women kept him solvent; at others, they kept him broke. When he was in luck, he was a prodigal buyer of furs, diamonds, and other antidotes to indifference. He held his own with the big spenders back in the pre-income-tax, champagne-for-the-house days. His resourcefulness in getting rid of money was illustrated by a front-page scoop in the *World* on December 19, 1912, describing a poker game played by Mizner, John Shaughnessy, Nat Evans, and George Young Bauchle. With stakes running into tens of thousands on the table, Mizner said, "I can't bear to spend Christmas in New York. If I win this hand, I'll take you all to Europe and show you around as long as the money lasts, provided you go to the boat with me as soon as the hand is played." Mizner won. He, Shaughnessy, and Evans hurried to the Mauretania and boarded it without baggage. Bauchle remained behind.

Evening it up with the *World,* the New York *Press* got a front-page scoop by cabling to Mizner on his arrival in London for an account of the expedition. It was an Iliad of hardship. According to Mizner, there had been only one toothbrush and one mustache cup among the three. He added that they were in a tramplike state because of their inability to buy clothes and other equipment in London on Christmas Day. "ALL THE STORES AND THEATRES, NOT EXCEPTING WESTMINSTER ABBEY, ARE CLOSED," he cabled. Serious trouble arose, he reported, because Shaughnessy's racial prejudice against Englishmen took the form of a blanket announcement at a big Christmas party: "If there's any battle of the Revolutionary War that remains undecided, I'd like to fight it over again."

Later, in Paris, Mizner took his guests out for a nine-course dinner at nine different restaurants, each course being something for which one particular dining place was especially noted. Correspondents in Paris and elsewhere on the Continent kept New York readers posted on such activities. Toward the end of the trip, Mizner was accused of trying to drive his companions home before all the money was spent. He failed to move them, even though he bribed orchestra leaders to play "Home, Sweet Home" incessantly. They stayed with him until his money was gone.

Because of his fame as a collaborator with Paul Armstrong on "The Deep Purple" and on "The Greyhound," Mizner was called in to doctor a London girl show. He filled it with strokes of genius from the American vaudeville stage; it was a success. When he heard cries of "Author!," he said, "There isn't room enough on the stage to hold all the authors."

Mizner became interested in the lobby advertising signs for this show. They were samples of a new German process for reproducing masterpieces. Even the roughnesses of the surface and the frayings of the canvas were imitated. Since his life in the Yerkes mansion, with its famous art collection, Mizner had been deeply interested in old masters. Although not a professional fence, he is supposed to have protected hot merchandise of this kind, holding stolen canvases until the owners had been induced to sell them for a fraction of their real value. Postgraduates in Mizner lore have credited him with "protecting" the "Mona Lisa" for a time after it was stolen from the Louvre; he is said to have received it rolled up in a cardboard cylinder and to have held it for a year or more without knowing what it was. This report, however, is widely at variance with the orthodox "Mona Lisa" story.

Mizner's first step toward exploring the possibilities of the new German process was to take one of the reproductions to a pawnbroker, who, with gleaming eyes, made an extravagant loan on it. His next step was to send his friend E. Ray Goetz with samples to America to raise money to acquire the American rights to the invention. New York customs officers seized the samples in the belief that they were originals; on this showing, Goetz had no difficulty in borrowing fifty thousand dollars, which he cabled to Mizner. There was a battle in London between various interests that wanted to control the invention in the United States. The European promoter of the process, an inexperienced and bashful individual, had just made the discovery that there was a whole sex composed entirely of women. Mizner closed the deal by using half the chorus of his show as his negotiators.

Mizner opened the Old Masters' Art Society, on Fifth Avenue near Forty-second Street, in 1913. The reproductions were sold at upward of a hundred dollars apiece. One hotel bought several hundred and hung them in the bedrooms. For a year or so, business was good, but then it began to suffer from competition with cheaper processes. Mizner was forced to cut prices. He came down to sixty-five dollars for da Vinci's "Last Supper," but would not budge further. "I won't take less than five dollars a plate for it," he said.

Mizner's merchandising manners were not of the best. Neither were those of his general manager, an ex-bartender named Bert. The salesrooms formed a labyrinth, in which visitors occasionally got lost. The lighting was controlled by a master switch. Once, when a customer tried to beat down prices, Mizner said, "Bert, turn off the lights and let this son of a bitch find his way out."

At about the time Old Masters folded, Mizner had another inspiration. He established a tipster service in New York in collaboration with Tod Sloan, the disbarred demigod of the turf. The jockey's great contribution to racing had been his method of cutting wind resistance by stretching himself along his horse's neck. Jeered at when he introduced his monkey-on-a-stick style in England, he was taken more seriously after he had ridden twenty-one winners in his first season. Sloan constantly whispered in his horse's ear, and it was widely supposed that they had secrets. At one time, he was bitterly assailed for making unethical promises to horses. But the thing that gave him highest prestige as a tipster was the fact that he had been ruled off the turf on a charge of complicity in a betting ring. The combination of the bad reputations of Sloan and Mizner caused a rush to buy their tips. But after three days, in which they failed to pick a single winner, business fell off, and the tipster service was soon discontinued.

The Millionaires' Club was another of Mizner's New York enterprises. Among its appointments was a three-hundred-pound man with a resemblance to William Howard Taft, who at the time had only recently left the White House. This man was always seated in a huge armchair in the reading room, with a highball in his hand and a newspaper before his face. As people could tell at close range that he was not Taft, strangers were led to the door of the room for a look but were requested not to enter. They were told that the old fellow hung out there because it was the most exclusive club in town and the one place where he was sure of not being disturbed. Although chief owner of the club, Mizner posed as a casual patron so that he could bring suckers in without embarrassment. He had steered in a gorgeous prospect one evening when the place was suddenly thrown into an uproar; Taft had sunk a knife into a waiter for persistently bringing him highballs with hardly any whiskey in them. During the turmoil, the sucker fled. Meeting him a few days later, Mizner said, "Can you beat it, the way they kept that story about Taft out of the papers?"

Mizner was a star witness on March 14, 1918, at a John Doe inquiry into gambling in the Court of General Sessions. According to the *Sun*, which treated the inquiry with some flippancy, it all started when a German baker, who had lost thirty-five thousand dollars to Mizner at *chemin de fer*, started to pay off in doughnuts. The *Sun* asserted that tens of thousands of doughnuts were piled up in front of Mizner's apartment, on West Forty-third Street near Sixth Avenue. One of the questions put to Mizner was how long he had played *chemin de fer*. "Since infancy," he said. The investigators, learning very little from Mizner and other witnesses, concluded the inquiry without indictments.

Mizner denied on the witness stand in a Magistrates' Court on August 28, 1918, that he lived entirely by gambling. He testified that he had a half interest in a tannery in Newark and did scenarios on the side. The charge against him was that of assaulting Herman Frank, an actor, in a Times Square restaurant. Frank had accused Mizner of stealing a Ziegfeld beauty from him. According to the testimony, Frank had sent Mizner a challenge to a duel in Van Cortlandt Park and Mizner had neglected to reply. On cross-examination, Mizner said that he didn't write scenarios but that he telephoned them. Referring to a screen drama of which Mizner was the author, the opposing lawyer said, "Do you mean to say that you gave that to the motion-picture company by telephone?" "Yes," said Mizner, "and they paid me by telephone." Like most of the criminal charges against Mizner, the assault charge evaporated somewhere in the judicial processes.

Mizner occasionally called together his close friends for an opium-smoking party, a social diversion that was smarter a quarter of a century ago than it is today. It was the practice of opium-smokers to cover doors and windows with wet sheets, partly to keep the fumes from escaping and partly to exclude fresh air, which opium-smokers regarded as a dangerous gas. Mizner was entertaining friends in a hermetically sealed room in a hotel on Times Square one day in November, 1918. One of the guests complained of a tingling in his ears. Before long, he said that it amounted to a positive jingling. Others experienced the same thing. One asserted that he could almost swear he heard sleigh bells. They attributed it to an impurity in the opium and forgot it. Some hours later, Mizner went out. He came back with news of the armistice.

At one time, Mizner added the sniffing of cocaine, or "snow," to his amusements. Instead of concealing little failings of this kind, he always exploited them for their comedy value. He was seated at a table playing faro in a New York hotel when a man entered in a fur coat covered with white flakes. "It's snowing hard," said the newcomer. Mizner hailed a bellboy. "Boy," he said, "take my nose and hang it out the window."

After intense suffering, Mizner broke himself of the drug habit. It was asserted that in his later life he was a "social drug-taker." A Los Angeles police physician is quoted as asserting that Mizner was the only man except Sherlock Holmes who could take drugs or let them alone.

One of Mizner's few innocent pastimes was the singing of sentimental lyrics. He loved the old songs, especially those that glorified the simple virtues. In his younger days, he had a fine baritone voice. It became rusty and squeaky in his later years but still had some command over pathos. Among his favorites were "The Chairs in the Parlor All Miss You," "When I Leave the World Behind," "The Curse of an Aching Heart," and "The Mansion of Aching Hearts." In Hollywood, he spent many evenings in Jane Jones' Little Club, the headquarters of old songs. He maintained a deep attachment for his singing companions of earlier days. In autographing a picture of himself, he would usually write something like "Wanted in every state and welcome in none," but on a photograph sent to his fellow-ballad-singer Hype Igoe, the cartoonist, he wrote, "To my little pal Hype, who spans the abyss between the boresome present and the beautiful past with a bridge of old cherished melodies."

Mizner's fondness for Igoe was based partly on the fact that they were both pre-earthquake San Franciscans. When writing dialogue for Warden Lawes' picture "Twenty Thousand Years in Sing Sing," Mizner gave a touching exhibition of his sentiment for the cartoonist. Not having seen Igoe for years, Mizner used the sound track to convey an affectionate remembrance. It was comparatively easy to hail the cartoonist through this medium, as "Hype" is a unique first name. Igoe is the only man in the world to be named after a hypodermic needle. When he started to work on the San Francisco *Examiner,* at the age of fifteen, he was undersized, emaciated, and deathly pale. The Negro elevator man affected to believe that nothing but the hypodermic needle could reduce anybody to such a state. Whenever the boy approached, the elevator man would issue a prolonged cry of "Hy-y-y-pe!" and go through the motions of giving himself a shot in the arm with a gigantic needle. Others took up the name, and the cartoonist has answered to it for more than forty years. In writing the Sing Sing picture, Mizner took advantage of this to give Hype a surprise greeting. He wrote in a scene showing a popular murderer leaving the condemned cell for the electric chair. The condemned man called, "So long, boys," to his fellow-inmates in the death house. They chorused back, "So long, Hype."

Men who were in Wilson's confidence tell of the wide range of devices by which he raised money. A rich young man of Seattle, on a visit to New York, complained to Mizner of a hangover and a complete inability to remember the events of the preceding night. Mizner hopped over to confer with the maître d'hôtel of a reigning lobster palace, concocted an itemized bill for nearly two thousand dollars, to be split two ways, and had it collected from the Westerner, who was informed that during the period about which his mind was a blank he had thrown one of the biggest and wildest parties of the season. Once, on a visit to a prosperous underworld establishment, Mizner faked the symptoms of scarlet fever. A confederate, masquerading as a physician, notified the proprietress that he would have to quarantine the place for a month. He settled, however, for a thousand dollars. On one occasion, Mizner sold a selling-plater for ten times its value by the simple device of moving back the six-furlong post in an early-morning workout, thereby shortening the course so that a stopwatch indicated the horse had broken the six-furlong record.

He was twenty-five or twenty-six when he executed one of the most profitable of his coups. A close pal of his was a member of a San Francisco family that had gained enormous wealth in Nevada silver mines. Mizner took the young scion of the Comstock Lode to New Orleans; their mission was to clean out a poolroom with the help of inside racing information. What the young silver millionaire didn't know was that the poolroom, with its entire personnel, customers and all, had been organized by Mizner solely for the purpose of getting a slice of the silver millions. Mizner's net profit at the expense of his bosom friend was more than $100,000, and in those simple days it lasted him more than a year. Mizner never had the slightest compunction about this informal method of redistributing the wealth. On their return to San Francisco, the young silver millionaire became suspicious and accused Mizner of fraud. Mizner gave him a beating, after which they became comrades again.

On other occasions, Mizner opened poolrooms and gambling houses, each for the purpose of fleecing a man of great wealth. For the exclusive benefit of the son of one of New York's richest bankers, he rented a house in Great Neck and installed a small stock company of underworld characters, who went through the motions of gambling for large sums in order to make the sucker feel that he was only one of many wealthy patrons. The Great Neck establishment failed with a considerable loss. The sucker had lost more than $200,000 when the operator applied too much magnetism and arrested the roulette ball in mid-career. The sucker grabbed his money. Mizner fled.

A trip on an ocean liner usually produced a substantial bank roll for Mizner, whether he played honestly or otherwise. On rare occasions, he picked the wrong man. He once drew a simple-looking stranger into a poker game and let him win for a while. Suddenly they began raising each other wildly, and the stakes became enormous. Mizner laid down four queens and reached for the pot. The stranger laid down four kings. Mizner pushed the pot back across the table. "You win, stranger," he said, "but those are not the cards I dealt you."

Although Mizner preyed on suckers most of his life, he was never appreciative. He seemed to have a genuine hatred of them. He regarded them as a corrupting influence. He never showed regret for his misspent life, but his bitterness on the subject of suckers apparently reflected a deep conviction that he would have been a credit to society if he had not fallen into their company. He asserted that confidence men did not discover suckers. The suckers, he said, hunted up the confidence men and usually brought them suffering and disgrace. He regarded the sucker as an unconscious *agent provocateur*. The police were never known, he asserted, to catch a confidence man until the suckers found him for them.

Mizner had a social philosophy on this subject. He particularly objected to Gold Coast punks who dangled inherited bank rolls before the eyes of resourceful men, and he disapproved of a government that allowed such things to be. He said that he had already been "sucker-sour" at the age of twenty-two. Texas Guinan's "Hello, sucker" was borrowed from Mizner. Other lines of his on this subject were "A sucker is born every minute, and two to take him" and "Boost a booster, knock a knocker, and use your own judgment with a sucker." Some authorities credit him with "Never give a sucker an even break," but this is disputed.

Besides commercializing his underworld lore in writing, Mizner gave it away to his friends. A member of his set in San Francisco years before was a young fellow who sold burnt-leather novelties to local merchants. The merchants beat down his prices until he could barely make a living. This was back in the days when the big executive cultivated the glare of a wild boar and fixed his blazing eye on an inferior to test his character. The superstition then was that if a man could not look you in the eye, he was dishonest. The executive usually had his desk about twenty feet from the door, so he could break a visitor down with his death-ray eyes before he had time to take a seat and start a conversation. The young leather salesman was defeated the moment he entered one of these offices. He sat there convicted of larceny while the merchant took the burnt leather at his own price. Mizner was up in arms on hearing of this situation. He had learned an antidote for the glaring eye of authority from a friend of wide penitentiary experience. He taught the young leather salesman never to look a man in the eye but always to fix a sober gaze on a spot between his eyes, just above the bridge of the nose. "When you learn to do that," said Mizner, "no man can outstare you. He thinks you are staring at him, and you are not even aware that his eyes are on you."

Mizner's convict friend had made this discovery after losing optical duels for years with detectives, district attorneys, turnkeys, and wardens. The young burnt-leather man practiced the trick until he found himself staring the most ferocious merchants into helplessness. The price of burnt leather soared.

As his impudence increased, the salesman became a writer. He is today one of the best-known motion-picture scenarists in Hollywood. Recently he was in conference with an executive noted for his menacing eye. As the conference proceeded, the executive nervously opened drawer after drawer in his desk and fumbled among their contents. Then he inspected his shoes. At last he burst out, "For God's sake, man, stop looking at me like that!"

This recipe for changing a slave into a tyrant has been a closely guarded secret for years. Until very recently, it is said to have been known to only eight people.

Chapter Twelve

THE BOOM

THE FLORIDA BOOM OF 1924 and 1925 made temporary multimillionaires of both Addison and Wilson Mizner. They promoted the gaudiest of all the subdivisions, Boca Raton—Beaucoup Rotten, as rival real-estate men called it. Boca Raton was the Bride of the Gulf Stream, the Anteroom of Heaven, the Miznerized Venice. It had a built-in ocean to carry electrically driven gondolas, steam yachts, and Cleopatra's barges to your doorstep. It had Palm Beach, a few miles north, for servants' quarters. Boca Raton became a blaze of tropical splendor as Addison dipped his maps and sketches in the colors of paradise. The parks and gardens of the ocean-front estates were to flow rhythmically into one another, according to Addison's master plan. The whole coastline was to unroll like a Persian rug, causing people on passing steamers to scream with delight. The Mizner brothers sold eleven million dollars' worth of lots the first day their property was offered to the public. The Miami *News* compared the stampede of the wealthy into Boca Raton with the foot race of the original Okies into the Cherokee Strip when it was thrown open to homesteaders in 1893. Cash money—"immediate filth," as Wilson's old partner in crime Dapper Dan Collins called it—rolled into the Mizner headquarters in Palm Beach.

"As you stagger out of Palm Beach with millions revolving in your mind, the fact remains that Wilson Mizner is $3,000,000 to the good,". wrote a *Variety* correspondent. "Come in, little suckers, come in," wrote Jack Hughes in the same publication. "It's a platinum sucker trap," said Wilson, describing the subdivision to Ashton Stevens. Wilson told Edgar Leslie, author of "Get Out and Get Under" and other song hits, that he and Addison had between forty and fifty millions salted away. He raised the ante still higher in a conversation with Arthur Hopkins, the Broadway producer, at Bradley's gambling house in Palm Beach. Wilson was talking about the family resemblance between the Florida boom and the glorious visions of his opium-smoking days. "When it's all over," he said, "I'm going to write a book about it, and the title will be 'How I Ran a Habit Into a Hundred Million Dollars.'"

The public relations of the Mizner promotion were handled by Harry Reichenbach, the most gifted mob psychologist since P. T. Barnum. Harry's battle cry was "Get the big snobs, and the little snobs will follow." The weakness of the other Florida promotions, as Reichenbach saw it, was that they sought to attract the middle classes. It was his conviction that nobody wanted to belong to the middle classes. The keynote of his advertising was that it was impossible for any member of the middle classes to get within rifleshot of Boca Raton. He spent millions hammering home the idea that nobody but bluebook celebrities and you could get into Boca Raton. He addressed all his advertising to you. You were Reichenbach's beau ideal of an exclusive super-patrician. It was obvious to him that you would fit in beautifully with the dukes, earls, and countesses, the Vanderbilts, Wideners, and Whitneys of the Mizner colony. One of Reichenbach's master strokes was a committee that acted as the Supreme Court of American Society and maintained the exclusiveness of Boca Raton by ruthlessly weeding out everybody except the cream of the international set and you. Reichenbach may have been in a slight hurry when he organized the committee, for Wilson Mizner was named to spearhead it, but in the miraculous year of 1925 few were surprised at anything that happened in Florida. Nobody complained when the social czar turned out to be the Underworld Abe Lincoln, as he was nicknamed by Bob Hopkins. Nobody squawked because the leader of high society in Boca Raton had been the leader of low society in Nome and on the Barbary Coast. In the delirious atmosphere of Florida, it seemed natural that the new drawing-room king should be the old sweetheart of Diamond-Tooth Gertie and Nellie the Pig, the lieutenant of Soapy Smith, the pal of Two-Toothed Mike and the Half-Kid, and the accomplice of the female world's heavyweight champion, Charlotte Poillon.

Damon Runyon commented in his column that Wilson had long been suspected of being "a spat-wearer at heart," but apparently nobody else commented at all. Wilson didn't let his sudden social glory go to his head. While he was supposed to be showering blackballs on Newporters and Palm Beachers who were striving to crash Boca Raton, he was actually holding nostalgic reunions with felonious old buddies, who turned up in Palm Beach in no small numbers during the boom. "Arthur," he telephoned to Arthur Somers Roche one evening, "I want you to come over to my house and meet an old girl of mine. She's the greatest pickpocket in the world. She can steal a grand piano from the room and you'll never miss it." Whether an authority on the blue-blooded gentry or not, Wilson was an authority on the light-fingered gentry. Praising the dexterity of one eminent professional, he said, "He could walk across the bottom of the Hudson River with an armful of eels without losing one;" denouncing a clumsy pretender, he said, "That fellow couldn't dip his hand in the Hudson River without knocking over the Palisades." It was probably no coincidence that at the very time when Wilson's old chums were swarming down to visit him, Warren Irwin, Palm Beach correspondent of the New York *Times,* wrote that an epidemic of thievery had broken out and that "women who used to be loaded with jewels are now wearing imitations."

Wilson was a critic of prizefighters as well as of dips and débutantes. A West Palm Beach preliminary fighter stopped him on the street one day and asked, "Mr. Mizner, do you think

I'll ever get anywhere as a fighter?" "My boy," said Wilson, "you'll never be anything but a catcher, and if you don't stop now, you'll be walking along the street slobbering out of both sides of your mouth instead of only one." Illustrious colleagues of Wilson joined the rush to Florida, where, according to John Henry Strosnider, one of the rascal heroes of D. W. Maurer's book "The Big Con," it became necessary to drive suckers away with clubs. The boom attracted some of Wilson's competitors in the old Mann Act shakedown racket, one of these being Jackie French, who harvested three hundred and forty-eight thousand dollars in Florida in con games in one week, according to Maurer. "More of Wilson's ragamuffins," exclaimed Addison joyously as he greeted a Mr. and Mrs. Earl, all-round sharpers and confidence people who had worked the steamship lanes with Wilson. Hailing from some obscure corner in Wilson's past was a sensational Palm Beach beauty who had once done a bit for infanticide. A protégé of Wilson's was installed as butler for Harry Reichenbach and his wife. Mrs. Reichenbach thought her new major-domo a little clumsy for one who had served all the dukes and millionaires mentioned by Wilson. Giving an engagement party for Maurice Fatio, the architect, and Eleanor Chase, she was surprised to find that her new butler, instead of serving café diablo, was sitting Buddhalike on the floor worshipping the flames. "Oh, he's all right," said Wilson, "he's only had a little too much cut glass." ("Cut glass" was what members of dope rings called their merchandise when making deliveries.) Mrs. Reichenbach discovered later that her butler was an old Barbary Coast chum of Wilson's and had recently finished a term for manslaughter. Two of Wilson's boom-time friends were famous in Palm Beach as "the best-kept women in the world," their boy friends being two of the richest men in America.

Wilson paid little attention to his high office of generalissimo of society. He was never known to weed out anybody who wanted to buy a lot in the Mizner subdivision. On the first day of her employment in the Mizner office, a lady was startled at hearing a bullfrog voice growl, "Don't ever let me hear of your turning down any money." She looked around to see an un-

shaven giant in a dirty linen suit, with his toes leaking out of
woven-leather sandals and a small, thoughtful monkey in the
crook of his left elbow. She was astonished to learn that the un-
shaven monster was Wilson Mizner, social monarch of Boca
Raton and her new boss.

The Mizners were slow to get interested in the boom. Addison, at the height of his vogue as society's architect, had no reason for fooling around with subdivisions. Wilson hated legitimate business, and the boom in its early stages was legitimate.
"You don't have to work hard to make a fortune at legitimate
business, but you do have to work *continuously*," he said. He
could work furiously in spurts, but he abhorred the idea of sustained effort. He thought better of the boom as it took on fraudulent aspects, but it still wasn't sufficiently in his line. Highly
trained in the art of fleecing one sap at a time, he had had no
practice at taking saps by the thousand, and he was as confused
as a fly-caster among the seine fishermen on the Grand Banks.
The boom flew in the face of all crook experience; it was a shell-
and-pea game in which the swindlers and suckers were both
making money. In spite of these baffling features, the boom gradually broke down the resistance of the Mizners, and in the end
they contracted one of the worst cases of subdivision fever.
Stronger heads than theirs were spinning like tops down there
in the tropical atmosphere. The Florida boom was far more in-
toxicating than the stock-market boom. Roger W. Babson, the
Calamity Jane of Wall Street, was the Pollyanna of Florida. The
boom had the remarkable power of converting skeptics into true
believers. Cornelius Vanderbilt, Jr., started out by writing that
the Miami surf was full of man-eating sharks and that you could
boil eggs in the breakers; a few days later, he called Miami the
Magic City and announced that he was going to run a new railroad and a new steamship line down to it. T. H. Weigall, a
British journalist, wrote home to London that Miami was probably the ghastliest hole on earth; then he spent a year ballyhoo-
ing it as a garden strip of paradise. George Horace Lorimer
scented the truth about Florida and tried to blow the lid off the
boom, but his hardboiled debunking *Saturday Evening Post*

writers could produce nothing but blurbs about our American tropics. Colonel Jake Ruppert, of the Yankees, hated the boom because it took the minds of his athletes off baseball during the spring-training season, but he bobbed up in due time with one Ruppert Beach and three Ruppert Islands down there. Trailing some crooks to Florida, Raymond Schindler, the private detective, remained there to engage in the manufacture of islands by pumping sand into steel frames in Florida bays. One enemy of the boom, a Kansas City banker who went to Florida to collect evidence that the whole thing was a snare and a delusion, rushed into the office of Joe Copps, a real-estate man, one day and bought a hundred and eighty thousand dollars' worth of Miami Beach lots. Ben Hecht and J. P. McEvoy travelled to Florida to get gags for a W. C. Fields laugh riot about the crazy supersalesmen of rapidly growing nonexistent cities. They forgot W. C. Fields and became supersalesmen themselves of one of the most stupendous of all the rapidly growing nonexistent cities.

At the beginning of the boom, the Mizners had the Palm Beach psychology. The typical Palm Beacher, having amassed or inherited his wealth long ago, found it tiresome to watch the middle and lower classes scrambling for their first million. But it was hard to maintain an attitude of boredom in the face of the daily reports of huge killings. Even actors were making money. Val C. Cleary, a strolling player with the Pickert Stock Company, was rudely awakened from sleep one afternoon and forced to take a profit of $150,000 on his Miami property. Weigall wrote about a bank clerk who, needing money to marry his boss's daughter, went to Florida and made an acceptable nest egg of $375,000 in three weeks. A Mrs. Mary O'Dwyer, of Toledo, got $165,000 for nothing; her husband had said "Count me in" on a Florida real-estate deal and had died suddenly without putting up any money, but his honest partner handed over $165,000 as her late husband's share of the profit. The columnist Frederick J. Haskin told of a schoolteacher who collected $6,000,000 on an investment of $3,500. Will Payne, in an article in the *Saturday Evening Post*, wrote that a man was getting $10,000 a year in rent for a property that had cost him $10,000.

Harry Block related in the *Times* that one lucky operator had made $9,000,000 on a $20,000 investment. Nobody was too young or too old to scoop in that Florida money. Seventy-four-year-old John S. Collins had started the whole excitement with his Miami Beach real-estate operations, and, according to the Miami *News,* eleven-year-old Gray Singleton, of Fort Meade, swung a $100,000 deal singlehanded. Sackcloth-and-ashes literature began to appear—the bleats of those who failed to close their fists when fortunes came within their reach. Paul L. Kinkhead told in *Liberty* how his lack of the gambling spirit caused him to spurn opportunities for untold wealth, even while he was watching one man who ran two bottles of synthetic gin into $75,000 in real-estate profits and another who became rich by shutting up his house in the North and investing his winter's coal money in Florida lots. Kenneth Roberts, the novelist, asserted that J. W. Young, the promoter of Hollywood-by-the-Sea, paid $65,000 to get back a lot he had sold for $800 a couple of years before. *Variety* testified that E. F. Albee, the vaudeville king, after having refused to pay $10,000 for a piece of Florida property, was now refusing to pay $4,000,000 for it.

The boom had originated in Miami, and Palm Beach looked down on Miami as Bar Harbor looks down on Coney Island. It was impossible, however, to keep on sneering when the boom finally hit Palm Beach. Samuel Untermyer, the keen-witted New York lawyer, pocketed a $700,000 profit on his Palm Beach property. Mrs. Francis Cragin sold for $1,750,000 a Palm Beach tract that her father had reluctantly accepted in settlement of a debt of a few hundred dollars. The Mizners were shaken out of their complacency as verifiable tales of Florida riches continued to circulate—$2,000,000 picked up by an aged railroad employee, $4,000,000 by a former hot-dog man, $8,000,000 by a minor poet, $10,000,000 by an old bicycle racer.

Nobody in Florida could very easily ignore the boom. The late Mark Sullivan, author of "Our Times," said that none of our earlier gold rushes, oil booms, or land booms could compare with the Florida excitement. The London *Times* gave part of the credit to British capitalists. George W. Seaton, a travel writer, called it "the most fantastic land boom since the Mississippi Bubble." The Miami *News* said that the rush of "prospects" into Florida constituted "the greatest migration since the Crusades." The New York *Times*, discussing the boom in an early stage, said that three hundred thousand "pioneers de luxe" had already settled in Florida in two years—more than had settled in California in the ten years following the arrival of the forty-niners. At the height of the jamboree, it was figured out that more than two million people had invaded Florida since it started, and they were regarded as only the vanguard of the approaching host. Roger W. Babson computed that six million farmers lived close enough to Florida to hibernate there easily, and he added that they were swarming in because they liked those bona-fide Florida profits after having been painfully stung by blue-sky mining stock and wildcat oil shares. Newspapers quoted a prominent "economic statistician" who found that fifteen per cent of the country's population, or twenty million people, had money enough to build winter homes in Florida—forty billion dollars' worth of homes, at the modest rate of a ten-thousand-dollar house for each family·of five. A Miami real-estate editor wrote that everybody expected one solidly built-up city seventy miles long to develop between Miami and Palm Beach. Charles Donald Fox, author of "The Truth About Florida," made the city a hundred and fifty miles long, the south end of town consisting of the islands, or keys, between Key West and the mainland. Mark Sullivan said that the subdivisions were already almost continuous from Jacksonville to Miami—or a three-hundred-mile-long city. Theodore Dreiser wrote that Florida was wholly dedicated to luxury and grandeur and was preparing estates, clubs, and casinos for twenty million multimillionaires. A Chicago broker calculated that the town lots in Florida would provide for eighty million people, or more than half the population of the United States. He was eclipsed by a baseball statistician who figured that the Florida subdivisions would take care of slightly more than three hundred million people, or a little less than the population of India.

The Florida rainbow had a particular appeal for the eco-

nomically disinherited. The boom was full of Dick Whittington
stories—reports of sudden riches coming to poor boys who invested the equivalent of a cat. There were various easy ways of
starting penniless, acquiring a little cash, and parlaying it into
wealth. One short cut was to get up early and stand near the
head of the line in front of a real-estate office that was opening
a new world capital; somebody was pretty certain to come along
and offer you fifty or a hundred dollars for your place in the line.
One man padlocked himself to an office door to make sure that
he would have first choice of lots. When a sale of lots on the
Davis Islands, in Tampa Bay, was announced, a customer set
up a cot in front of the office two days in advance and waited in
comfort. Another source of quick money was selling life mem-
berships in fake yacht clubs. Peddling was still another means
of earning a stake; thousands of people in cars were held up by
traffic jams in Miami, and itinerant merchants with trays of neckties, stockings, and other notions burst into the cars, displaying
their merchandise and shouting that it was "the bee's knees" and
"the rooster's boots"—phrases of the twenties for supreme excel-
lence. According to Thomas J. Pancoast, a leading citizen of
Miami, some of the newcomers got their start by selling forged
deeds to desirable properties. Others got off to a flying start by
honest methods. A British journalist sold ten-line poems at fifty
dollars a poem. P. Jocelyn Yoder, the Coral Gables publicity chief, walked into a barbershop one day and inquired
for his regular man. "Oh, he quit," Yoder was told. "He's
a millionaire now." The barber had saved up eighty dollars in
tips and, by prudent investment, made himself a rich man in a
few weeks. A New York taxi-driver drove down a party who
couldn't get rail accommodations to Miami, started to speculate
with his fare and tip, and was soon in the higher brackets. Anybody who knew a building trade could quickly earn a down payment, or starting money, by working two shifts at premium rates.
The old rules for getting rich didn't apply to Florida. The man
who investigated before he invested might save himself a fortune but he couldn't make himself a fortune; any promising
property was sure to be sold five or six times while he was inves-

tigating. The wild man with a shoestring fared better than the careful investor with a bank roll.

Editors, bankers, and businessmen all over the country were alarmed by the stampede of their neighbors to Florida. "Literally thousands of persons," said the Indianapolis *Times,* "are leaving the state in search of something for nothing in the land of oranges and speculators." The Massachusetts Savings Bank Association reported that more than a hundred thousand Florida-bound depositors had withdrawn money from Massachusetts banks. Seven bankers of Columbus, Ohio, raised a fund and ran big advertisements in Middle Western newspapers, saying, "You are going to Florida for what? To sell lots to the other fellow who is going to Florida to sell them to you?" This was blasphemy, and James M. Cox, a former Governor of Ohio himself, reported that Florida was boycotting Ohio products because of the Ohio bankers' propaganda. Florida credit men passed a resolution calling for the dismissal of an executive of the National Association of Credit Men for applying the word "levitated" to Florida land values—"levitating" being the term used by spiritualistic mediums for causing chairs and tables to rise into the air without apparent motivation. When W. O. McGeehan, the sports editor, gently kidded the boom in the New York *Herald Tribune,* the Ku Klux Klan put on a parade to warn him and a St. Petersburg paper printed an editorial headlined "SHUT YOUR DAMN MOUTH." The proprietor of a novelty store in Miami was sent to jail for ten days for complaining that rents were too high in town.

The anti-Florida statement of the Ohio bankers was "a nefarious attack" on "the intrinsic mobility of capital," according to a proclamation issued in Palm Beach by the Duc de Richelieu. The Duke was just one of the many titled Europeans who became champions of the boom. Prince Michael Cantacuzene was another. He was developing twenty-six thousand acres near Sarasota. The Countess Marie, daughter of the Duke of Wittelsbach, was still another. The Miami *News* said that a fortune had been made in Florida real estate by the Countess, lineal descendant of Otto the Great, and the "only woman in the world who knows the inside story of the tragic death of Prince Rudolph and his mistress at Mayerling." Arcadia Gardens announced that thirteen blocks of its subdivision had been bought by Prince Habibrath of India, while large chunks went to Countess Boutonni of Biarritz, Countess Rica des Leontine, and Countess Juanita de Lavalette. The Mizner boys specialized in American celebrities. The Boca Raton list included not only Paris Singer but General T. Coleman du Pont, F. V. du Pont, Harold Vanderbilt, the Reverend Maitland Alexander (known as "the multimillionaire clergyman of Pittsburgh"), Elizabeth Arden, Mme. Frances Alda, J. L. Replogle, Jesse L. Livermore, H. H. Rogers, Lytle Hull, Irving Berlin, Herbert Bayard Swope, James M. Cox, George Whitney, Matthew C. Brush, and Marie Dressler —who became known as the Duchess of Boca Raton. The Mizners had some fairly good foreign titles—Lady Diana Manners, Countess Salm, Lord Ivor, Charles Spencer Churchill, Lord Glenconner, the Duchess of Sutherland, and the Princess of Ghika, from Rumania. In addition to contributing royal background, the Princess Ghika joined the staff and sold lots. Employees of the Mizner office in Palm Beach still remember the day the Princess burst into the office shouting, "Where's my money? If you think I'm in this goddam plebeian swamp for my health, you're crazy as hell." Harry Reichenbach was more than satisfied with Boca Raton's list of celebrities until a rival promotion, Floranda, came along with the Earl of Lauderdale and his wife, Gwendoline, Countess of Lauderdale, author of the statement that "the blue-and-gold climate of Florida beats Capri," as well as Lord Thirlestane, Prince Paul of Greece, and the exiled King George of Greece. Reichenbach's competitive spirit was violently excited by the announcement that the King was to make his winter home at Floranda, and he fought desperately to get a monarch or two for Boca Raton. He even tried to kidnap the King of Greece from the opposition. Reichenbach was still combing the Old World for a couple of exiled potentates when the boom busted.

The Riviera was reported to be almost deserted because of the rush to Florida. The New York *Times* quoted M. Aletti,

"the uncrowned king of Nice," and M. Comouche, of the Cannes Casino, as blaming the exodus on the unparalleled climate of Florida, but predicting that the old customers would be driven back to the Riviera by the unparalleled prices of Florida. The British were well represented in the boom. Cecil Roberts, an English author, wrote a book in which he tells about his quest in Florida for Alcantara Heights, the loveliest city ever turned out by a printing press, and about his discovery in a forlorn wilderness of a broken entrance arch on which "A cant a" was still legible. One London writer was lured to Florida by a photograph of a dumb-looking youth who made two hundred and fifty thousand dollars in four weeks in Florida real estate. But the greatest migration came from the nearby Southern states. "Cities below Mason & Dixon's Line are being depopulated by the rush to Florida," said *Variety*. Both *Variety* and *Billboard* reported a terrific slump in the motion-picture business all over the South because so many former patrons were headed for Florida. Georgia suffered the greatest loss of population. In a speech in Miami, the Governor of Georgia said, "You're going to have a great state here in Florida if the population of Georgia holds out." The policemen, firemen, and other city employees of Miami resigned to become realtors, and the city recruited new employees among the immigrants from the Tobacco Road sections of Georgia. No men ever loved their occupation better than the Georgia crackers loved being Miami policemen. They rattled their handcuffs meaningfully at passersby. Their greatest toys were their revolvers, which were constantly leaping from their holsters at the smallest provocation. One Georgia cracker in brass buttons opened fire on a pedestrian for attempting to cross a street on a red light and winged an old Miami resident who was sauntering along on the sidewalk a hundred feet away.

Addison Mizner had every reason to keep out of the boom. After spending most of the early part of his life dodging sheriffs and collection agencies, he had no urge to risk his sudden Palm Beach wealth on anything speculative. "Don't you worry about me, Phil," he told Philip Boyer, an old friend who had known him during his penniless days. "I have a million dollars put away in government bonds, and you can rest assured that I'll never touch a penny of the principal." Solvency had been forced on Addison. For the first time in his life, money poured in faster than he could spend it. Even with his large staff of assistants, he found it difficult to handle all the business that was offered him. One day, a wealthy Palm Beach woman caught him lying on a beach. "This is a nice way to treat me," she said. "You claim you have no time to do a house for me, but you have plenty of time to loaf in the sun." "Dearie," said Addison, "here it is." Taking a stick of driftwood, he started to draw in the smooth, wet sand. He sketched the front, rear, and wings of a Mizner Spanish house, and the client gave her approval on the spot. A Mizner draftsman copied the sketches, and the house was built largely from the designs in the sand. Money rolled into Addison's pockets from three sources—first, architectural fees; second, the sale of roof tiles, glazed decorative tiles, wrought iron, carved wood, stained glass, and other products of the Mizner workshops in Florida; third, his antique-buying tours in Spain. Addison loved architecture, but he was a junkman at heart. According to him, he, with nimble assistance from Wilson, had started robbing cathedrals in Guatemala when they were boys. He owned a remarkable private museum of crucifixes, his love for hallowed relics having been stimulated by his thefts when he was a youngster. On his trips to Spain, Addison took pride in the hard bargaining by which he obtained church relics and other antiques for a small fraction of their value. One of his secretaries said that she had known the great man to buy a worn-out Oriental rug in Spain for two dollars and sell it for two thousand dollars in Palm Beach. One of Addison's victims was Sam Harris, the Broadway producer. Sam, a great friend of Addison and Wilson, took a fancy to an old refectory table that the architect had acquired in Spain for seventy dollars after furious haggling. He had expected to sell it to a Palm Beach sucker for between fifteen hundred dollars and two thousand. The articles in Addison's antique display never had a price tag; the first duty of a Mizner salesman was to find out how ignorant and how rich the customer was and to measure the price accordingly. Discovering that Harris was a complete ignoramus about the value of old Spanish pieces and that he was in a spending mood, a salesman extracted four thousand dollars from him.

Writing about Addison, Karl Kitchen said that home building and home furnishing were being done on the "sight-unseen" principle in Palm Beach. In January, he said, a client would give the architect a huge check, and then have nothing further to do until the following January, when he would take possession of his place. Addison did some of his best work on that basis. He worked on his architectural plans during the first few months of the year, dashed off to Spain for a freebooting expedition during the late spring and summer, then came back to Palm Beach to supervise the work on his buildings in the fall. On one trip to Spain, Addison had letters of credit for nearly a million dollars from clients who were buying Mizner-built and Mizner-furnished houses. He knew Spanish art and Spanish history. Alex Waugh described one or two of the architect's exhibitions of Spanish lore. Mizner and Waugh were being shown over the Church of San Juan de los Reyes, in Toledo, by the local historian. Addison caught the historian in one inaccuracy after another and then, according to Waugh, "pinned the man into a choir stall and really told him the history of his church, his town, and his country." On another trip, Addison, Mrs. Joshua Cosden, and Peggy Thayer, later Mrs. Harold Talbott, were guests of the Duke of Alba, the leading connoisseur and collector in Spain. The Duke and Addison got into a violent argument. The nobleman had been explaining an ancient battle-painting in the castle, and Addison flatly contradicted him. The Duke sent for the history books, then made a low bow and apologized for setting up his meagre knowledge of the chronicles of his country against the attainments of a real scholar like Addison. The Duke and other grandees furnished the architect with letters of introduction to landowners and churchmen. Spain was poor, the dollar was all-powerful, and Addison filled three warehouses in Madrid with stuff to be shipped to Palm Beach—paintings, sculpture, ironwork, carved wood, ceilings, walls, floors, tapestries, rugs, and gorgeous ecclesiastical needlework.

The greatest of all Addison's trophies was the fourteenth-century panelling from a chamber in the University of Salamanca—the very chamber, it was asserted, in which Ferdinand and Isabella commissioned Columbus to discover the New World and in which they issued the decrees for expelling the Jews and Moors from Spain and for setting up the Spanish Inquisition. The panelling consists of low-relief profiles of great churchmen and statesmen. Addison panelled his own dining room on Via Mizner with these Spanish saints and heroes. A new process was developed in one of his workshops for reproducing wood carvings. A plaster cast was made of the carving, and the cast was filled with a damp composition of plaster, wood pulp, and fibre. After the mixture hardened, it was stained an ancient color. Former employees of Addison's say that eleven excellent reproductions of the Salamanca panelling were built into eleven Mizner palaces, giving rise to a confused idea that Ferdinand and Isabella issued their historic decrees from twelve sections of Palm Beach. King Alfonso was said to have aided the architect in acquiring the original panelling and shipping it out of Spain. Addison planned to build himself a Boca Raton palace that was to become a center of Spanish culture in America. He already owned Goyas, Murillos, Zuloagas, and other Spanish masterpieces, and he said that he hoped to accumulate vast treasures of Spanish art with the help of Alfonso. "That little son of a bitch will do anything for me," he added. One of Addison's trophies was a massive wood-and-iron door that he brought from Spain to be the entrance of the Mizner palace-museum in Boca Raton. The ancient portal was equipped with three ancient knockers—one for short men, one for tall men, and one for men on horseback.

The Mizner Renaissance in Palm Beach attracted famous artists, including the Spanish painters José María Sert and Ignacio Zuloaga. Sert's masterpiece in Palm Beach was a series of murals for the ballroom of Playa Riente, the huge show place that Addison built for the Joshua Cosdens. The murals were colossal illustrations in red, silver, and black of the tough experiences of Sinbad the Sailor with rocs, leviathans, elephants, and other real and fabled monsters of the Arabian Nights. One of the most delicate tributes ever paid to a painter was a news item alleging that the Cosden servants had refused to serve refreshments in the ballroom because they were unnerved by the terrifying Sert animals and birds. Playa Riente was one of Addison's greatest triumphs, both socially and architecturally. Critics placed it at the top of his creations. It emphasized the fact that a fine Mizner house in Palm Beach was a royal road to social eminence. The building of Playa Riente was, in fact, the final maneuver of the Cosdens in their campaign for social leadership.

The Cosdens were proof that social climbing is a waste of time and that people with brains and money can simply walk in and take charge of high life in America. Josh Cosden, a former streetcar conductor of Baltimore, was endowed, according to his admirers, with a personality like that of Charles M. Schwab, who could charm the bird from the tree; Mrs. Cosden was a handsome woman and a smart hostess. Cosden made a fortune in Oklahoma oil and became one of the greatest gamblers of the era, at cards, commodities, and stocks. He was reported to have made a million in cotton while sitting in a rocking chair on the porch of the Breakers, in Palm Beach, and to have taken a pot of eight hundred and seventy-five thousand dollars in a poker game with Harry Payne Whitney, J. L. Replogle, and some others who would never miss a sum in only six figures. Cosden had a well-defined gift for becoming head man wherever he was, and when he found himself in society, he didn't fool around at the tail end of the procession but went right after the grand marshal's place at the head. The Cosdens discovered one great social secret—that the English aristocrats, used to dating things from 1066, were not impressed by the venerableness of the old families of America; that they regarded all Americans as delightfully new; and that their interest was in the quality of the entertainment, not in whether their hosts had been in society for one year or a hundred. So the Cosdens set out to corner the market of titled Englishmen and plied them with fun, excitement, victuals, drink, and, according to some authorities, Wall Street tips. They made Knickerbocker and Newport society look foolish in 1924, when they took possession of the Prince of Wales, Lord Louis Mountbatten, and the rest of the Buckingham Palace set and had them as guests on Long Island. The blaze of Cosden publicity was redoubled when Lady Mountbatten was robbed there of several hundred thousand dollars' worth of jewels. Next to the Prince of Wales, the greatest landmark in Cosden social history was their Mizner Palm Beach house, the gayest of the pleasure domes built by Addison. The social panic caused by the sudden rise of the Cosdens did Addison no harm. Owning the biggest Addison Mizner house had become the touchstone of social supremacy, and Mrs. E. T. Stotesbury, long the reigning hostess of Palm Beach, called Addison in and had him build additions to her El Mirasol until it was unmistakably bigger than the Cosdens' Playa Riente.

Among the artists attracted to Palm Beach during the Mizner period were three young brothers who became interesting figures in the decorative side of the boom. They were Achille, Alberto, and Frederico Angeli, members of Italy's leading family of imitators of old masters. The father of the three young painters was the president of the Copiers' Guild of Florence. According to Addison, half the museums in America displayed Angeli reproductions as old masters. The Angelis were honest craftsmen. They sold their work as copies for a few dollars a picture, and it was none of their business if unscrupulous art dealers palmed them off on clients as work "of the school of" or "attributed to" Giotto or some other great name. The Angelis were mass producers. In the busy season, their factory in Florence turned out ten or twelve distinguished, ancient-looking paintings in a day. In their spare time, they rode around buying decrepit barns, to supply ancient wooden backs for their ancient-looking paintings. The star of the Angeli family was Frederico, who could knock off a life-size "Flight Into Egypt" in six hours, but Alberto was no slouch at a "Flight Into Egypt," either. While still in Italy, he was commissioned to do one for Mrs. William Crocker, of San Francisco, and he did it so well that the art authorities of Florence refused at first to clear it for export, as they suspected a plot to smuggle out an old master disguised as a modern copy.

Frederico and Achille were the first of the Angelis to arrive in America. Stopping over in New York on the way to Palm Beach, they were told that the best way to see the city was to ride on top of the Fifth Avenue buses. They found themselves peering into the second-story shopwindows, which at that time formed practically one long art gallery on the Avenue. The young Florentines had been on their first bus only a few minutes when Achille exclaimed "Frederico!" and pointed at one of the windows. Then Frederico exclaimed "Achille!" Again and again, they uttered wild cries. At least twenty times, according to Achille, they discovered rapid-fire masterpieces of theirs in positions of honor among the second-story merchandise. They were best represented by their small Italian primitives and their big eighteenth-century Roman landscapes, the latter being, for some unaccountable reason, particularly popular among the second-string art patrons of the twenties. Arriving in Palm Beach, the Angeli brothers went to work at the Cosden house, where they reproduced the fourteenth-century frescoes of the dining room of the Davanzati Palace in Florence. Frederico was the discoverer of the famous Davanzati murals. After scraping off twelve coats of whitewash, he had detected traces of painted plaster dating back to the time of Boccaccio, and he made a more or less imaginative restoration that attracted wide attention. The imitation Davanzati room was considered one of the triumphs of Playa Riente, and the Angeli brothers were a sensation in Palm Beach.

Achille became rather noted during his first season there because he unwittingly got involved in one of Addison's social feuds. Addison's feuds were among the delights of his existence. He had always loved the slander, libel, and character assassination that went on in the highest circles, but it was not until the twenties that he could afford to take a leading part in them. Biting and gouging affrays with his Palm Beach clients became his hobby. He built one of his finest houses for Major Barclay H. Warburton, son-in-law of John Wanamaker, and then, in a fit of temper, groomed Johnny Brown, his monkey, to run against the Major for the post of Mayor. The Palm Beach code of etiquette was like that of a Western mining camp, where decorum required feudists to check their shooting irons before going to a party, and Addison was always suavity itself when he met his bitterest enemies socially. He had once instructed his lawyer to sue a woman client for a fee of eleven thousand dollars, and a few days later telephoned to say, "Make that eleven thousand dollars and seventy-five cents. I won seventy-five cents at backgammon from that bitch last night, and she didn't pay that, either."

E. Clarence Jones, a wealthy old bachelor known as King Jones of Baden-Baden, was one of Addison's clients and mortal enemies. Old Baden-Baden hated all the Mizners, because in 1906, while he was laying siege to the rich Fifth Avenue widow Mrs. C. T. Yerkes, Wilson called in a parson and swiftly tied up the matrimonial deal for himself. But an emergency compelled the old monarch to build a Palm Beach house with great speed, and he had to get Addison's help. The Eighteenth Amendment was the emergency. As King Jones grew older, he lived for only one thing—an enormous drinking party that he gave annually at the Coconut Grove, in Palm Beach. Every year, he spent six months looking forward to this party and six months looking back on it. He felt that prohibition would abolish him if it abolished his annual spree. Somebody told him the way to beat prohibition was to build a cellar and stock it up with enough stuff to last the rest of his lifetime, so King Jones commissioned Addison to build a huge cellar with a superstructure just large enough to house the one bed that was necessary to make it a legal residence. But you can't have a cellar in Palm Beach. The ocean seeps in as fast as you excavate. Old Baden-Baden's project became an architectural problem of the most difficult type. Addison had to build an aboveground cellar, and for the sake of his own reputation he had to put a decent-looking top on it, so the house—now the Patio Restaurant—cost three times the estimate. King Jones cried robbery and screamed that Addison had built two other houses out of the surplus lumber. Addison sat up nights devising droll stories of how the Widow Yerkes had spurned Jones in favor of Wilson and how Jones had accumulated his wealth by plundering his benefactors. For a while, the two men spent their spare time walking the streets looking for fresh audiences for their scandal. Dr. Preston Pope Satterwhite, who had an Addison Mizner house, was resolved to carry out a medieval notion of having a bas-relief of the architect built into it. C. Percival Dietsch, the sculptor, had trouble executing the job because Addison insisted on being pictured thumbing his nose at King Jones, whose cellar home was across the way.

Addison never became directly embroiled with the Cosdens, but he exploded with indignation at Captain Alastair Mackintosh, the grand vizier to the Cosdens. Mackintosh, a royal equerry in England, had transferred his allegiance from the Court of St. James's to the Court of Josh Cosden. He incurred Addison's undying enmity by making a suggestion about bathrooms. The knowing courtier put his finger on the architect's weakness. Addison was steeped in medieval Spanish architecture, but his medieval scholarship furnished no clues on the subject of bathrooms. With no precedents to guide him, Addison was lost. His genius deserted him at the bathroom door, and it was his practice to give carte blanche to the plumber. Captain Mackintosh started to propagandize for more exalted bathroom fixtures for the Cosdens. Addison was forced to yield, but he never forgave him. "You!" he roared. "You who have stood in line for hours in the corridors of Buckingham Palace waiting for your weekly chance at the tub—you dare to come over to this country and tell us about bathrooms?" Wilson felt called upon to amplify. "An Englishman never bathes," he said. "He is born wearing a sack suit, which they have to pry off him after death with a cold chisel."

The stateliest of Addison's vendettas was with his great patrons, the Stotesburys. It was in this feud that he used Achille Angeli as an instrument of revenge. Fee trouble was the origin of the quarrel. Addison wanted the architect's usual ten per cent. E. T. Stotesbury loathed all architects. His wife's passion for building had, in spite of his wealth, been bleeding him white. He insisted that five per cent was enough and that Addison could take the rest in boasting that he had worked for the Stotesburys. This was not unreasonable, for the Stotesbury cachet was invaluable, but Addison was furious and talked of suing. He changed his tune when Stotesbury, a veteran financier, picked up several promissory notes on which Addison had raised money to start his workshops. Addison would have been thrown into bankruptcy if immediate payment was demanded. He agreed to the five-per-cent fee, and the notes were extended. Addison was bitter, but nevertheless remained the court architect and the court favorite of the Stotesburys.

Mrs. Stotesbury was annoyed one day to discover her husband and the architect absorbed in a game of pinochle during one of her big recitals. "You sneak away when Rachmaninoff is playing!" she exclaimed to Addison. "I thought it was the piano tuner," apologized Addison. The architect had to wait a long time to square accounts with the Stotesburys, but he finally succeeded in making Mrs. Stotesbury the object of a season's tittering. The young Italian artist came into the plot when she decided to build a loggia with frescoed walls as part of her counterattack on the Cosdens. She sent a note to Achille asking him to call on her. Achille, still so new to the Western Hemisphere that the name of Stotesbury meant nothing to him, took the note to Addison. Addison said that it would be a twenty-thousand-dollar job. As he was talking, Wilson dropped in. He got Addison aside, and they held an earnest conversation. Returning to Achille, Addison told him that rich, famous Americans liked to hear their names pronounced in a loud, ringing tone and that it was necessary to pronounce the name of any really great man or woman at least once in every sentence. Achille, with his feeble grasp of English, practiced saying "Stotesbury." "No, no, no," said Addison. "It's *Strawberry! Strawberry!*" Achille found this a tongue twister. Wilson finally led him into Addison's library and drilled him for half an hour until he could rattle off "Strawberry" like a native. Achille kept the appointment to see Mrs. Stotesbury, and came back crestfallen. "Did you get the job?" asked Addison. "No," said Achille. He said that the great lady had received him with cordiality, but had gradually grown colder and finally called the major-domo to see him out. He added that she kept exclaiming, "Stotesbury! The name is Stotesbury!" Achille took credit for self-control at one moment during his interview with Mrs. Stotesbury. Showing him her art collection, she had pointed out a small Madonna, saying, "This is a Madonna of the Giotto school." Achille said he was just about to shriek, "Oh, Mrs. Strawberry, I painted that myself!" but he checked himself just in time. Addison gave a dinner in honor of Achille and invited the entire anti-Stotesbury faction of Palm Beach. He made Achille tell the story of the visit over and over again. The young artist had enough ham in him to be pleased at making everybody laugh, even though he didn't know what people were laughing at. When he finally began to understand, he was not too impressed with a joke that had cost him a twenty-thousand-dollar job. Addison squared things, however, by getting him a twenty-thousand-dollar order to do the frescoes in the dining room of the Everglades Club.

Chapter Thirteen

VISION

ADDISON AND WILSON MIZNER built the broadest highway in the world during the Florida boom of the early twenties. This was El Camino Real, or the King's Highway, which led to the Mizner principality of Boca Raton, the most snobbish of all the Florida real-estate subdivisions. El Camino Real was two hundred and nineteen feet wide and had twenty traffic lanes, or enough to deliver several hundred thousand people a day to the most exclusive spot on earth. Harry Reichenbach, the highest-paid publicity man on earth, exhausted the national bank of superlatives in describing the widest road on the planet. He found that the Mizner highway took first place in seven or eight respects among the world's arteries of traffic. It was, for example, the most extravagantly landscaped. The parks and gardens and promenades of El Camino Real were patterned after those of Avenida Beira Mar, which stretches around Botafogo Bay, in Rio de Janeiro, but the Mizner boulevard was broader and better. One of the novelties of El Camino Real was indirect illumination. Drawing on his experience as a Broadway playwright, Wilson Mizner lit the road from the wings, using concealed lights in the curbs in place of lampposts. El Camino Real was waterscaped as well as landscaped. Down the middle ran the Grand Canal of Venice, with Rialtos, ornamental landings, and electrically driven gondolas. These romantic vehicles were actually made in Venice. The great Florida boom had touched off many minor booms, one of them being a burst of activity in gondola-making circles on the Adriatic. At a meeting of the Boca Raton directors, Wilson Mizner, a fanatical perfectionist, fought for an appropriation to import Venetian gondoliers, in costume, to sing and play on guitars. An economy-minded director objected that a genuine gondolier was superfluous in a gondola that had batteries and a propeller. He argued also that the gondolier might cause accidents by poling it in one direction while the man at the wheel tried to steer in another. "We'll have

him use a fake oar," said Wilson. "Then the son of a bitch can't do any harm."

El Camino Real had certain defects. Addison had set his heart on having beautiful blue water in the Grand Canal, but it persisted in being muddy. The architect was furious. No man was ever so exasperated with a body of water since Xerxes scourged the Hellespont. Addison kept scores of workmen busy cleaning out mud and silt, but more kept seeping in. The harder they tried to make the canal blue, the muddier it got. The trouble was that, the canal being at sea level, the tides kept bringing soil in. Addison was fighting the Atlantic Ocean, and he was as badly overmatched as the Mrs. Partington who fought a tidal wave with a mop. Another trouble was that automobiles kept

Reginald Marsh

diving into the canal. But the chief defect of the commodious thoroughfare was its length. While it was the widest road in the world, it was also the shortest. The great boulevard ran from the Dixie Highway to Lake Boca Raton, a distance of slightly less than half a mile. Also, whereas El Camino Real was twenty lanes wide on the east side of the Dixie Highway, it was hardly two lanes wide on the west. All the world-beating effects disappeared on the west side, El Camino Real becoming a mere trail in the sand. Two cars could barely pass without becoming entangled in the branches of the scrub pines on either side. In boom maps and blueprints, El Camino Real rolled its twenty traffic lanes past a series of colossal nonexistent cities. In real life, it died away in brambles and swamps.

El Camino Real was not of much use as an artery of traffic, but it had a vast power of suggestion. The two million lot-buyers in Florida were all seeking clues to the subdivision that had the most sensational future. El Camino Real was a startling piece of evidence. Just as a scientist can reconstruct dinosaurs from one giant fragment of bone, so the Florida sucker was able to forecast the tremendous future of Boca Raton from the giant fragment of road. London had no twenty-lane highway; Paris, Rome, New York, and Chicago had no twenty-lane highways. As investors studied the implications of El Camino Real, the corner lots in Boca Raton jumped in value from a few hundred dollars to a hundred thousand dollars. When enthusiasm was running wild, Wilson Mizner offered fifty thousand dollars for a choice Boca Raton lot owned by Lytle Hull, the well-known society man. Hull was insulted. He wouldn't talk to Wilson for two weeks. He hung on to the lot until after the Florida bubble had exploded, and then found that it was worth about two hundred dollars by the new scale of prices.

Boom-time Florida had many El Camino Reals of one kind or another—expensive improvements intended as appetizers for the sucker imagination. Other subdivisions had ornamental boulevards—not quite as wide as the Mizner highway but almost as short. Steel skeletons of hotels and office buildings shot up in uninhabited regions. Most of the big and middle-size promoters believed themselves to be Romuluses and Remuses about to found another world capital. They thought all they needed to start a stampede toward their new Eternal City was a building or some other showy improvement to proclaim that the new seat of empire was off to a flying start. Promoters were willing to throw large sums into one imposing structure, in the hope of setting off an orgy of construction. That first structure was the queen bee of the building industry; it was supposed to have the power to lure swarms of buildings to settle on all sides of it, until the subdivision had a metropolitan skyline. The real-estate sections of the local newspapers showed hundreds of subdivisions with a background of the jagged outline of New York as seen from the Bay. Anybody with a haircut and a lead pencil could turn out a metropolis with a Manhattan silhouette; making sketches of the horizon of downtown New York for advertisements was one of the busiest callings in Florida.

After the crash, Florida had something new to offer in the field of archeology. The state was dotted with unborn ghost cities, the picturesque remains of places that had never had an inhabitant. The crash came so suddenly that New Yorks, Chicagos, Biarritzes, and Monte Carlos were abandoned before a single building had been completed. Sometimes the hardhearted bankers stopped construction while the concrete was still being poured. Florida became the richest country in the world in fresh ruins. One pompous relic of the boom, a source of astonishment to people on passing ships, was a seven-story hotel on Singer's Island, just north of Palm Beach. This majestic pile was built by Paris Singer, who planned to make it the aristocratic headquarters of the world. Designed by Addison Mizner, decorated by the Duchess of Richelieu, this structure was to be the forerunner of a family of gorgeous palaces that, according to the boom-time theory of the propagation of buildings, would multiply like guinea pigs until Singer's Island made Palm Beach look like a slum. Suites in this blue-blooded caravansary were reserved for the gilded popinjays of two worlds, but the bankers called off the contractors when the place was nine-tenths finished, and the apartments of dukes and princes were taken over by thou-

sands of sea gulls and pelicans. The Singer establishment was
the most expensive roost for wild fowl in the world. The most
expensive roost for tame fowl was a hotel that dominated a wide
stretch of landscape near the Miami airport and became a familiar sight to thousands of air travellers. This conspicuous landmark was built as a luxury hotel for human beings, but the crash
turned it into a luxury chicken coop for a hundred and sixty
thousand domestic fowl. The hotel was supposed to start the
magic transformation of a cow pasture into a great city. The promoters had bought a dairy farm, chased the Jerseys off the broad
meadows, and divided the area into business districts, Gold
Coast residential districts, and civic centers. The fine six-story
hotel was erected on the boom theory that once any area in
Florida was inoculated with steel and masonry, it would break
out in a rash of noble edifices. The bubble exploded before the
windows and interior furnishings had been installed. Unfit for
human habitation, the hotel was turned into the most modern
and probably the most populous of hen hotels. One of its features was a gravity system that caused an egg, as soon as it was
laid, to roll down felt-lined runways to a central collecting point.
In addition to an enormous output of eggs and broilers, this
Waldorf of henneries sent thousands of day-old chicks to all
parts of the East. The basement was used for growing mush-
rooms. During the war, the Army took the place over, and it is
now a private aviation school.

Many of the expensive relics of the boom were not really
sucker traps. Some of the million-dollar mistakes were monu-
ments of public spirit. All the big-calibre promoters became victims of a furious urge to build proud cities. They ceased to be
businessmen and turned into creative artists, using municipalities
as an artistic medium. They had the instinct of Frémont, whose
campfires became the sites of towns and cities. Rolling up fortunes for themselves was secondary to the passion for civic accomplishment. Probably the most impressive of the semi-ruins
was the University of Miami, sponsored by the promoters of
Coral Gables. The English writer T. H. Weigall, who was involved in the university project, has left an account of some con-

ferences with the head men of Coral Gables. They demanded
one of the world's greatest seats of learning for Coral Gables, not
as a selling point for real estate but as a glorious institution
worthy of the glorious subdivision. They confidently expected
that their university would take its place beside Athens and Alex-
andria in the history of the human mind. Making use of the
balmy climate, they planned to steal a little academic thunder
from Plato, Socrates, and Aristotle by holding many of their
classes in the open air. Publicity releases announced some of the
departments, particularly that of the drama, in which the new
university was to lead the world. More than fifteen million dollars was subscribed for the ambitious school, but the crash came
before much of it was paid in. Collectors couldn't collect a cent
from one man who had subscribed a million dollars; they found
him waiting on table in a Miami restaurant. Many other big
contributions also vanished. The main building was not completed for twenty years, but the stricken university held classes
in a stricken hotel, and gradually developed into a high-grade
institution.

During the boom, the big Florida promotions were constantly
playing follow-the-leader. Coral Gables was in some ways the ring-
leader of the developments, and when it got itself a university,
other big subdivisions had to have their universities, too. Fulford-by-the-Sea announced something along the lines of the University of Chicago. Hollywood-by-the-Sea was meditating something like the Sorbonne. The Mizners planned a great Spanish
cultural center for Boca Raton. The city of Upton announced
Upton University, but the promoters, on being questioned about
their publicity by the Better Business Bureau, explained that
Upton University was a typographical error. Some of the great
universities of the East were reported about to move to Florida,
and for a while it was almost impossible to buy a lot without
finding yourself in a college town. Seth Clarkson, a humorist on
Miami Life, was inspired to write about a premonition he had of
the final struggle for supremacy between the ghost elevens of
two ghost universities at the climax of the football season in the
Ghost University League. The game took place under difficul-

ties, for old grads crowded on the field to buy and sell lots, while cheerleaders led the audience in college yells and real-estate slogans. The Joe College trimmings of the subdivisions disappeared the moment real-estate prices began to totter. Only the University of Miami survived.

The bewildering final stage of the boom was dominated by what was known in Florida as "vision"—a gift that enabled an observer to mistake spots before the eyes for magnificent cities. "Vision" was a word that stirred the imagination and caused abundant streams of sucker money to gush forth. The greatest disgrace that could befall a man in Florida was to be suspected of not being a man of vision. You were in danger of having your vision doubted if you failed to see a coming Babylon or Baghdad in any body of land or water that was being cut up into building lots. You qualified as a man of vision the moment you saw the Manhattan skyline rising out of an alligator swamp. The realtor's standard question for testing a man's vision was "Can you imagine a city *not* being here?" The state was peppered with Chicagos. Forty-second-and-Broadways were so numerous that in 1927 the Florida Chamber of Commerce, decribing the state's remarkable comeback after the Florida crash, boasted that cabbage patches and truck gardens were flourishing where the Forty-second-and-Broadways used to be. The most spectacular of the men of vision was Barron Collier, a New York advertising man, who bought more than a million acres in Florida and announced plans to replace the lights of fireflies with the lights of happy homes. "Barron Collier has more vision than any man since Cecil Rhodes," said the Miami *News*. "Vision" eventually became a synonym for lunacy, fraud, and robbery, but the real pioneers of the boom actually had vision up to a point, and their first crop of visions came true. Skylines popped up like jack-in-the-boxes in Miami and Miami Beach. Miami inevitably got the nickname of the Magic City when lovely islands climbed up out of the mud and hotels, parks, office buildings, and fine residential districts emerged from dense jungles. An exclusive shopping district arose along a path where, a few years earlier, a panther had chased Miss Hattie Carpenter, a Miami schoolteacher, who escaped by furious pedalling on her bicycle. "Miami," said William Jennings Bryan, "is the only city in the world where you can tell a lie at breakfast that will come true by evening." Tens of thousands of people had seen visions harden into reality. Millions of others had seen the "before" and "after" photographs of the miracles—yesterday's bogs, today's millionaire suburbs. The only fallacy was the popular belief that because some visions had come true, all delusions and hallucinations must also come true.

"Boom" was a word the boomers hated. They argued that Florida was having not a boom but a development. "It's just a catching up," was the standard explanation. In one of his double-page advertisements, Harry Reichenbach clarified the situation by a parable. On a certain island in the Indian Ocean, the benighted heathens thought that pearls were worthless beads, but one day they woke up to find themselves filthy capitalists. "This was not a boom," said Harry. "It was a recognition of value." The wonders of Florida had, in fact, been overlooked. Americans had been backward about appreciating their own subtropics for a number of reasons. Spanish rule had continued in Florida until 1819. Then came the Seminole Wars, the Civil War, and Reconstruction. Although the state began to pick up late in the nineteenth century, most Americans thought of it as a remote playground for the very rich. It took the automobile and improved roads to bring about the real rediscovery of Florida. In 1920, the Tin-Can Tourists of the World, forerunners of America's trailer-home population, established themselves in Florida. Elderly people found out about the "actinic rays" of the Florida sun, which were believed to have an extraordinary ability to unharden the arteries. Folks of moderate means began to master the secret of the winter vacation just when the bull market was providing them with the extra money to pay for it. Under the impact of the rush to the "last frontier," Miami real estate became lively in 1922, highly animated in 1923. Vacationers returned North with tales of gigantic profits, and in 1924 the boom was unmistakable. Its frienzied final stage was blamed, by Frederick Lewis Allen in "Only Yesterday" and by Kenneth

Ballinger, a boom historian, in "Miami Millions," on the confidence inspired by the overwhelming Republican victory in the national election of 1924.

The original men of vision of Miami Beach had the vision of becoming millionaires by raising coconuts. That was back in the eighties, when a mild coconut mania hit many Southern beaches. The coconut planters of Miami Beach hired New Jersey lifeguards to come to Florida at the end of the summer-resort season in the North. Loading small boats from a mother ship, the lifeguards rowed ashore and sowed coconuts in the sand and jungle back of the beaches. Tens of thousands sprouted, but the young plants were nearly all eaten up by rabbits, raccoons, water rats, and other pests. When the coconut experiment began to get shaky, early in the century, John S. Collins, who had been a horticulturist in Moorestown, New Jersey, switched to avocados. His first young plants were cut to pieces by sand blown from the beaches. He wrapped his later plants in burlap, grew rows of corn as protection from the flying sand, and planted thousands of Australian pines as a windbreak. Then, around 1910, Collins had a new vision, this one to the effect that Florida's best crop would be winter vacationers. He and some associates began to build small hotels and boarding houses near Miami Beach. The only connection between Miami Beach and Miami was by boat. A bridge was needed to bring in the vacationers swarming to Miami by buggy and automobile, and Collins raised money to build one across Biscayne Bay. In 1913, the money gave out, before the bridge was finished. The elderly Collins' game struggle on behalf of Miami Beach attracted the attention of Carl G. Fisher, who was vacationing in Florida. Fisher furnished the money to complete the bridge, and soon succeeded Collins as the chief promoter of Miami Beach. Starting out as a newsboy, Fisher had become a professional bicycle rider, then sold acetylene lamps for bicycles and automobiles, and eventually headed the Prest-O-Lite Company. He had disposed of his business interests for six million dollars just before coming to Florida. After finishing the bridge, he began building hotels, roads, parks, residences, and golf courses in Miami Beach. He reclaimed thousands of acres of swamp and then began pumping sand into frames to build islands in Biscayne Bay. After a shaky start, Fisher's enterprises were enormously successful.

George Merrick, of Coral Gables, J. W. Young, of Hollywood-by-the-Sea, and D. P. Davis, of Davis Islands, in Tampa Bay, were among the other boom chieftains—the Mohammeds who led millions of the faithful in the holy war to get rich without work. Their aims and methods were imitated by nearly all the other promoters. Even the Mizners, who affected to scorn their competitors, lifted ideas from Merrick and Young. The most familiar vision of the boom—the idea of taking an undeveloped expanse and spreading a ready-made city over it—was originated by George Merrick. He was the son of the Reverend Solomon Merrick, who left his pulpit in Gaines, New York, and started a citrus grove near Miami in the nineties, calling his place Coral Gables. George Merrick's first ambition was to be a man of letters, but after winning a prize in a short-story contest and writing a volume of poems, he gave up literature and devoted himself to oranges and grapefruit at Coral Gables. Around 1913, when he was in his early twenties, Merrick had the vision of replacing his citrus plantation with a city. His Coral Gables was not a get-rich-quick scheme but a real adventure in city planning and city building, and much of the boom revolved around this gigantic project. It was the boom's answer to skeptics. Merrick's accomplishments shut the mouths of those who denied that wonder cities could be produced by magic.

Most of the Florida promoters learned lessons in aggressiveness from J. W. Young, who started the practice of invading the North with boisterous expeditions of merrymakers and salesmen. He had been a newsboy in San Francisco, and was once president of the Newsboys' Union there. He must have learned about shanghaiing sailors in San Francisco, for he used a similar technique on investors, plying them with gaudy entertainment and then whisking them off to Florida in his fleets of buses. Young's advance agents held grand balls and banquets in Northern cities, hypnotized the revellers with tales of everlasting youth and unheard-of profits, and then herded them South by the thousand. Others followed Young's example, and during the peak of the boom hundreds of buses and dozens of special trains were carrying suckers and their bank rolls to new heavens on new Rivieras. Young had a vision of a city like Coral Gables, and he constructed it on an unlikely area twenty miles north of Miami. Some of the women captured by Young's raiders and taken to Florida were terrified by their first glimpse of the site of Hollywood-by-the-Sea. The Florida landscape can be unnerving. Twisted by hurricanes, the trees are gnarled and contorted. The undergrowth carries thorns that are the size of small daggers and are accused of attacking men without warning. The ground is covered with savage saw and sword grass. The tendrils of the vines and the branches of the trees point accusing fingers, and the general effect is ferocious. As a bus was passing through one tropical scene of horrors, a woman started to shriek. In a few seconds, all the prospects were screaming hysterically, and they had to be treated for shock before they could sign up for lots in the baleful wilderness. Yet in spite of a little trouble at the start, Young's city was a great success.

Ex-newsboys seem to have had more than their share of boom-time vision. Fisher and Young had sold papers, and so had D. P. Davis, one of the great subdivision showmen and the most spectacular of the island builders. Davis sold extras during the Spanish-American war in Tampa, rose to become the Frankfurter King of Jacksonville, and returned to Tampa, where he created three artificial islands that were rated among the finest accomplishments of the boom. Davis was in the front ranks of the subdividers. The crash caught him in the midst of an island-making project off St. Augustine. Like all the big figures of the boom, he was wiped out by the crackup. He disappeared from an ocean liner, and was generally thought to have taken his life, but Raymond Schindler, the detective, insisted that he had gone through a porthole merely as an oratorical gesture. Davis used strange rhetoric after he had had a few drinks. Once, in New York, when an opponent was unimpressed by his logic, he crawled out of a seventeenth-story window in the Commodore and clung by his fingertips until his antagonist conceded the point. According to Schindler, Davis, who had been reasoning with a lady in his stateroom, crawled through the porthole to clinch an argument and was drowned when his fingers slipped. Newspapers hinted at foul play. Some people maintain, however, that Davis has since been seen in Paris, Bangkok, and South Africa.

In the footsteps of the newsboys and other pioneers came a multitude of promoters and boosters, ranging from some of the leading men of America to scallawags, mail-fraud artists, and all varieties of Get-Rich-Quick Wallingfords. At one end of the scale was General T. Coleman du Pont, the chief bottleholder for the Mizners; at the other was the most notorious swindler in the country, Charles Ponzi, who ran a real-estate clip joint called the Charpon Land Syndicate. Most of the promoters had an honest enthusiasm for Florida, but as the boom reached full speed, they tended to lose their equilibrium. They developed a language of their own; "near" meant "far," "high" meant "low," "great" meant "small." Cosmic City had no inhabitants. Textile City didn't even have a spool of thread. Reflected-glory cities came into existence. Their attraction was that they were "near" some well-known place. Ponzi's city, sixty-five miles from Jacksonville, was advertised as being near Jacksonville. The promoters of Manhattan Estates invented a city in order to make their subdivision a suburb of it. "Near the prosperous and fast-growing city of Nettie," said the advertisements, although there never was a city in Florida named Nettie. The promoters of Manhattan Estates justified themselves on the ground that they had been told that there was an abandoned turpentine camp named Nettie in the vicinity and that they were entitled to a little real-estate license.

Florida was sensitive about the fact that it was the flattest state in the country except Delaware, and it attempted to achieve altitude by playing games with words. Okeechobee Highlands was twelve inches taller than the country around it, according to Kenneth Ballinger. Any twenty-four-inch altitude constituted "heights," according to Ralph Henry Barbour, another Florida chronicler. Baldwin Heights was found by the National Better Business Bureau to be under water. Any unevenness of surface was likely to become a cliff or a bluff in boom literature. Florida has Mount Pleasant, Mount Dora, Mountain Lake, Iron Mountain, and other titles of altitude, but the highest peak in the state is less than four hundred feet above sea level. The magazine *Suniland* made the resounding claim that Iron Mountain (altitude, 325 feet) was "the pinnacle between New Jersey and Mexico." One series of little molehills was described as the Berkshires of Florida even before the realtors took over the language. The real Berkshires are ten times as high as their Florida namesakes, but a nine-hundred-per-cent exaggeration was modest in 1925. In the general reshuffling of the Florida vocabulary during the boom, "the Berkshires of Florida" became, said Professor Homer B. Vanderblue, the economist, "the Alps of Florida," and would probably have been promoted to the Himalayas if the boom had continued into 1926. "By-the-Sea" was a curious piece of subdivision slang that meant "far back in the hinterland." Fulford-by-the-Sea was a huge promotion several miles inland from Miami. One of the standard jokes of 1925 was "Did you hear the news? They've hired a hundred salesmen to push Fulford by the sea." J. W. Young's original city site was a considerable distance from the sea, so he called it Hollywood-by-the-Sea. When, by addition and expansion, he reached the Atlantic on a broad front, he was embarrassed by "by-the-sea," which implied to the knowing that his city was a backwoods community, so he changed its name to just plain Hollywood.

Almost anything—a nearby city, a new hotel, a civic center, a mountain, a bay, a lake, or an ocean—became a talking point for a development. A resourceful promoter could make almost anything do for a landmark. Charles Ort, a promoter known as the King of the Keys, was sold a tract on Key Largo by a realtor who didn't mention that it had been a quarry and was full of deep holes. Ort looked ruefully at the hollows and chasms, but then snapped his fingers and danced wildly about, shouting, "Sunken Gardens! Sunken Gardens!" He doubled the price of the lots with the deepest abysses. The promoters of Wyldewood

Park, near Fort Lauderdale, had difficulty finding a talking
point to wrap their subdivision around. There were no startling
geographical features, no skyscrapers, coliseums, or campaniles.
But there was an interesting tree—a large banyan, which had
dropped branches into the ground to become new roots, until
the tree was beginning to look like a small forest. A big sign,
"$2,000,000 Tree," was hung on it, and it became the logical
argument for buying homesites in Wyldewood, the claim being
made that a banyan-crazy Yankee had once offered two million
dollars for the tree if it could be moved to his home up North.
The tree is still one of the points of interest in Florida—the most
famous botanical item next to the Senator, a cypress alleged to
be three thousand years old.

Promoters who couldn't find even a tree or a quarry to rave
about took refuge in the word "proposed." A newspaper advertisement or a sign was the only immediate expense required for
a "proposed" improvement. Kenneth Roberts has told of a group
of capitalists who hired a painter to do a sign reading, "A Million-Dollar Hotel Will Be Erected Here," but the capitalists
couldn't raise the eighteen dollars to pay for the sign, so the
painter sold it to another group of capitalists. In order to save
buyers from going to see their purchases, promoters had relief
maps of their subdivisions done in papier-mâché. The investor
merely had to point at a lot and say, "I'll take that one." The
most elaborate of these models was D. P. Davis's forty-foot
miniature of his proposed island off St. Augustine, the bay and
ocean being represented by water a foot deep, in which miniature electric yachts and steamers sailed. Thomas W. McMorrow,
who specialized in fiction with a fact basis, wrote of a fancy
raised map of a subdivision, which was delivered after all the
land had been sold. It was so beautiful that suckers insisted on
buying lots in it even though there was no land to go with it.
Next to maps and signs, the cheapest substitute for splendor was
the triumphal arch. The principle of the tail wagging the dog
was so prevalent in Florida that any stately arch was confidently
expected to attach a stately city to itself. The countryside is still
strewn with heaps of disintegrated stucco, slats, rusty chicken

wire, and other debris of imperial entrance gates, once used as yardsticks for measuring the imperial communities projected by realtors' imagination. The word "proposed" was considered important enough to carry whole cities on its coattails in the last stages of the bubble. Billions and billions of dollars' worth of "proposed" architectural and engineering feats were placed before the investor. "All of these here lots," said Will Rogers, plugging for his own imaginary world capital, "are by our Proposed Ocean." The humorist's Proposed Ocean was outdone by reality.

The ocean was not only proposed, it was built into dozens of subdivisions. "The sea is actually being brought back into the heart of the pine woods," wrote Rex Beach in "The Miracle of Coral Gables." Coral Gables, which is several miles inland, advertised "Forty Miles of Waterfront," but the forty miles bordered on canals cut through to the ocean. The idea of working a synthetic coastline into the subdivisions came from the brain of a resourceful realtor named C. G. Rodes. He was shaking his head mournfully over an unlovely drainage ditch when an idea came to him. "The Grand Canal of Venice!" he exclaimed. He beautified the drainage ditch, added a network of ditches to it, and gave the name of Venice to the subdivision, which is on the Gulf Coast of Florida. The idea of gliding along on canals had a mysterious appeal to railroad men, and the Brotherhood of Locomotive Engineers threw away more than ten million dollars on the Florida Venice. After Rodes made his historic discovery, nearly every slough and open sewer in Florida became a romantic piece of water. Islands were popular with the suckers, and the promoters found that, instead of paying millions to build islands by pumping sand, they could produce cheap ones by digging ditches around low-lying properties. The banks of any ditch that held a few gallons of brine became "waterfront" or "oceanfront" property, and the postal authorities, no matter how fervently they tried to prevent fraudulent advertising from going through the mails, couldn't do anything about it. Some buyers of ocean frontage were astonished to learn that the Atlantic was hardly big enough for a duck to turn around in. Abandoned canals, choked with vegetation and lined by decaying little Rialtos, are still to be found in the old boom country.

Paper cities on paper oceans, paper universities, paper race tracks, coliseums, and casinos marked the overripe phase of the boom. One of the last great sensations was the paper migration of the motion-picture industry from California to Florida. Paper studios sprang up everywhere. "PICTURE PROMOTERS IN FLORIDA STIR UP STATE," said a *Variety* headline, the article adding that "the magnates are plugging Florida as an ideal successor for Hollywood." In an earlier day, Florida had been a greater motion-picture land than Hollywood, and the magnates were always threatening to go back there unless the Hollywood pay-roll behaved itself. "COAST AFRAID OF FLORIDA," said *Variety* of September 2, 1925. There was good reason for Hollywood's agitation. Enough paper studios had started up in Florida to make ten times as many pictures as Hollywood ever turned out. Tens of thousands of lots were offered in the great cinema cities where you could live next door to the stars and probably get your young before the camera at a salary of three thousand dollars a week. One of the first magnates to turn up in Florida was H. M. Horkheimer, who announced Film City, covering a hundred acres near Miami. Horkheimer, husband of Jackie Saunders, a movie belle of the silent days, had made himself famous in Hollywood by putting a sheriff, who had come to seize his studio, into an important part in a Western. The most imposing magnate to go to Florida was Lewis J. Selznick. Selznick, once a diamond merchant, had become a film executive when, a total stranger, he slipped into the Universal offices in New York and issued orders to everybody. Everybody obeyed, and after a short period as a comic-opera magnate Selznick mastered the business and became a real magnate. Selznick arrived in Florida in 1925, accompanied by reports that he was about to start the world's greatest picture company there. He considered locating in Picture City, an eleven-thousand-acre cinema capital started by Felix Isman, a Broadway magnate, a few miles north of Palm Beach. Picture City was calculated to make Hollywood tremble. Although there were no buildings in

Picture City, there were towering signboards announcing, "Studio H-3," "Studio K-19," "Studio J-H-6," and other indications that Paramount and Metro were soon to be left in the lurch. The Chamber of Commerce of Fort Myers, Edison's winter home, announced that the biggest studio would be located there. The birth of a great picture industry was announced in Ocala, with a Ku Klux Klan leader as the top magnate. Winter Haven claimed that it was actually shooting an epic—a romance of the boom, with a realtor for the hero. The promoters of Sun City, near Tampa, did build a studio, said to be the biggest on earth, and claimed that production was going to start with "Rain," under the direction of Sam Wood. In 1925, Van Sweringen was the biggest name on the railroad map, and Sun City placed a Van Sweringen in charge of things. The great Van Sweringens were M. J. and O. P. Sun City had H. C., an obscure brother of the famous railroad men, but Florida suckers were in no mood to quibble about their Van Sweringens, and H. C. was just as good as M. J. or O. P. for subdivision purposes. Of all the film metropolises in Florida, Sun City was the only one that left a respectable monument behind. Its studio became the Sun City schoolhouse. In 1940, Sun City had a population of eighty-five—a remarkable showing for a boom city fifteen years after the blowup. A score of pupils were then attending classes in the enormous old studio. The school's proudest possession was a huge painted panorama of Sun City as it was expected to look when it had superseded Hollywood as the world's entertainment center.

Addison Mizner was not content with building a road as a token of Boca Raton's future immensity. He built the Cloister—since enlarged into the Boca Raton Hotel—an airport, a polo field, two golf courses, a yacht basin, a church for his brother the Reverend Henry Mizner, and several other buildings. As fast as sucker money rolled in, Addison threw it into his citadel. He had the richest and nobbiest backers in Florida, but they all evaporated when the boom exploded. Addison's career was ruined, and his admirers blamed his troubles on Wilson. The architect's greatest mistake, as his friends saw it, was bringing

Wilson to Florida in the first place. Addison's ruling passion
was family affection. He had made almost a lifework of attempting to reform his scapegrace brother. The Boca Raton promotion
was said to be just one of Addison's devices for trying to keep
Wilson out of mischief.

Addison's goal in life was high social position, and Wilson
was always on the verge of making it impossible for him to reach
it. Throughout his career in New York, Addison's social standing was continuously damaged by Wilson's antics. He went to
Palm Beach in 1918, and quickly became a social potentate
there. But in 1921, when Wilson was poverty-stricken and dan-
gerously ill, Addison, yielding to a surge of brotherly devotion,
invited him South, hoping that he would not create too much
havoc. One of Addison's flourishing Palm Beach industries was his
tile workshop, where he turned out handmade roof tiles and ornamental terra cotta. He placed Wilson in charge of the workshop. Most of the employees were colored. Wilson discovered
that many of them were good singers. He took a portable organ
to the factory, collected his workmen around him, and played
while they sang. One or two hours spent melodiously disrupting
the workshop schedule constituted a hard day's work for Wilson.
Addison had invented the Mizner Senior Chair, an eight-hun-
dred-dollar seat for a man of two hundred and fifty or three hundred pounds, and Wilson nearly bankrupted him by making
gifts of these chairs to fat friends in New York. To his middle-
size ones, Wilson sent Mizner Junior Chairs, costing six hundred dollars. Addison was happy, however. He felt that Wilson
was making great progress toward rehabilitating himself and
becoming a useful member of society.

In 1919, Wilson had been convicted of running a gambling
house on Long Island. He received a suspended sentence, but
the reports that drifted to Palm Beach were that he was freshly
out of Clinton Prison. Instead of bothering to set people right,
Wilson shaved his head, looked as hangdog as possible, and
spent much of his time inventing tales of his imaginary life in
Clinton Prison with which to horrify Addison's aristocratic
friends. He was especially enthusiastic about his cellmate, an

Australian actor, who had deserted his wife and newborn child to come to America. She cabled, "SEND MONEY, BABY AND I ARE STARVING." He cabled back, "EAT BABY." The fastidious society dictator, Paris Singer, shuddered at some of Wilson's Clinton stories. "Do you believe that Wilson was ever really in prison?" the Duchess of Richelieu asked him. "I think he must have been; he has such an intimate knowledge of the plumbing," said Singer. Actually, the end of Wilson's long Broadway career had been hastened by a terrific beating, which left him with a multiple fracture of the jaw and other injuries. "What did they hit you with?" a detective asked when Wilson recovered consciousness. "I think it was St. Patrick's Cathedral," he replied. The reason for the beating is still unknown; underworld ethics kept Wilson silent on the matter. Times Square lore tells the story three ways—girl trouble, dope-ring friction, a difference of opinion about a gambling debt. Wilson told the Duchess of Richelieu that his assailants had contracted to murder him but that they were paid only half price, and they felt that they couldn't afford to deliver anything better than mayhem under the circumstances. He said that he got to taking heavy doses of morphine while in the hospital. During his last years in New York, everything went wrong for Wilson. His old sources of income dried up. Unable to make a living by gambling and confidence games, he was forced to declass himself by doing honest work, and he became a scenario writer for the Oliver Film Company, which had a studio on the East Side. He was apparently dying of shame and other infirmities when Addison had him come down to Palm Beach. Addison called specialists from New York to cure Wilson of the dope habit. For a while, Wilson made only lukewarm efforts to give up the needle, but one day an odd conversation caused him to really start fighting against his slavery to the drug. In search of amusement, he had gone to an undertaking establishment in West Palm Beach; he had always asserted that any normal man would rather see a morgue than Tiffany's window. The embalmer apologized for the quality of his work but blamed it on the subject in hand. "He was a hophead," he said. "What difference does that make?" asked

Wilson. "Hopheads won't set up," said the embalmer. "What do you mean, they won't set up?" asked Wilson. "Well, they just won't set up," said the embalmer. Wilson never did get a precise definition of the phrase, but he was appalled by the possibility that someday an embalmer might criticize him for not "setting up," and he went resolutely at the job of getting over his addiction. He told Ashton Stevens that by using scopolamine he cured himself without much suffering; he told others, however, that his agonies were unimaginable and that at times he chewed on rugs in the effort to distract himself. After he had given up drugs, it was for some time his custom to start the day with a highball spiked with laudanum. He nevertheless put on weight and was soon in fair shape.

In Palm Beach, Wilson worked for a time on a book called "The Wilson Mizner Story." For years, people had been urging him to do his autobiography. In 1916, he told Djuna Barnes, the novelist, that he had been offered twenty-five hundred dollars a week to write a motion picture based on his career and act the title role, but he refused to go on after seeing how he looked in a screen test. "I photograph like a bloodhound with the mind of a Pekinese," he said. Ray Long, editor of *Cosmopolitan,* was determined to print Wilson's autobiography, and legend says that he offered him fifty thousand dollars for his confessions. Wilson called in Charles Speer, a Palm Beach journalist, and started to dictate, but soon abandoned the project, claiming that he couldn't tell his story without implicating old confederates. Some years later, Speer telegraphed Wilson, who was then in Hollywood, suggesting that they resume work on his memoirs. "WHERE WOULD I GO THEN? CHINA?" Wilson wired back.

Possibly because of promises made to Addison, Wilson didn't turn to bootlegging or confidence games, both of which were tremendously lucrative vocations in Florida in the twenties. One of his Florida pals, though, was Bill McCoy, the most famous of rumrunners. He kept Wilson supplied with free Scotch, apparently just out of friendship. Wilson decided to look for graft in Addison's architectural office. Once, when Addison went on a trip to Europe, he left his office in charge of Howard Major,

later a well-known architect in Palm Beach. Major called for
sealed bids on a job, but Wilson told him to disregard the figures and award the contract to a contractor pal of his. Major
refused. Wilson, who had fixed judges, district attorneys, prizefights, horse races, and foot races, was outraged that he couldn't
fix a sealed bid in his own brother's office, and he succeeded in
making things so unpleasant that Major resigned. As the boom
began to hit a wild tempo, Wilson picked up some money dab-
bling in lots, and Addison began to take an interest in the real-
estate uproar. Addison and Wilson had been in the Klondike
gold rush together, and they now plunged into the Florida boom
together.

Chapter Fourteen

WHEN FISH BECAME BIRDS

At the start of the Florida boom in the twenties, the state
suffered from certain drawbacks. It was poor in raw
materials. It lacked important industries. It was a semi-
ghost state when its winter playgrounds were boarded up, from
April to November. But by 1925 it was believed to have suddenly shaken off all its major infirmities. Mob scenes in July
proved that it had overcome the summer slump. Printer's ink
testified that boundless stores of raw material had been discovered and that the state was rapidly being industrialized. In
advertisements, interviews, magazine articles, radio talks, and
ordinary conversation, Florida began to teem with mines and
quarries, factories and foundries, smelters and rolling mills,
looms, laboratories, and assembly lines. The weaknesses disappeared. The black clouds all vanished. Prices got their second
wind and soared wildly. It was rash not to buy anything at
any figure; everything in Florida became "a steal." The usual
spring migration from Florida to the North was reversed in
1925. Instead of being depopulated during the hot months, the
state actually gained a couple of million inhabitants. The Dixie
Highway was jammed with the automobiles of newcomers. Some
slept in their cars; others in railroad stations, on beaches, and in

parks. The shortage of rooms was acute. No other department of
the boom quite equalled the hotel-building mania. Permits to
build hotels were issued at a rate of more than a hundred a
month. Yachts, barges, and steamers were turned into lodging
houses. The Mississippi excursion boat Harry G. Drees became
a luxury hotel in Tampa Bay. The North & South Floating Inn
Co., Inc., was organized in Massachusetts to ransack the ship
cemeteries for ancient vessels that could be towed to Florida to
solve the housing shortage. Three citizens of Miami bought a
century-old warship from the Danish Navy and brought it to
Biscayne Bay to serve as an American-plan hostelry. The moni-
tor Amphitrite, pride of the American Navy in 1893, was sold
under the Disarmament Treaty to the Modern Hotel Corporation. Converted into a seagoing night club, it cruised along the
Florida coast until, after being converted into a hotel, it settled
down to become one of the show places of Fort Lauderdale.

Florida had violently broken out of its old April-to-Novem-
ber lethargy. A glance at any street corner proved that. The evidence that it had suddenly become an inferno of industry was
less convincing, but it was good enough, and the miracle of industrialization was not much harder to swallow than other
Florida miracles. Skeptics were discredited. Childlike faith paid
off. Millions rolled into the pockets of those who couldn't grasp
the distinction between big talk and big achievements. For years,
people had dreamed that Florida's vast jungles and wastelands
would someday become productive. Dreams became convictions
in 1925. It was firmly believed that mills were making wonder
cloth out of swamp-grass fibre. Silkworms had been raised in
Florida for fun, and a few yards of silk had been woven as a
hobby, so the clatter of silk mills began to echo through the subdivision propaganda. The hair-raising claim was made that
Florida was the richest region in the world in diatomite—a substance that contains the fossils of more than two million plants
to the cubic inch and makes an excellent substitute for meerschaum in pipes. Rex Beach, who was devoting his literary talents to the praises of Coral Gables, announced that a hundred
thousand acres were to be devoted to peanuts to produce millions

of gallons of peanut oil for use in the arts and industries. Bamboo was being planted to produce lumber for gay little cities in the Polynesian style of architecture. Guano deposits were reported on the Florida Keys. A bright future was seen in gathering conch shells for amplifiers in radio sets. Important forests of gumbo limbo, the sap of which is reputed to be an incomparable aphrodisiac, were discovered on Key Largo. Oil strikes were reported on the mainland. J. W. Young, father of Hollywood-by-the-Sea, published a thick, heavily illustrated slick-paper monthly magazine about Florida's steel mills and automotive factories, and about its rubber, leather, and cement industries. "Acres of Diamonds—in the Everglades" was the title of an article in *Suniland*, the boom magazine, which reported vast deposits of Everglades peat yielding between forty and fifty important byproducts. Of all the typewriter-created industries, rubber was the greatest. It had the magic name of Thomas A. Edison behind it. His experiments, which had the backing of Henry Ford, in Fort Myers, Florida, showed that rubber could be made from the sap of the sunflower, the goldenrod, and hundreds of other plants that grew in subtropical America. Harvey Firestone was cheering both men on, and the printing presses began to groan with hundred-thousand-acre rubber plantations. The newsprint shortage was about to be solved by using Florida saw grass in place of wood pulp. Being close to South and Central America, Florida, with its enormous new manufacturing capacity, was certain to go in for producing gadgets, gimmicks, fizgigs, and whigmaleeries for Latin-American consumption. J. W. Young called in General George W. Goethals, digger of the Panama Canal, to dig a deep-sea port that would get first crack at that lucrative Latin-American trade. Real-estate subdivisions quit being Biarritzes and Deauvilles in order to be Smoky Cities. Joe Tinker, the famous shortstop of the Tinker-to-Evers-to-Chance combination, came out with two great developments—Tinkerville, the aristocrat's playground, and Longwood, the center of heavy industries. Tinker advertised "No Venetian Lagoons for Longwood," explaining that guitars and gondolas wouldn't harmonize with the blast furnaces and the roar of mighty machines. It be-

came bad form to mention Florida's industrialization as a thing
of the future. The present tense was used in the best boom literature. "LAKELAND HAS SEVENTY-FIVE INDUSTRIES," said one headline in *Suniland*. "PENSACOLA HAS NINETY-SEVEN INDUSTRIES,"
said another. The enthusiasm rose as other cities produced similar statistics. Cool heads turned hot, enthusiasts became fanatics,
lunatics became maniacs.

While all this was going on, Addison and Wilson Mizner

were occupied in promoting their own subdivision, Boca Raton.
But even they paused in their work to buy large acreages to provide an industrial background for their imperial city.

The oddest of the new industries was digging for doubloons,
moidores, louis d'ors, pieces of eight, and just plain bars of bul-
lion. Somebody had dreamed of buried treasure, and the state
was swept with an epidemic of "pirate gold." Florida was full of
press agents, all stealing ideas from one another. Any inspired

flash was quick to achieve general circulation, and the business of dredging for the loot of ancient pirates became one of the most highly advertised sources of wealth. The corsair superseded the bathing beauty as the emblem of Florida. Commercial artists specialized in buccaneers with earrings, cutlasses, and bandaged foreheads, all burying chests of treasure in the big subdivisions. The Mizners claimed that their Boca Raton was the ancient headquarters of Captain Teach, or Blackbeard, a formidable old scourge who was credited with having mastered the difficult art of mounting lighted candles in his beard to scare coastal towns at night. Harry Reichenbach and Wilson Mizner buried some doubloons and some fake relics of Blackbeard in Boca Raton Inlet, and they were disinterred amid wild excitement. The Mizners had no monopoly on buried treasure. A big haul of ancient Mexican money was announced at Grassy Key. A Portuguese fisherman broke into print with a report that he had fished up near Miami an iron chest weighing a couple of hundred pounds, but the fishing line had broken and he could never find the old chest again. Captain Kidd was dragged in to boost the new industry. So were Sir Henry Morgan, the Laffite brothers, Black Caesar, Gasparilla, and Sir Francis Drake. The greatest center of pirate legend was Key Largo. Seventeen galleons with cash and jewels were sunk off Key Largo in one sentence by one Florida writer.

National interest was excited in the finds of pirate gold in the Key Largo City subdivision of Charles Ort, one of the most brilliant shooting stars of the boom. Ort, who arrived broke in Miami when the boom was already approaching a climax, took options on a city dump. Covering the ashes, tin cans, broken bottles, old kitchen sinks, and rusty bedsprings with blazing tropical flowers, he sold the enchanted oasis for millions and then poured his wealth into Key Largo City, a combination of Tahiti and Newport. No ordinary press agent was good enough for Ort. He hired the famous novelist Ben Hecht and the Broadway author J. P. McEvoy to handle his public relations. Their imagination was promptly captured by pirate gold when two ancient crocks filled with doubloons were dug up in the sands

of Key Largo. Hecht telegraphed accounts of the discovery to
hundreds of newspapers. Herbert Bayard Swope, of the New
York *World,* who won the Pulitzer Prize for his reporting of the
First World War, wired that he planned to hurry down to
chronicle the amazing discovery himself, but he demanded
Hecht's guarantee that the thing was on the level, and his telegram was ignored. Hundreds of people poured into Key Largo
to dig for treasure. The two crocks of doubloons had been dug
up by a fisherman named Captain Chester, and Hecht then
spent a week helping the Captain find adequate words to describe his discovery to newspaper reporters. The Captain became the worst victim of the pirate fever. Calling in his thirteen
grandchildren, he kept them digging for weeks after the other
treasure hunters had departed.

Pirate gold was the gilded frame of the new Florida—Florida
the workshop of the nation, Florida the great stamping ground
of capital and labor. The famous Florida climate had become a
kind of loony gas. Everybody was successful, and success went
to everybody's head. Subdividers hired poets to write odes in
their honor. Shoestring operators named cities after themselves.
The Mizners lost their sense of humor for a while, both becoming Napoleons—Addison the Corsican of city planners, and Wilson the Bonaparte of finance. Addison also began to feel old-
master blood in his veins. He had always been proud that he
was, according to the family genealogical chart, a collateral descendant of Sir Joshua Reynolds. He now frequently managed
to find openings in the conversation for ringing in allusions to
his relationship with the great portrait painter. Earlier, however,
he had made Sir Joshua the butt of little jokes. When, in his
youth, Addison was picking up a meagre living in San Francisco
as a miniature-painter and society clown, the San Francisco
gossip weekly, *Town Talk,* told of a quaint argument Addison
had put forward to prove the far-reaching effects of heredity.
"I'm a descendant of Sir Joshua Reynolds," he said, "and I josh
and I paint." But in the boom atmosphere Addison took the tie
between himself and his great-great-great-uncle more seriously.
Over the head of his bed he hung a painting, almost life-size,

with a brass plate that said, "Sir Joshua Reynolds. Self-Portrait." Addison seemed impressed when writers who were not on his payroll compared him to the great architects of Athens and Rome, and he purred contentedly when Harry Reichenbach, who was on his payroll to the tune of three thousand dollars a week, called him the Poet of Architects and the Thinker of the Future. At times, Addison went into artistic trances. Once, when he was seated in a huge chair, stroking a chow and gazing into space, Reichenbach rushed excitedly into the room to tell him one of the crookeder of the executives connected with the Boca Raton project was about to skip to Europe with a quarter of a million dollars belonging to the Mizner Corporation. Addison, still stroking the chow, turned a faraway look on the publicity man and said, "Oh, Harry, don't bother me with these things."

The boom intoxication, which made Addison a dreamer, made Wilson a man of action. He became the personification of big business. He dashed around the Boca Raton offices barking short, sharp orders and undermining the morale of the employees. The publicity and advertising staff was the particular target of his outbursts. Archibald McNeill, formerly a state representative in Connecticut, was in charge of Boca Raton ballyhoo before Harry Reichenbach joined the organization. One day, McNeill contracted for a hundred thousand dollars' worth of advertising space in the Miami *Herald* and a hundred thousand dollars' worth in the Miami *News* without a penny of cash outlay, the papers taking their compensation in Boca Raton stock and Boca Raton lots. Wilson's lip curled when he heard of this coup. "You made a wonderful deal—a wonderful deal for them," he said.

Wilson was the secretary and treasurer of the Mizner Corporation—a dignified climax to a lifelong career of larceny. There was as much as ten million dollars in down payments in the treasury at one time, but apparently very little of it stuck to Wilson's fingers. He occasionally cut up an unethical melon for himself and his friends, but so did nearly every other subdivider in Florida. A "melon party" was always held at Wilson's house in

Palm Beach on the eve of a public sale of Boca Raton lots. Wilson and his friends would study the blueprints and pick out for themselves the properties that had the best talking points. It was a certainty that investors would bid extravagantly for these lovely locations and that the prices would double and treble. Boca Raton property was in such demand at first that not only did the Boca Raton lots skyrocket but the stock in the Mizner Corporation jumped from a hundred dollars to a thousand dollars a share. There were few sales of stock, the stockholders clinging to their Mizner blue chips in the belief that they were safer than government bonds. One of Wilson's chores as watchdog of the Mizner treasury was signing checks. Miss Bess Hammons, a brand-new employee, was startled when the big, hoarse-voiced Secretary-Treasurer said, "Oh, Bess, I'm tired of putting my autograph on chicken feed. Bring me a million-dollar check to sign." Miss Hammons was somewhat flustered. Her first day in the Florida environment had been trying. She had left a routine Wall Street job to join the Boca Raton organization. On her arrival in Florida, she was greeted by Irving Berlin, who drove her to the Mizner headquarters, where she was greeted by a monkey, which jumped out of a window and wrapped its arms around her neck. Half stunned by her two unexpected welcomes, she was shown to her office, a completely bare room. When she asked about furniture, she was told that such things as desks, chairs, and filing cabinets were not to be had in Florida. She sat down on a window ledge, put her typewriter on a packing case, and typed contracts until after midnight.

Wilson's assumption of the chairman-of-the-board manner was a surprise to those who had regarded him as merely a jester at the court of King Addison. Ex-Mayor E. Tinsley Halter, of Palm Beach, Hugh Dillman, former president of the Everglades Club, and other Palm Beach notables reported that they laughed themselves into a state of helplessness at Wilson's conversation, but only a meagre anthology of his Palm Beach wisecracks has survived. In Hollywood and on Broadway, there were Mizner circles that memorized Mizner lines, but Palm Beach didn't bother. Addison was Wilson's chief Boswell. He repeated Wilson's sallies with such gusto that they always won laughs. Addison used to tell how he and Wilson had lost their bearings on an automobile trip. Wilson stopped and asked a farmer how far it was to Palm Beach. "Nine and three-quarters miles," said the farmer. "An educated son of a bitch!" Wilson exclaimed. Wilson was the official abuser of Addison's enemies. Addison was raving about the rascality of a Palm Beach contractor, and Wilson helped out by saying, "He's so crooked he'd steal two left shoes." Addison was discussing a former carpenter who had become a slightly illiterate celebrity in Palm Beach society, and Wilson said, "Every time he opens his mouth, a handful of shingle nails drops out." Once, when Wilson and some friends stopped at a hotel near Sebring, Florida, the manager telephoned several times to complain of the noise. "Listen, you bastard," said Wilson, "if you bother us again, I'll get a pair of scissors and cut your goddam hotel to pieces." The most familiar phrase in the boom period was "As of one, two, and three years," since practically all deals called for a small down payment plus three annual installments. Wilson used the phrase to get a laugh at a wedding in Addison's Palm Beach house on the Via Mizner. As the bridegroom repeated, "With all my worldly goods, I thee endow," Wilson's stage whisper boomed out, "As of one, two, and three years." Addison built a fine house in Palm Beach for Wilson. He once gave a small dinner there for Irving Berlin. Berlin and some other guests bribed Wilson's chef to sabotage the meal. Asafetida was sprinkled on the anchovies. The steak was a thin slice of the toughest meat on the market, and holes were burned clear through it. The worst possible botch was made of the strawberry shortcake. When Wilson tasted the anchovies, he exclaimed, "They died of convulsions in a septic tank!" At the sight of the steak, he said, "It's a blacksmith's apron." And on the strawberry shortcake he commented, "It's first-class surgery." But comedy and horseplay occupied a smaller and smaller part of Wilson's life as he began to look on himself as the driving force behind a gigantic enterprise and one of the pillars of the American economy.

Wilson's career as a big executive touched its peak the night he stole the ocean from the Finns. In addition to Boca Raton, the Mizners owner the Mizner Mile, a nine-hundred-acre strip near Boynton, fifteen miles south of Palm Beach. Addison had drawn up plans for a ten-million-dollar hotel of Mizner Spanish architecture, to be operated by the Ritz-Carlton chain, and the rest of the Mizner Mile was to be cut up into exquisite little estates for people of great wealth. There was one defect in the Mizner Mile. The highway ran between the Mizner property and the beach. The region was inhabited largely by Finnish farmers, who spoke of the beach as "our beach" and of the ocean as "our ocean." Their views clashed with those of the Mizners, who planned to advertise that every estate had the Gulf Stream in its front yard. Wilson and Addison took it as a personal affront that a public highway should presume to cut off their subdivision from direct access to the water. If the highway were allowed to remain there, the people who built their palaces on the Mizner Mile would have to cross the road to get to the beach, and then they would probably find the surf alive with Finlanders. It was a very pretty real-estate problem, and it received a spirited solution at the hands of Wilson. He stole the ocean from the Finns by the simple process of tearing up the highway after laying a new one on the west boundary of the Mizner property, which was several hundred yards away from the ocean. A report of a riot in Boynton reached the Palm Beach newspapers late one night, and a local columnist named Emilie Keyes was sent to cover the excitement. She found a shouting mob of Finns and their allies brandishing clubs, pitchforks, and shovels, and preparing to rush a wooden barricade that had been placed across the highway. On the other side of the barricade, a huge machine was tearing up the highway. By the illumination of road flares and automobile headlights, Miss Keyes could see Wilson Mizner shaking his fist at the Finns and cursing them savagely. One thing that struck her was that Wilson was wearing a silk hat, white tie, and tails. Palm Beach is an informal place, and in her account of the Boynton battle Miss Keyes wrote that never before had she ever seen a Palm Beach resident in a swallowtail coat. Wilson had either just left some function

268 · *The Legendary Mizners*

of unparalleled exclusiveness or else he had rigged himself in that fashion in the hope of unnerving the Finns. It may have had that effect, for the Finns, despite their superiority in armament, finally stood still and looked on in openmouthed stupefaction at Wilson's plug hat and coattails. Having worked on a Palm Beach newspaper for years, Miss Keyes had seen arrogance in her day, but she had never, she said, witnessed anything half as high and haughty as Wilson Mizner. She felt, she said, as if "A Tale of Two Cities" had come to life and she was looking on an uprising of the sans-culottes against a particularly obnoxious young nobleman. Her sympathies were with the rabble, and she was hoping that some Finn would wing Wilson with a little load of buckshot, so that her story would be worth big headlines, but the Finns allowed themselves to be stunned by Mizner's haberdashery and vocabulary. Wilson had mixed with Finns in the Klondike and Nome, and was able to abuse them with the vilest epithets in their own language. When the matter eventually got into court, the issues were lost sight of as the judge, jury, lawyers, and spectators became absorbed in watching the lady court reporter trying to cover her face with one hand while she recorded the awful language with the other.

Wilson's rough work in Boynton did not especially outrage public sentiment. The general feeling was that the region had been built up by big Northern millionaires and that the big Northern millionaires were entitled now and then to grab something they wanted. Wilson had the standing of a Northern colossus, as Harry Reichenbach had just spent a million dollars in a campaign to make the name Mizner impressive, and it was regarded as poor taste for a bunch of Finns to cling selfishly to their ocean when a man like Wilson Mizner had a mind to it. Florida had been changed from a poor state to a rich state by three generations of Northern spenders. The year-round population owed most of its prosperity to the annual migration from the high latitudes, and it was grateful. The soak-the-rich policy never made any headway in Florida, which is the original don't-shoot-Santa Claus state. All laws that interfered with the fun of solvent Northerners were dead letters in Florida. The Volstead

Act went into the ash can, and so did the anti-gambling and anti-race-track laws. Rich Northerners had a particular dislike of state income taxes and state inheritance taxes, and Florida adopted an amendment to its constitution to forbid the legislature to levy such taxes. Some of the Florida statutes were personal compliments to outstanding Northern benefactors of Florida. Henry M. Flagler, the greatest patron the state ever had, wanted to divorce his first wife, on the ground that she had sent jewels to the Czar of Russia because the Ouija board said he was in love with her. That did not constitute a legal reason for divorce in Florida, so the legislature passed what was known as the Flagler Law, specially drawn to authorize the Flagler divorce, and then repealed it, so that nobody else could take advantage of it. When Barron G. Collier became the largest landowner in Florida, the legislature carved a huge area out of Lee County and named it Collier County in his honor. Some sections of Florida even ruined themselves by voting bond issues for roads and other improvements to help visiting capitalists with their subdivisions.

The idea of showering favors on illustrious Northerners was gradually broadened to showering favors on anybody who put money in circulation. Florida courts and lawmakers turned the language inside out to help deserving interests. "Wild" became "tame," "salt" became "fresh," and "fish" became "birds." Florida is the richest state in the country in wild hogs, but every one of these ferocious animals was tamed by an act of the legislature. They have been running wild since the old Spanish days, and they think nothing of attacking a man. According to Marjorie Kinnan Rawlings, they know how to line up in football formation and crash through the door of a granary. They are locally called "wind-splitters" and "the Devil's right bowers," because of their speed and savageness. But the hog-raising industry complained that hunters were always shooting tame porkers and evading damages by claiming to have mistaken them for wild ones, so to correct this situation the legislature pronounced all wild pigs tame. Fresh water became salt to oblige the fishing industry. The fisheries wanted to catch black bass all the year round in Lake Okeechobee, a gigantic fresh-water lake, but there was a closed season on black bass in fresh waters. The legislature declared the fresh water of Lake Okeechobee to be salt water, thus making bass-fishing legal twelve months out of the twelve. Fish became birds to solve a similar problem. The fisheries wanted to catch mullet with seines in Lake Okeechobee. The taking of fish with seines in inland waters was illegal. The courts, however, decided that a mullet had a gizzard and that no creature with a gizzard was a fish. Thus mullet joined the bird family, and there is no law against taking birds with seines.

Private interests were generally favored over public interests in Florida, and big grafters given the preference over little grafters. Some coast cities claimed to own the bays they were situated on, but they were beaten in court when they tried to oppose subdividers who invaded those waters to manufacture islands. Big squatters had the right of way over little squatters. Barron Collier grabbed thousands of acres of Marco Island, but when little squatters tried to follow suit, they were chased off by the sheriff. Important private interests were occasionally discomfited, but only when they clashed with still more important ones. Addison Mizner and Paris Singer suffered a mortifying defeat when they attempted to steal a landscape. Singer and Addison were planning to subdivide Singer's Island, which is just north of Palm Beach. Singer's Island was a barren sandspit. Paris had a mental picture of how beautiful the place would be if it were adorned with colonnades of royal palms, serene and stately trees that, because of their air of meditation, have been called the philosophers of the vegetable kingdom. There was only one way to get enough royal palms to decorate Singer's Island, and that was to transplant them from Royal Palm Way, a magnificent thoroughfare in Palm Beach. Paris and Addison started out by ridiculing the grave deportment of the Platos of the botanical world, calling them "stiff," "ungainly," and "pompous." Addison caused his capable assistant Byron Simonson to produce a color drawing of Royal Palm Way that made the majestic trees as repulsive as possible. Then Simonson turned out another drawing, showing how elegant Royal Palm Way would be when beautified with lovely little shrubs. Addison and Paris now tried to rush the authorities into ordering this grand civic improvement. They were on the verge of running off to Singer's Island with the whole lot of royal palms when the Garden Club of Palm Beach became alarmed. The Garden Club represented billions, while Paris and Addison represented only millions, and the plot was frustrated.

It was easy enough, however, to purloin land or sea when the only opposition came from Finns or the People. One man pilfered a furlong of coastline in Palm Beach itself. Miami Beach residents woke up one day and found that a long stretch of their ocean had been misappropriated, but nobody could do anything about it. Wilson Mizner wasn't half as barefaced as some of the other ocean burglars. Wilson never believed in doing anything by violence that could be done by knavery, and he acquired a magic document to justify his seizure of the surf and shore at Boynton. Boynton happened to have a lame-duck administration, its officials having been swept out of office by a reform wave at the last election. They listened to reason. A few hours before their terms of office expired, they held a secret meeting at which they voted in favor of a motion to "abandon" the beach roadway and "accept" the substitute that ran back of the Mizner property. This action was denounced as nefarious, and Wilson was arrested. At his trial, an attempt was made to prove that Addison was back of the whole business. Wilson was accused of evading questions on this point. "You love your brother, don't you?" demanded the prosecutor. Wilson gazed contemptuously at his questioner. "Answer me!" shouted the lawyer. "You love your brother, don't you? You have a great affection for him, don't you?" "I have a vague regard for him," said Wilson. This and some other replies of Wilson struck the jury as funny, and they rapidly acquitted him. The Finns never got their ocean back.

Another of Wilson's achievements in his new role as a titan of business was paying a record price for a piece of property in Miami. The Mizners wanted a Miami headquarters, and Wilson took over Ye Olde Wayside Inn, on Flagler Street, at a price said to be higher than any ever paid for a property of equal size on Broadway or Fifth Avenue. "You've ruined me!" exclaimed Addison when he heard the figure, but Wilson quickly convinced him that it was "a steal." The inn, decorated in Mizneresque Spanish, with fresco murals and ancient doors and fixtures imported from Spain, is familiar to tens of thousands, for it became the Childs Restaurant of Miami after the boom. Addison's remodelling of the place was quite an accomplishment; artists, electricians, and carpenters worked on the walls and ceiling while mobs of salesmen and customers milled about on the floor. The terrific cost of the property created a blaze of publicity for the Mizners. It was a landmark in the boom. Money talks, and the Mizner deal said emphatically that Miami was rapidly overtaking New York, if it was not already ahead of her.

The price paid by the Mizners was soon eclipsed by bigger and bigger prices for Flagler Street property. One lot was reported priced at seventy thousand dollars a front foot—a figure unheard of in New York or in any world capital. Prices were running wild all over Miami. It was said that one speculator figured out that he would have to build a two-hundred-story building to earn a decent return on the fabulous sum he had paid for a Miami lot. But the speculator was not worried. He was sure that he could unload the property—"pass the baby," in boom dialect—for a figure that would compel the next man to erect a two-hundred-and-twenty-story building. In the first stage of the boom, it had been thought necessary to discover or invent a justification for a staggering price tag. Buyers stampeded this way and that as millions of dollars in real-estate values were created by confidential whispers—a new railroad station here, a multimillionaire colony there, a super-Rue de la Paix on this avenue, a big brother of the Woolworth Building on that. But in the later stages of the boom rumors and inside tips went out of fashion. The boom ceased to be speculation in real estate and became gambling in pieces of paper called options or contracts to buy. You put money down on an option as on a roulette number. Whispering campaigns were unnecessary.

Nearly everybody in Miami was involved in the boom. There were fifty-nine hundred and seventeen real-estate dealers in Miami in 1925, and they had tens of thousands of assistants, known as "sniffers," "spotters," "cappers," "pointers," "touts," "scouts," or "bird dogs." Invalids going to Florida for their health found real-estate profits a sovereign cure for a great variety of maladies. One woman, apparently dying of grief because of her husband's death, was sent to Florida, where she mourned for a day or so, then bought and sold real estate like mad, forgetting all about the deceased. The psychology of the Florida boom was fundamentally identical with that of earlier real-estate booms. It was the old monkey ancestry of the human race asserting itself in the presence of unlimited peanuts. But the Florida madness was ahead of its predecessors in several respects. It was the first full-fledged mania of the gasoline and electronic age. Automobiles made it possible to concentrate millions of suckers in the boom area, and radio gave powerful aid to depriving them of reason. The Florida boom was also the first lunacy to feel the full power of the press agent. All previous feats of publicity were topped by what happened in Miami. Press agents have been known to crow over getting twenty-two words in a newspaper; P. Jocelyn Yoder, the public-relations man for Coral Gables, got twenty-two whole pages of publicity in one issue of a Miami Sunday paper. In 1925, the Miami *Herald* printed more advertising than any other paper in the world; the St. Petersburg *Times* came second. In the years before the boom, the Miami newspapers almost faded out of existence in the hot weather, but in the summer of 1925 they achieved their greatest size, the issue of the Miami *News* on July 26th containing five hundred and four pages and weighing seven and a half pounds. *Suniland* became one of the fattest periodicals in the country; its issue for November, 1925, ran to two hundred and fifty-six pages. Before the boom, there was one advertising firm in Miami—Loomis, Bevis & Dummer; at the peak of the boom, there were thirty-three advertising firms in Miami; after the boom, there was just Loomis, Bevis & Dummer. Some authorities attributed the enormous sale of Florida real estate—computed at seven billion dollars in 1925 alone—to brilliant new advertising devices, but *Advertising & Selling* was not impressed. In its issue of November 4, 1925, that publication said, "Motion-picture scenery, trick photography, impressionistic art, distorted and unscaled maps— every twist and turn of fake advertising from the Year One appears in the Florida advertising of the unscrupulous promoters."

Miami was swamped with buyers and sellers. Shoppers were prevented from entering stores by mobs of men and women with maps, blueprints, and contracts, and the Miami authorities had to break up the congestion by forbidding the completion of real-estate deals on the sidewalks. Dealers then made their offices under beach umbrellas set up on lawns and in vacant lots. Areas between buildings were roofed over and cut up into realtors' headquarters. The porches of private houses became real-estate marts by day and bunkhouses by night. One large hotel dismissed its restaurant staff and rented the tables in the dining room for realtors to use as desks. Real-estate offices were seething with activity up to and sometimes after midnight. Rex Beach told of lawyers working all night long and drinking gallons of black coffee in an effort to keep up with their real-estate business.

Religion, sports, and entertainment were all involved in the boom, one way or another. On Sunday mornings, William Jennings Bryan conducted, on the grounds of the Royal Palm Hotel, the world's greatest Bible class, with an attendance of eight thousand, but as the benediction was said, the audience disintegrated into hundreds of little groups of realtors and bargain hunters. Charles Ort built a tabernacle on Key Largo and hired a battery of evangelists as salesmen. The New York *Times* of September 28, 1925, printed an item about one Presbyterian minister who was suing another Presbyterian minister for fraud in a Miami real-estate deal.

Gene Tunney accepted the post of manager of the Hollywood Pines Estates. Baseball stars were important in developments around St. Petersburg and Sarasota, mushroom cities having streets called Wingo, Daubert, Roush, and Coveleskie— names that, in 1925, were on every infant's tongue. Big promotions had sales organizations built around famous golfers. D. P.

Davis imported leading professionals from England and Scotland to aid him in marketing Davis Islands, in Tampa Bay. Retinues of salesmen followed golf stars around the links and sold lots to spectators between strokes. W. O. McGeehan, of the *Herald Tribune,* said of a golf-and-realty-selling match in Sarasota that Walter Hagen had "outplayed, outtalked, and outsold" Bobby Jones, winning the bout by four business lots and eight bungalow sites.

Broadway celebrities played a big part in the final months of the boom. Vaudeville headliners, opera singers, and bands were in great demand as promoters put on costlier and costlier shows to lure the crowds away from rivals. Wells Hawks, the famous press agent, and executives of the Hippodrome were brought down to Miami Shores to stage a stupendous show called "Fountania." Wilson Mizner worked on "The Pirate," a musical show that was to open the Cloister, the hotel and clubhouse in Boca Raton. Big subdividers hired songwriters to compose lyrics of the national-anthem type for their properties. The most successful was "On Miami Shores," which was written for Miami Shores, Inc.; its chorus had a finish line that was pronounced "On Mi-am-bam-bammy Shaw-haw-haw-haws!" Wilson Mizner brought the gifted songman Grant Clarke to Florida to grind out verses on Boca Raton. One of the ballads about the Mizner promotion was "Boca Raton, You Have a Charm All of Your Own." Mme. Alda was the official prima donna of Boca Raton. Chaliapin was Miami's greatest operatic star. Miami became the headquarters of many of the popular bands of the country. Coral Gables had the greatest of them all—Paul Whiteman's. Publicity chief Yoder said that a little temporary slump in the realty market caused mild consternation among the Coral Gables people, so they hired Paul Whiteman, at a staggering fee, to play martial music in order to put the do-or-die spirit back into the hearts of the salesmen. Evelyn Nesbit, the heroine of the Harry Thaw-Stanford White case, sang at a combination real-estate office and night club. Realty headquarters and cabarets became almost indistinguishable, the offices presenting vaudeville acts between sales talks, while the cabarets served as rendezvous for big real-estate operators. Ruby Keeler and Walter O'Keefe were entertainers at Texas Guinan's Miami night club, where the price of a glass of cracked ice was two dollars and fifty cents. Helen Morgan, Fritzi Scheff, and Elsie Janis sang and danced and chattered for Hollywood-by-the-Sea. Elsie Janis, the highest-priced star of the boom, was paid a hundred dollars a minute.

The paid-by-the-hour orator, a familiar figure in earlier booms in California and the Middle West, was employed on an unprecedented scale in 1925. Experienced hell-fire preachers were found to be among the best sales-talk artists, and the Bible Belt was combed for them. Anybody who could shout and keep on shouting—sideshow barkers, auctioneers, soapbox orators, jury pleaders—could command a minimum of ten dollars an hour for shouting in favor of subdivisions. They fulminated from buses, trucks, and platforms, in vacant lots, and at roadside barbecue shacks. Passengers arriving at Miami by ship were met by small boats with bands playing, real-estate banners flying, and orators screaming. Skywriters scribbled real-estate slogans overhead. Elephants, acting as sandwich men, with real-estate billboards dangling from their sides, hauled the baggage of steamship passengers along the piers. Red-liveried buglers, standing on top of buses, blew till their eyes stuck out, and then brazen-throated lecturers jumped up and started to rave about a new metropolis or projected archipelago. There were hundreds of lecturers working long hours at the height of the boom. Some of the new subdivision millionaires went crazy with self-admiration and, under the pretext of boosting new suburbs, delivered orations on themselves. Coral Gables was the leader in orators, as in nearly everything else. One of the celebrated real-estate demagogues was Joe Mitchell Chapple, the editor of a collection of verse and prose called "Heart Throbs" and an apostle of optimism. He threw people into fits of avarice with his hysterical outbursts on the moral duty of doubling and trebling your money by investing in Coral Gables. Chapple made his appearance at the town's Venetian Pool and addressed crowds seated in bleachers around the water. In his loftier moods, he climbed up to the high-diver's platform to deliver his messages. The greatest of all the lecturers was William Jennings Bryan, three-time Democratic candidate for President of the United States. Coral Gables hired him to turn loose his blazing rhetoric from a raft in the Venetian Pool, after which salesmen went to work on the crowds in the bleachers.

Chapter Fifteen

THE CRASH

GENERAL T. COLEMAN DU PONT was the man who killed the Florida boom, according to some authorities on the subject. The General was originally a champion of the boom. He had been the most influential backer of the Mizners. Trouble arose when the Mizners failed to show proper appreciation of their backer. In boosting their magic city of Boca Raton, the Mizners had spent millions to make their name important. They were convinced that Mizner was a bigger name than du Pont. Nothing but the Florida frenzy could have made business and financial bedfellows of T. Coleman du Pont and Wilson Mizner—General du Pont, for thirteen years president of E. I. du Pont de Nemours & Co., and Wilson Mizner, whose chief business experience had been running dubious hotels and steering wealthy suckers against cardsharps, con men, and shakedown artists. Usually, the General made the strictest inquiry into proposed business associates, but the carefree atmosphere of Florida persuaded him to neglect to brief himself on the subject of Wilson Mizner. The General was relaxing in Palm Beach when he caught the subdivision mania. Many of the celebrities of the resort were signing up with the Mizners' Boca Raton enterprise. The General joined the procession and was elected to the directorate. One of his fellow-directors was Jesse L. Livermore, famous for the Black Fridays and Blue Mondays he had caused by cornering the wheat market. Another was Matthew Brush, a major figure in Wall Street. The Mizners claimed a hundred millionaires among the backers of Boca Raton, but the General's name had ten times the sucker-drawing power of any of the others.

The General was a man of many quirks, foibles, and oddities, and these were partly responsible for his disastrous experience with the Mizner boys. He regarded himself as the Flo Ziegfeld of private life, and travelled around Palm Beach like a sixty-year-old Maypole surrounded by Queens of the May. As soon as he joined the Boca Raton project, he established himself in the Mizner headquarters as a mad wag and a tireless practical joker. He started by coming into the office with an air of excitement and handing an important-looking envelope to an employee. As the envelope was opened, a mechanical beetle darted out with a terrifying rattle and zigzagged around the room, causing the General to double up with laughter and slap his thighs explosively. He was a great handshaker; his palm usually contained a tiny device that inflicted an electrical shock, or a bit of sticky paper, so that when the victim drew his hand away, he pulled yards and yards of colored tissue paper out of the General's coat sleeve. He sometimes amused himself by putting on a deaf-and-dumb act. Once, when he was frantically making signs to a bootblack, an onlooker asked what it was all about. "He's deef and dumb," said the bootblack. The onlooker exclaimed, "Ain't he a big bastard!" The General was, in fact, six feet four, rawboned, and powerfully built. He was a familiar figure in Palm Beach in his white knickerbockers, knee-length silk stockings, and tweed coat, from the right-hand pocket of which he was constantly extracting a pack of cards, saying, "Take any card you choose." He could do card tricks by the hour. There was an affecting scene one day when the General, immediately after being reconciled with a du Pont cousin following a long estrangement, offered his deck of cards, saying, "Take any card you choose." His residence was equipped with telephone receivers that shot streams of water into listening ears, highball glasses that sprang leaks, matches that gave out sparks like Fourth of July flowerpots, unlightable cigarettes, and detonating cigars. His fame as a wit seems to rest mainly on a line inspired by a lady's nightgown that had been accidentally left behind by a previous occupant of a suite he stayed in at the Hotel Blackstone, in Chicago. Summoning the manager, the General handed him the garment, saying, "Fill it and bring it back." The great characteristics of the General, according to intimates, were that he was generally overflowing with animal spirits and that he "loved people." His comedy was, however, sometimes a little inhumane. He had a habit of offering a watch as a prize in all sorts of contests. When the winner came for his reward, the General would solemnly hand him an Ingersoll; the humor of the thing was the disappointment of the man who had expected a Tiffany or Cartier masterpiece from the frightfully rich old du Pont. The General was a friend of the late Senator Bankhead. He started the Senator's niece Tallulah on her career by lending her a thousand dollars to launch herself on the London stage, but he kept her on the anxious seat so long that she appraised him as a big-hearted, genial, but slightly sadistic old gentleman. The General's favorite fun machine was an electrically operated papier-mâché bulldog that he kept in a dimly lighted room. An almost invisible wire extended from the bulldog to the General's pants pocket, and by pressing a button he could cause the fierce-looking animal to growl and make short jumps in the direction of nervous visitors. When he had unsuspecting house guests, the General would start the day by raving about buckwheat cakes and maple syrup until his hearers were ravenous. Then a steaming platter of cakes would appear. In attempting to eat them, the hungry guests would make the hilarious discovery that they were composed of flannel dipped in batter. The General's chef concocted a marvellous sauce, the smell of which would drive a man mad. The General had it served on rubber frankfurters. One of his whims was taking parties of luxury-loving men and women in cold weather to his hunting lodge on the eastern shore of Maryland and watching their agonized expressions on discovering that there were no bathtubs, no running water, no electricity, no heat except from a log fire, which the General lighted by rubbing two sticks together, and no lavatory except an outhouse. Another of the General's uses of disappointment and consternation was his trick of seeming to lose his mind over a golddigger. When he had the poor girl dreaming of pearl necklaces and apartments overlooking Central Park, he would take her to a party and introduce her to his daughters, cousins, and nieces, the cream of the thing being her surprise and alarm at finding herself inundated with respectability and domesticity.

The General's frolics in Palm Beach made members of the Mizner organization suspect that his mind was going. They therefore considered it safe to take all kinds of liberties with his name. Wilson Mizner, who had had experience coaching witnesses, actors, and extortionists, acted as coach for the Boca Raton salesmen, and taught them to hammer home the point that T. Coleman du Pont was throwing countless millions into Boca Raton. The General's name was used in nearly every sentence of every sales talk. The wealth of the General and all his relatives could hardly have redeemed all the pledges that were backed by the sacred honor of T. Coleman du Pont. The fact that he was being exploited by word of mouth didn't come to the attention of the old capitalist, but one day the Mizner organization made the mistake of exploiting him in print. The General was in New York, in May of 1925, when he happened to see in the Palm Beach *Post* a publicity release announcing that "T. Coleman du Pont and others" were going to build Boca Raton hotels and theatres that would be among the wonders of the world. In a telegram to Addison, the General denounced the statement as a falsehood, and added, "PLEASE CORRECT IT IMMEDIATELY WITH AS MUCH OR MORE PUBLICITY AS WAS GIVEN FALSE STATEMENT. AM DEEPLY CHAGRINED BY STATEMENT AND FEARFUL OF OUTCOME OF A CONCERN THAT DOES BUSINESS THIS WAY. KINDLY WIRE ME WALDORF THAT ADEQUATE DENIAL HAS BEEN MADE." Addison promptly wired back a mollifying telegram that started with "I AM FRIGHTFULLY SORRY FOR SUCH A GRAVE MISTAKE AND MISSTATEMENT" and wound up with "EVERY CORRECTION AND REPARATION POSSIBLE WILL BE MADE." The General's peace of mind was restored, and in a letter to Addison he said, "Gee, I was glad to get your telegram. It took a load off my mind. You see, in Florida, I know from experience, advertisers are apt to exaggerate (I am putting it mildly) and I have always, in business, believed in being very, very careful not to make a statement that could not be backed up by facts in every way." The General went on to deliver a sermon on truth in advertising and suggested it be circulated among all the Boca Raton employees.

Wilson Mizner and his lieutenants had made the mistake of taking the General for a nut when he was only an eccentric. The General had a business reason for his clowning. His glittering success in life had been partly based on slapstick comedy and feats of legerdemain. He was a master at breaking down reserve, suspicion, and sales resistance and getting big men into big deals. The General's vaudeville talents and irrepressible boyishness had melted some of the icebergs of the financial world. The du Pont empire is based in some degree on the mergers effected by the General's boisterous personality and his bag of tricks. He was the headliner at du Pont employee outings, and a master of labor relations with his jokes and sleight-of-hand performances. He was, according to Marquis James, biographer of Alfred I. du Pont, a skillful pickpocket; he would now and then steal a watch from a department head and restore it with a solemn admonition to the man to keep a sharper eye on his department than he did on his valuables. As a preliminary to important business conferences, the General would perform card and coin tricks until everybody was in good humor; then, turning grave, he would pass the exploding cigars and call the meeting to order.

The General did not inherit his place in the du Pont dynasty. He belonged to the Kentucky, not the Delaware, branch of the family. Emerging from M.I.T., he started out as a common laborer in a coal mine in Central City, Kentucky. Before long, he was operating his own coalpit, and he later embarked on a career of reorganizing sick corporations, especially broken-down streetcar lines. He claimed to have made more than a million dollars in a single year while he was in his thirties. In 1902, he and two cousins bought the du Pont Company, which was about to be sold out of the family. For more than ten years, the General was the sparkplug, organizing genius, and supersalesman of the business. In 1915, not long after becoming a General in the Delaware Militia, he sold his du Pont stock for fourteen million dollars—a poor bargain, for eventually it was worth hundreds of millions. The General made the deal when he was in the Mayo Sanatorium. He believed he was dying, but an operation for adhesions made a new man of him. Someone said, "Now you've got your health and fourteen million dollars, what are you going to do?" "I'm going to burn up the pike," he replied. He began this project by running himself as the businessman's candidate for President of the United States. He got Delaware's thirteen votes at the Republican Convention of 1916. Later, he became United States Senator from Delaware. Making his headquarters in New York, he established himself as a stupendous old playboy. It was nothing for him to have the chorus of a Broadway show at one of his late suppers. For his outdoor parties at Nevis, his estate on the Hudson River near Dobbs Ferry, the General would borrow half the mechanical horseplay of Coney Island from his friend Barron Collier, who owned Luna Park. He introduced Western customs at dinners over which he presided. As toastmaster of the Rocky Mountain Club, he commanded silence by drawing a long-barrelled six-shooter and shooting up the frescoed ceiling of the Waldorf-Astoria. There were no complaints; the General owned the hotel. He had a business reason for nearly everything, and he became the Flo Ziegfeld of private life in order to perfect himself in the science of business administration. Experience taught him that bankers react to curves and dimples as well as to charts and graphs. The General had a personal catalogue of stage and screen stars, society and home girls, and he wired to all parts of the country for them whenever he had a big deal at the critical stage. He had learned the technique through an association, in the motion-picture business, with the meteoric French promoter Joe Godsol, who lavished great numbers of beautiful women on important business negotiations. Messmore Kendall, a colleague of both du Pont and Godsol, said in his autobiography, "Never Let the Weather Interfere," that the Miss Americas were so greatly in the majority at one Godsol party that most of them had no man to talk to. "Let them talk to Benjamin Franklin on the hundred-dollar bills they find under their plates," Godsol said. General du Pont never borrowed an idea without improving it. A member of the Mizner organization counted twenty-four girls and six men at one of the General's parties, and reported that every male got the illusion of being a Lord Byron in looks and a Dr. Johnson in conversational prowess.

One of the General's ambitions was to be the acknowledged champion at racing through New York traffic. He had certain advantages. He was one of the comical Deputy Police Commissioners who abounded during the administration of Mayor Hylan, and it was his custom to tip the traffic cops along his route with twenty-dollar gold pieces. His chauffeur, a master at dodging through traffic, was Alfred Sinkingson, a professional racing driver and former British champion. The General received a challenge from Leroy Baldwin, president of the Empire Trust Company, who claimed to have clipped several seconds off a du Pont point-to-point record. The two financial giants planned a race from East Sixty-eighth Street to Wall Street for a bet of a thousand dollars. Baldwin proposed that they trade automobiles for the race, so that the General would not have the advantage of his Special Deputy insignia. The General agreed, but he asked to make the trade twenty-four hours before the race. He said he wanted Sinkingson to familiarize himself with the strange car. Baldwin became suspicious and called off the bet. Later, he asked the General his real reason for wanting the car a day in advance. "I was going to paint it red and put a fire bell on it," said the old humorist. Too much fun was probably responsible for softening up the General to the point where he could become entangled with the Mizner promotion, but nobody could fool him for any length of time. Many go-getters made Wilson Mizner's mistake of taking him for an easy mark, but the General had an uncanny knack of seeing through flatterers and schemers. He was not dedicated to roistering. Even in his wildest days, he got up at 5 A.M., brewed himself quarts of coffee, and put in hours of thought on his business affairs. He had usually done a day's work before most of his Wall Street pals were up.

After his outburst against the Boca Raton management, the General was quiet for four months, but in September he was stirred to the depths of his soul by the discovery that he was being played for a sucker. Harry Reichenbach had become connected with the Mizner promotion. Sales at Boca Raton had been averaging only two million dollars a week, and Wilson Mizner was dissatisfied. He wanted a high-power brain to run the Boca Raton ballyhoo, so he lured Reichenbach to Florida. Reichenbach regarded great people like General du Pont as mere pawns for his publicity gambits. He looked on international situations as mere backdrops for press-agent stunts. One of the sorrows of his life was that Washington interference had spoiled his plan to have the screen vampire Clara Kimball Young captured by Mexican rebels and rescued by the United States Cavalry. Arriving in Florida, Reichenbach sensed that the real-estate market was being hurt by phony advertising. Gross exaggeration had made the public skeptical. The only thing Reichenbach could do was murder skepticism by choking it to death with hyperbole. The public discounted Florida advertising ninety-nine per cent. Thus, anything less than hundredfold exaggeration was an understatement. To make any impression at all, Reichenbach was compelled to rant and rave. He peopled the jungles and bogs of Boca Raton with the snootiest aristocracy ever assembled in one place since the time of Louis XIV. When the one complete structure in Boca Raton was a hamburger stand, he advertised, "No Existing World Resort of Wealth and Fashion Compares with Boca Raton." Reichenbach didn't ask you to take his word for it. Cautioning his artists not to be parsimonious with their palaces, temples, towers, and civic centers, he spread magnificent views of the imaginary city over double-page advertisements to prove his statement that "The Riviera, Biarritz, Mentone, Nice, Sorrento, the Lido, Egypt—all that charms in each of these finds consummation in Boca Raton." The skepticism of Rupert Hughes, debunker of George Washington, was beaten down by Reichenbach's pictures and text. He wrote to a national-maga-

zine editor suggesting an article on American genius and enterprise as exemplified by the glorious city of Boca Raton, but the
editor wrote back that he happened to have seen Boca Raton and
it was still a practically untouched wilderness. General du Pont
began his second attack on the Boca Raton management after
reading an announcement of the Mizners' hundred-million-dollar "development program" in the Palm Beach *Post* of September
11th. "We have no such program and should not have advertised
it," he wrote to Addison. On September 15th, the General sent
another letter to Addison, this one full of complaints about Harry
Reichenbach. He objected to modest little statements like
"Yachts discharge directly at the lake entrance to this hotel,"
when, in fact, there was no hotel and nothing bigger than a
large skiff could have landed at the proposed site of the proposed
hotel. By this time, the Mizners had begun to regard the General as a disgruntled old kill-joy, and they paid no attention to
his outcries.

Reichenbach's next move enraged the General. Reichenbach
had invented a sovereign cure for skepticism. As his advertisements grew more delirious, he included the following in each
one: "Attach This Advertisement to Your Contract for Deed. It
Becomes a Part Thereof." Under the heading of "A Declaration
of Responsibility" Reichenbach asserted that the sponsors of
Boca Raton guaranteed each and every statement made in Boca
Raton advertising. The General realized that the directors were
now liable if any preposterous claim about Boca Raton failed to
come true. Lining up Jesse Livermore and some other directors,
he started a crusade to fire Wilson Mizner, Harry Reichenbach,
and a couple of other Boca Raton executives. One of the General's bombshells was a photostat of a newspaper account of Wilson Mizner's conviction for running a gambling house in 1919.
Wilson retaliated by going to the county jail and inducing a girl
prisoner who had become a Palm Beach sensation as a bad-check
passer to sign a letter to the General saying, "You are responsible
for my pregnancy," and making other accusations. These were
sheer inventions, but Wilson thought it might be well to give
the General a new subject to think about. The General, how-

ever, was not to be diverted. Late in November, he dropped in to see Bess Hammons, who was a confidante of the warring factions. "I've got a press statement I want to read you, Bess," he said. "I'm getting out. I can't stand— Say, Bess, did you ever see this one? Take any card you choose." For half an hour, the General did card tricks, slapping his thigh with pleasure at her wonder and astonishment. Then he put the cards in one pocket and took a typewritten statement out of another. "I'm getting out, Bess," he said. "I've never been connected with a failure in my life, and this thing is sure to fail with these people in charge."

The General's statement, blasting the methods of the Mizners, was given out not only in Florida but in New York, and it was played up in the *Times* and the *Herald Tribune*. It later became the General's trump card in fighting innumerable lawsuits, as it proved that he had tried to stop the fantastic ballyhoo for Boca Raton. The Mizners issued a reply charging that the General had quit because he wasn't permitted to load the Mizner payroll with du Ponts. Before the General's statement was published, the Mizners had to keep their offices open until after midnight to handle the demand for Boca Raton lots; after the statement, the place was a tomb. The General's attack put a wet blanket on the whole boom. Russell Hull, whose firm dealt in lots in Miami and Palm Beach, said that sales in both places stopped completely after the General's blast. Charts of the Florida boom made by the economist Homer B. Vanderblue show the nose dive beginning at just about the time of the General's statement. Either the General started the collapse or he displayed perfect timing in getting out from under.

The Florida phenomenon, which had become vaster than the Mississippi Bubble or any other real-estate mania in history, had undoubtedly been threatening to explode for some time. During the summer and fall of 1925, the question that was constantly being asked was "When will it all end?" Some of the answers were buoyant enough. Charles Donald Fox, author of "The Truth About Florida," asserted paradoxically that there was no boom and that it would last forever. Paul O. Meredith, head booster of Lakeland, Florida, said it would all end "when the Gulf Stream ceases to flow." The New York *Times* quoted one T. S. Knowlson as estimating that it would last ten years. The intrepid prognosticator Roger W. Babson, namesake of Babson Park, which was being advertised as the Wonder City of Florida, predicted in *Forbes Magazine* that the boom would last four or five years longer. One realist, Walter C. Hill, of Atlanta, correctly predicted in print that the boom would end during the winter of 1925–26, because the way prices were heading, sucker money would not keep coming in. According to Kenneth Ballinger, author of "Miami Millions," the first weak spot in the boom appeared in August of 1925, when a lot on Miami Beach that had sold for fifty thousand dollars brought only twenty-five thousand on a resale. The price of other lots dropped in sympathy, but things picked up again and the setback was looked on as an accident. R. T. Herrick, head of the sales department of the great Coral Gables promotion, began to fear that the boom was overexpanded when, on one day, four men tried to sell him lots in his own promotion. Some authorities date the beginning of the decline of prices from a civil war that broke out between the old carpetbaggers and the new. The old carpetbaggers dealt in options; the new carpetbaggers dealt in "binders," or options on options. The usual Florida real-estate transaction started with a down payment of ten per cent. The next payment, anywhere from twenty to fifty per cent, came due after the title had been searched and the deed recorded. As the County Clerk was overwhelmed with work, there were long intervals between the down payment and the next payment. During those intervals, you could trade in options without putting up much cash, and it was then that the binder boys got in their work. Properties were sold dozens of times before the first large payment fell due. Some of the veteran promoters claimed that the wild gambling in binders was turning Florida into a bucket shop, and they deliberately slashed prices in subdivisions in which the binder boys specialized. According to some students of the boom, they not only ruined the binder boys but started a downward price movement that ruined themselves as well. Second-payment trouble began to hit the boom late in the fall of 1925. The *Wall Street Journal* reported that legions of people had cheerfully paid the down payment, but that they became very lugubrious when called on to hand over the next installment, and they defaulted by the thousand. The income-tax situation was another boom-killing factor. The Treasury Department ruled that taxes had to be paid on all paper profits. A man might, for example, have paid $100,000 in cash for a property and sold it for $300,000, taking $100,000 in cash and $200,000 in promissory notes. The income-tax people wanted their cut on the $200,000 profit represented by the promissory notes. This meant that tens of thousands of speculators, to raise cash, would have to throw their properties on the market or sell the promissory notes at a tremendous discount. The federal government later modified its attitude, but not until a wave of fear had caused Florida's whole price structure to totter.

In the summer of 1925, the boom was also hurt by a freight congestion. The Florida railroads were swamped when they were asked to deliver thousands of freight trains loaded with unborn cities. Embargoes had to be declared on building materials and on nearly everything else except food for the suddenly increased population in the state. Even cattle feed was embargoed. Fresh milk almost disappeared. Shortages of every kind were reported. In some towns and cities, ice could be obtained only on a physician's prescription. Hardware vanished from the market. Lucinda Reichenbach, wife of Harry, made a trip to New York mainly to buy a garbage can and bring it back to her house in Palm Beach as baggage. Postal service broke down. Theodore Dreiser reported long lines of stalled mail cars at Jacksonville. Florida-bound actors were advised by *Variety* to carry costumes, props, and essential scenery as hand baggage. The most desperate characters in Florida were the owners of ninety-nine-per-cent completed buildings. They were losing money by the minute because they lacked the few bricks, the few boards, or the small amount of glass necessary to finish hotels, apartment houses, and office buildings so they could throw them open to the public. Bootlegging methods were used to sneak building materials into the state. With the connivance of a couple of railroad men in New York, one contractor smuggled a carload of bricks to Miami by putting several tons of ice around the bricks and covering the freight car with placards that said "Lettuce." Glenn Griswold, of the Chicago *Journal of Commerce*, was surprised to see a large vacant lot in West Palm Beach completely covered with bathtubs; the lot had signs proclaiming it the site of the most beautiful apartment house in Florida, but the builder had been able to get nothing delivered except the tubs.

Most of the heavy material for the Hotel Alba, later the Ambassador, had arrived in Palm Beach before the embargo was declared. The builders had three shifts of workmen busy night and day and were paying huge overtime to get it ready before the 1925–26 winter season. At last it was completed, except for some tons of iron grillwork, ornamental doorknobs, and other fancy metalwork that had been made in Spain. These arrived in New York, but their shipment to Florida by rail was forbidden by the embargo. They were finally carried to Palm Beach as baggage, the total excess-baggage bill coming to more than seventy thousand dollars. Building material became so precious that highjacking blossomed into a regular business. Lumber, bricks, glass, and plumbing supplies couldn't be left unguarded at night because they would be spirited off to complete some almost-finished building.

Thousands of tons of material were brought in by ship. From Maine to Puget Sound, hulls were taken out of ship morgues and fitted up with sails or engines for one last trip. The profit on the cargo was usually several times the value of the vessel. A. Hyatt Verrill, writer and explorer, reported that the captains of decrepit craft had orders to sink, burn, or beach their ships after selling the freight. *Variety*, which gave special treatment to Florida because it had suddenly become a great national entertainment center, reported a new institution—Lumber Row. Rum Row, an old, established institution, consisted of ships riding at anchor off the Florida coast and selling rum to speedboats. Lumber Row consisted of ships, unable to dock because of the congestion, riding at anchor and selling lumber to builders and speculators who came out in fishing fleets to get a few feet of precious boards or a few bags of cement. The furniture for the great new Roney-Plaza Hotel, in Miami, could not be transported by rail. It arrived on a big ship and was transferred to motorboats, sailboats, and rafts, quantities of costly equipment being smashed, water-soaked, or sunk in the process. Dozens of ships were anchored off Miami awaiting their turns to thread their way through the difficult channel into Biscayne Bay. The Florida bubble, already shrinking rapidly, met with a real disaster on January 10, 1926, when the Prins Valdemar, an old Danish warship with its wooden hull pierced with portholes for cannon, capsized in the channel, barring the entrance to sixty-two ships waiting off Miami. The vessel had been discarded by the Danish Navy after long service as a training school and had been towed to Florida to be made into a hotel. The Miami channel was only eighteen feet deep, and all the ballast had to be thrown off the Prins Valdemar. The ship was then fearfully top-heavy, with three masts rising high over an empty hull. The owners wouldn't hear of removing the superstructure, since the masts and rigging made their floating caravansary picturesque. The quaint old war horse of the sea picked the exact middle of the channel to flop over on its side. The crew, taken by surprise, swam for shore, one seaman arriving with dice and money from a crap game still clenched in his fist. The ship couldn't be dragged out of the channel. Efforts to dynamite a new channel failed. It was necessary to cut away the steel masts with acetylene torches before the Prins righted itself. It never did serve as a hotel, but after being blown ashore by a hurricane it became the municipal aquarium of Miami. Because of the blockade of the harbor, builders defaulted, head contractors couldn't pay subcontractors, hotel men failed, subdividers went broke, and banks began to sway.

As the Boca Raton promotion disintegrated, Addison suffered another misfortune. The neo-Spanish architecture that was his specialty went into a decline. For years, all smart people had insisted on red-tiled roofs, the contrast of the red with the vivid green of the palms being one of the enchantments of the Florida

Reginald Marsh

scene. Spain and Latin America had been plundered for antique tile for homes in the American subtropics. The Cathedral of Trujillo, in Honduras, sported a tin roof because its ancient terra cotta had been shipped north to cover villas and palazzos in Florida. In 1925, Addison made a profit of a hundred and sixty thousand dollars in his Florida factory, which produced architectural materials, especially handmade tiles in the Spanish manner. The real Tile King was Dr. Cyrus French Wicker, of Miami. Dr. Wicker had been in the diplomatic service, and his career as a tile magnate started when he heard a Californian say that the beautiful old tiles in Panama would sell for a dollar apiece in Santa Barbara. Dr. Wicker bought the whole roof of the Panama Cathedral when the edifice was being repaired, and took the tiles to Santa Barbara, where he made a fair profit on them. His first coup during the Florida boom was the purchase of a hundred thousand tiles from the Convent of Santa Catalina, in Havana. These were snapped up so eagerly that Dr. Wicker went to Spain on a roof-buying trip and chartered several ships to carry his purchases to Florida. Boom-time Florida structures were dressed up with Spanish tiles that had covered Saracenic, Visigothic, Roman, Phoenician, and probably even Cyclopean architecture. The Spanish police charged that the American roof buyer was stripping Spain of priceless antiquities. Dr. Wicker's operations were resumed, however, after he had authorized the police to act as his purchasing agents on a commission of a cent a tile. The police glutted the market with the roofs of historic buildings. The Florida crash saved whole provinces of Spain from being unroofed. The crash also put an end to the demand for old Spanish furniture to go with the new Spanish houses in Florida. During the height of the Spanish rage, it was compulsory in Palm Beach to eat from tables once used by Spanish monks and to sleep in beds that had belonged to nobility or, preferably, to royalty. In one of his brilliant Palm Beach sketches, Joseph Hergesheimer tells of an aged Palm Beach husband who barked his shins every night because he never could remember that he had to scramble up a platform to get into his Spanish bed.

Addison's life was shortened by his loyalty to the Spanish influence that he had introduced into Palm Beach. He brought on a heart attack by hoisting his two hundred and eighty pounds every night into a very high Spanish bed—once the possession, it was believed, of Ferdinand and Isabella, and now on display in the Mizner Museum, at the Driftwood Inn, in Vero Beach. The peak of the Spanish vogue was reached, perhaps, when Señor Riano, the Spanish Ambassador to the United States and a devout Catholic, went to Florida to dedicate a monument of neo-Spanish architecture that turned out to be a Protestant Church. Others say that the high mark of the Spanish invasion was reached with the opening of the Hotel Alba, in Palm Beach. The Alba was Spanish right down to the waiters, who were dressed in the leather costumes of Spanish muleteers. The Duke of Alba, after whom the hotel was named, was expected for the opening, but he sent his regrets from Madrid. Nevertheless, all the Palm Beach notables were invited to meet him. They were presented to Harold Fender, a Ziegfeld Follies star, who wore false whiskers and sat on a gilt throne.

The first man to turn traitor to Addison Mizner's Spanish style was Wilson Mizner. One day, when Wilson was in bed with the flu, Dayton J. Kort, a Palm Beach contractor, paid him a visit. Kort was aghast to find white paint covering the dark Spanish frescoes with which Addison had finished the room. "Why did you do it?" he asked. "On account of the goddam mosquitoes," said Wilson. "You couldn't see 'em when they lit on those dark walls. I had it painted white so I can spot 'em and kill 'em." Society leaders who built homes for themselves in Palm Beach decided that they wanted to be pioneers of a new architectural trend instead of tailenders in an old trend, and they began to order houses in any style but Spanish. It became fashionable to say, "After all, our ancestors were Anglo-Saxon." Smart young architects reversed the Mizner style at every point, introducing the lightest of blond woods as a contrast to the gloomy Miznerian interiors. In his earlier days, Addison had built log houses in the Klondike, bamboo houses in the South Seas, bungalows in California, rustic lodges in the Adirondacks, and Chinese, Japanese, and English houses on Long Island, but he was convinced that everything in Florida should be Mizneresque Spanish. "I can't bring myself to do this Colonial and Georgian stuff," he said. George Merrick, the builder of Coral Gables, was almost as Hispanic as Addison. He wanted Coral Gables to be a Spanish city, with nothing but red-tiled roofs. Near the end of the boom, however, he let a contract for a hundred houses in South African Dutch Colonial and other new modes. Harry Reichenbach sensed the drift away from Spanish; in some of his advertisements he housed the Boca Raton gentry in Elizabethan inns.

As the boom started to sag, some of the boomers tried to prop it up with increased advertising and wilder claims than ever. An Inventory Congress was held by the realtors in West Palm Beach to take stock of the situation, and the speakers generally contended that more vision was needed. Have-Faith-in-Florida Clubs were organized in other parts of the country. Frank Winch, a circus and theatrical man, attended a boosters' get-together in Miami. The guest of honor was a highly groomed and monocled Prussian, who pledged tremendous reserves of European capital to put the boom back on the upward spiral. The Prussian Croesus said that he and other financial giants of the Continent had been compelled to recognize that Florida was the coming playground of the world, and were planning to invest huge sums in Boca Raton and other great developments. The realtors left the rally exhilarated. The trend, however, continued downward. One day, when the crash was about complete, Winch was in West Palm Beach with Samuel Gumpertz, who was then running Ringling's Circus. Directed by a policeman, they went to a speakeasy. The proprietor was not especially well groomed and he wore no monocle, but he was unmistakably the Prussian hero of the boosters' get-together. After a few drinks, Winch began to ask questions. "Oh," said the speakeasy man, "I did that for Wilson Mizner. I used to be a steward with the Hamburg-American Line. I met Wilson when he was crossing the Atlantic. He was a big tipper and a fine fellow. When I came down here, he loaned me the money to buy a seaplane to fly rum in from Bimini.

When he wanted me to be a Prussian capitalist, I was delighted to do it for him. I'd do anything for Wilson Mizner."

Addison tried frantically to pump oxygen into the dying Boca Raton, but he met with one disappointment after another. Once, Arthur Somers Roche found him crying. "Oh, it's my dear little baby brother—it's Mama's Angel Birdie," said Addison. He always spoke this way of Wilson when the gigantic scapegrace had been up to some particularly distinguished piece of mischief. Addison had hooked a financial leviathan from New York, in the hope that he would put fresh capital into Boca Raton. When the deal seemed to be nearing completion, Addison asked Wilson to take the big capitalist and his wife to dinner. The wife turned out to be an old acquaintance of Wilson's. After dinner, the party adjourned to Wilson's house. His cellar happened to be out of Scotch, and the prospect went out to get some. When he came back, he found his wife sitting on Wilson's lap. Wilson had an icepick, and he and the lady were trying to pry a huge emerald out of its setting in her ring. The husband was deaf to Wilson's efforts to clarify the situation. He dragged the lady from Wilson's house, telephoned a bitter complaint to Addison, and broke off negotiations.

When Boca Raton finally sank, Harry Reichenbach sank with it. Svengali had hypnotized himself. Carried away by his own high-pressure publicity, Harry invested heavily in Boca Raton, and he was $118,000 in the hole when he left Florida, in spite of his salary of three thousand dollars a week. The crash came just in time to save him from still heavier losses, as he had planned to spend $250,000 on a Boca Raton castle. Mrs. Reichenbach had been alarmed for some time about the whole thing, and her alarm was increased when a Wurlitzer salesman dropped in to ask her if she wanted a $25,000, $35,000, or $45,000 electric organ. "I don't want any organ," she said. "Why, you have to have an organ," said the salesman. She called up Addison. "Why, of course you have to have an organ," he said. "You're going to entertain on a large scale, and you can't do without one." Mrs. Reichenbach continued to hesitate, however, and she was still in a state of indecision when the Florida bubble burst.

Addison and the Wurlitzer salesman were only following what appeared to be the dictates of common sense in boom-time Florida. High-priced organs were eclipsing yachts as indispensable marks of wealth and good taste. Addison and other architects helped to promote the organ business. They got a ten-percent commission on every one they foisted on their clients. Church choirs all over the country are singing today to organs formerly owned by Florida spenders.

Ben Hecht was the literary man of the boom. He showered the blue diamonds of his vocabulary on Key Largo City. It is impossible even now to read his prose without feeling an urge to rush South and invest a couple of hundred thousand dollars in the tidal swamp that once was the town's Millionaires' Row. The one man who had no trouble resisting Hecht's prose was Hecht. He wouldn't buy a nickel's worth of land in Key Largo or anywhere else in Florida. He was convinced not only that Florida real estate was no good but that Florida banks were no good. As a reward for barking for subdivisions in the style of Robert Louis Stevenson, Hecht received twenty-five hundred dollars a week, which he instantly stuffed into his pockets. People remarked that he was putting on weight, but in reality he was padded with rolls of bills. Refusing to deposit a cent in any Florida financial institution, he kept all his wealth concealed about his person. When he finally left Florida, he was bulging with $30,000 in currency. Hecht worked for Charles Ort, the man who started with a city dump. Ort was worth $30,000,000 at the peak of Florida prosperity. When this had shrunk to $800,000, Hecht counselled him to take the cash and skip. "I can't," said Ort. "Someday this will all come back, and what a fool I would look like with a measly eight hundred thousand dollars!" Ort wound up penniless. All the large-scale operators, including the Mizners, had a childlike faith in their promotions. When Florida capsized, every one of the big fellows went down with the ship. Carl Fisher, who could have sold out for $100,000,000 at the height of the boom, left an estate of $53,000. George Merrick, who once measured his wealth in nine figures, supported himself after the boom by running a fishing lodge on Upper Matecumbe Key. Joseph W. Young, whose Hollywood-by-the-Sea was given a $300,000,000 rating by the *Wall Street Journal,* found himself a comparatively poor man. Barron Collier, the biggest landowner in Florida, got a moratorium from the federal courts on $17,000,000 of debts. D. P. Davis, a spectacular operator, disappeared mysteriously from an ocean liner.

On January 13, 1926, less than two months after General du Pont had turned against the Mizners, *Variety* stated, under the headline "FLORIDA SLIPPING," that everybody was anxious to unload. The Mizners put on a brave front at a housewarming in February for the Cloister, the clubhouse and hotel at Boca Raton, but it was fighting after the bell. In March, W. O. McGeehan, in a dispatch to the *Herald Tribune* from the training camp of the New York Giants in Sarasota, wrote that destitute realtors had been caught disguising themselves as Giant rookies, so they could get free meals by signing checks at a restaurant that catered to the ballplayers. The *Times* reported that a hundred and fifty-four men stood in line in Miami to answer an advertisement for one night watchman. Most of the little speculators charged the big speculators with fraud. "The good people went in for a gamble," said Wilson Mizner, "and they are full of moral indignation because they lost." Lawsuits were filed by the thousand. When the sheriff came to Wilson's house to serve a paper, Wilson pulled open a drawer, revealing a stack of complaints and subpoenas. "Sheriff," he said, "would you like this on top or in the middle of the deck?" In a letter to Arthur Somers Roche, he wrote, "I never open my door but a Writ blows in—Assumpsit, Damages, Nudum Pactum, and old Lis Pendens. When the bell rings, I open the door, automatically stick out my hand, admit being Wilson Mizner, and accept service. I spend my evenings shuffling these fearsome documents and can already cut to any complaint I desire. This proficiency may prove valuable, should the judge wish to decide by chance what case to try next."

Wilson hated the ways of the Florida courts. He had always regarded a lawsuit as a contest in which rival raconteurs took the witness stand and tried to outnarrate one another. He was hurt because the Florida Judge gave the preference to written instruments over the most talented testimony. In his letter to Roche, Wilson expressed the deepest regret about his failure to imitate the wisdom of the lame Confederate general who, on seeing disaster ahead, said, "Boys, things look tough. But remember, the eyes of Dixieland are on you. The beauty and chivalry of the South know our desperate plight and thank God for it, as only in extremities like this are heroes made. The hated Yankees are preparing to charge—let them come! Don't shoot until you see the whites of their eyes and feel their fetid breath on your cheeks. A volley at such close range should wreak havoc. Then, my brave fellows, take to the bayonet and fight it out hand to hand, until the case is hopeless. Then you can retreat—but, seeing I'm lame, I'll start now."

Wilson didn't start to retreat until 1927, and then he didn't stop until he reached Hollywood, where he became a restaurant man and screen writer. Addison, who had demonstrated his faith in Boca Raton by assuming personal responsibility for the debts of the company, lived mainly on loans from wealthy friends during the last years of his life. When he died, in February, 1933, his estate was found to be insolvent.

Chapter Sixteen

THE MAIN EVENT

THE FLORIDA CRASH wiped Wilson Mizner out completely. When he went to Hollywood, he posed as a millionaire idler, but he was really looking for a job. His Florida experiences had broken his spirit to the extent that he was willing to do honest work. His friend Lew Lipton, who was then producing pictures, got him a job as a writer. Sound pictures were just coming in. Mizner scored heavily with the dialogue he wrote for "One Way Passage," one of the most successful of the early talkies. Deciding to settle down in the picture colony, Mizner joined H. K. Somborn, one of Gloria Swanson's former husbands, in opening the Brown Derby restaurant.

While Wilson Mizner devoted much of his leisure to the denunciation of suckers and chumps, his routine evening in Hollywood consisted of coming to the Brown Derby, of which he was part owner, with a thick roll of bills and giving them away a few at a time to professional moochers. By midnight, he would be reduced to getting his paper from his newsboy on credit. He offered a feeble resistance to some of the demands on his purse. Once, when a borrower asked for fifty dollars, he said, "Here's twenty-five dollars. Let's both make twenty-five dollars."

When a burglar came to him for a loan, he said, "Doesn't it get dark any more?"

For Mizner's protection, special glass was put into the front doors of the restaurant; a man inside could see out, but a man outside couldn't see in. With the help of this device, Mizner occasionally escaped. Once, he jumped up at the sight of a small-loan nemesis and hurried to the washroom. The knob of the washroom door was loose. It turned round and round in his hand and prevented his getaway. Mizner called to Robert Cobb, one of his Derby partners, "Hey, Bob! Take this knob and put it on the safe in your office. Jimmy Valentine couldn't crack it in three days."

Brusque and blasphemous in his own coterie, Mizner would put on an unctuous, ingratiating, Dale Carnegie manner at the approach of a stranger who appeared prosperous. His hope of finding new suckers to trim never deserted him. He would even stop eating a sizzling beefsteak in order to fawn upon a possible chump. In his later years, he had almost entirely lost the sensation of taste; heat gave him an illusion of flavor, and his chief pleasure of the table was a blistering-hot sirloin. His regular crowd always preserved silence until he had consumed it. One night, he was half through a hot steak when a well-groomed stranger appeared and offered to bet that Mizner couldn't remember him. Mizner sized up the stranger as a confidence man's dream. He forgot all about the steak and began to pour on the fraudulent camaraderie in his best how-to-win-friends manner. Didn't I meet you at Palm Beach? No. Monte Carlo? Wrong. Saratoga? Wrong again. Now I remember—Deauville? Still wrong. "Where was it?" Mizner finally demanded. "At the Hotel Ambassador last Wednesday," the man said. "Don't you remember? I showed you the samples of my new shirtings." Mizner picked up his steak knife, struggled to his feet, and chased the stranger into the night.

Most of Mizner's motion-picture work was done on the Warner Brothers lot. He was a writer who never wrote. His method of collaboration was unique. At the studio, he slept most of the time in a huge red plush chair, which so closely resembled an archiepiscopal throne that he was called the Archbishop. When Mizner's literary partners needed some lines or ideas from him, they would shake him gently and start him talking. After half an hour or so, they would order him back to sleep while they sat down at their typewriters and worked up his conversation into script form.

After thirty-five years of a strictly nocturnal life, he was a dormouse in the daytime. One afternoon, his collaborators moved his throne to a door commanding the corridor and assigned him to watch the fun they were having with an English writer. The Englishman was considered aloof. To shake him out of his insularity, one of the collaborators had forged an executive's signature to a note advising the Briton that his private life had caused unfavorable comment even in broadminded Hollywood and inviting his attention to the morals clause in his contract. Running past Mizner, the Britisher rushed into the executive's office and punched him in the nose. Mizner slept through it all.

The only time Mizner was ever known to show excitement in Hollywood was when his friend Jack Johnson, the former heavyweight champion, arrived at the Warner lot to play a small part. To most people, Johnson was just an old colored man, but Mizner threw his arms around him and kissed him on both cheeks. He introduced the fighter with great ceremony in order to make sure that the heads of the studio realized how much they were being honored.

There were large gaps in Mizner's pose of being the hardest, coldest, and most callous man in the world. He used to visit narcotic hospitals to cheer up old pals. He had a real talent for comforting a friend in distress. One day, he became greatly concerned over a change he saw in an old acquaintance, a screen writer who believed himself to be suffering from incipient insanity. The scenarist had just tried to introduce a man he had known for twenty-five years to another whom he had known for ten years. He had forgotten the names of both of them and was sure that his mind was cracking up. "I've known you for thirty years," said Mizner, "and that is the most hopeful sign I've seen in you. Now you're going to amount to something. Don't you know that when you forget your wife's name, your telephone number, and where you live, you're getting somewhere? Where would you be if you knew all the Vice-Presidents by their first names? You'd be getting thirty dollars a week. I wouldn't give a quarter for a son of a bitch with a memory."

In conversation, Mizner did his best to suppress the instincts of humanity. His later comic style was largely ridicule of all sentiment and feeling. Although at times he could be soft in his behavior, he aimed at being as satanic as possible in speech. He and his brother Addison both maintained a pose of being completely divorced from human emotion. Anything shocking or saddening was made to order for their wit. Death was the finest of all comedy subjects, because it provided the largest amount of emotion to be deflated. When Wilson and Addison were living together in Palm Beach, Addison came in one day with the news that another brother, Lansing, a San Francisco lawyer, had been killed in an automobile accident. "Why didn't you tell me before I put on a red tie?" said Wilson.

A young woman with whom Wilson had quarrelled threw herself from the eleventh floor of a Palm Beach hotel. The hotel clerk telephoned the news to Addison, who broke it to Wilson. Wilson picked up his hat and cane. "Where are you going?" asked Addison. "To Bradley's," said Wilson. "I'm going to lay a bet on No. 11. You can't tell me that isn't a hunch." This, to some of Wilson's admirers, was proof that his heart was broken.

He was working in Hollywood early in 1933 on a picture called "Merry Wives of Reno" when he received word that Addison was dying. He wired, "STOP DYING. AM TRYING TO WRITE A COMEDY."

Singularly enough, the best-known and probably the greatest of Mizner's sayings is the only emotional line in his entire anthology, and it bears on the subject of death. In 1910, when Mizner was managing Stanley Ketchel, the great middleweight who lasted twelve rounds with Jack Johnson and who was the embodiment of the fighting spirit, news was telephoned to Mizner that Ketchel had been shot and killed. "Tell 'em to start counting ten over him, and he'll get up," said Mizner.

Fatal illness was almost as happy a subject of merriment as death. One of Mizner's closest friends was Grant Clark, the songwriter. Like most other songwriters, Clark lived chiefly on advances from publishers. Shortly before his death, he tottered up to Mizner's table in a restaurant. He wanted to borrow twenty dollars. "I'll tell you what I'll do," said Mizner. "I'll take you around to Campbell's funeral parlor and get an advance on you."

Mizner got all possible comedy value out of his own last illness. In March, 1933, in his fifty-eighth year, he had a heart attack at the Warner studio. When he recovered consciousness, he was asked if he wanted a priest. "I want a priest, a rabbi, and a Protestant clergyman," he said. "I want to hedge my bets."

His heart attack, President Roosevelt's inauguration, the bank holiday, and a California earthquake came at almost the same time. Mizner criticized this piling up of climaxes. "Bad melodrama," he said.

Told that death was only a few hours away, Mizner rallied strength to send a postcard notifying a friend. "They're going to bury me at 9 A.M.," wrote Mizner. "Don't be a sucker and get up."

When they arranged a tent over him for the administration of oxygen, he said, "It looks like the main event."

Coming out of a coma shortly before his death, he waved a priest away disdainfully. "Why should I talk to you?" he said. "I've just been talking to your boss."

The priest gently reproached Mizner for levity at such a time. He told the sick man that his death might come at any moment. "What?" said Mizner. "No two weeks' notice?"